JoJo Marie Schillaci

MY MISSING PEACE

JoAnna (JoJo Marie) Maria Antoinina Schillaci
My Missing Peace
© 2020, JoAnna (JoJo Marie) Maria Antoinina Schillaci
Self-published
simplyjojomarie.com
simplyjojomarie@gmail.com
All rights reserved.

Cover artwork by Michael Hankus.
michaelhankus@gmail.com

Author photo by Neha Patel.

No part of this publication may be reproduced, stored in a retrieval system, stored in a database and/or published in any form or by any means, electronic, mechanical, photocopying, recording or otherwise, without the prior written permission of the author.

My Missing Peace

JoJo Marie Schillaci

"Once you live in peace, you will never accept chaos."

JoJo Marie Schillaci

JoJo Marie Schillaci

Dedication

This book is dedicated to my humble and gracious son Joseph, whose never-ending belief in me sustained me through the darkest times and inspired me through to the brightest. Joseph, you have used every challenge as a stepping-stone towards achieving greatness and you are everything I aspire to be when I grow up. I love you always and forever...

And to my mother, who taught me through example to never give up, to push through and that every day is better with lipstick on.

JoJo Marie Schillaci

Acknowledgments

My rebirthing was not by the work of one woman, but by an entire village. A village of love, compassion and unshakable dedication and support.

My special heartfelt thanks to:

My son Joseph. There are not enough words in the English language to describe what you mean to me and my gratitude for all you have done and continually do. You never gave up on me, you stayed by my side and showed me by example that "I can do it." Thank you for holding me accountable from the day you gifted me a set of bookends in 2014, with the sole purpose to one day hold my book. You make me want to be a better person by watching how you live your life, how you carry yourself and how you treat others. I am forever grateful for the Universe seeing fit to bring you to this world through me. You are the greatest gift and I am so grateful for all your help to bring this project to the finish line.

My mother Antoinette Amodeo. You epitomize the word strength. Thank you for being both mother and father to the three of us and for always giving us all you had each and every day. You have been my lighthouse, my support and the reason my son and I made it through. I am forever your Rosie.

My great grandmother Giuseppina Schillaci. You taught me that a gracious life comes from gracious living and that our lips are better served in prayer than gossip.

My grandmother Antonina Badali. You taught me to never give up, to be stubbornly determined and you showed me through your own living love story that true love does in fact exist.

My Auntie Rea who left this world forever young. I thank you deeply for teaching me to appreciate every little thing in life, to dress and act like a lady and that if you have to crawl, crawl gracefully.

My brother Anthony Amodeo. You never stopped believing in me, you held my hand and told me I was beautiful despite what your eyes were seeing. You brought music and laughter where there was silence and stood by my son every step of the way.

My Uncle Joey Amodeo. Your words have guided me and echoed in my mind my entire life. I am grateful that you stand beside me today as you always have. I thank you for every card, every phone call and for always making me feel like I matter.

My cousin Cosmo Pusateri. You taught me to believe in the Universe and in the powers we cannot see. You answered every call and exemplify the word family.

Rizwana Jafri. You never left my side. You are my constant protector and my loudest cheering section. You always said there was nothing I couldn't do.

Sharon Ross-Marzano. I thank you for always seeing and speaking the truth, for being my voice when I had none and for loving Joseph and I through it all.

Dr. Ric Levenston. Thank you for your kindness, love, compassionate care and insights that finally diagnosed me and for a most beautiful friendship.

Dr. Peter Gaibisels, You have been my parental guide and support through it all. Through the years you helped me uncover my core truth and your wisdom has guided me to fierce independence. You have always been there and supported me every step of the way. You define the word compassion.

Katherine Liberatore. I thank you for answering the call despite the odds and logistics, for showing up and giving 110% to this case and for doing so in the most selfless compassionate way. For every day off you spent with me, I am forever grateful.

Joon Nah. I thank you for your patience and expertise that took a terrified upside down brain and made it right again.

James Noronha. You took my son and guided him through the storm with the most compassionate and sincerest heart of any human I know. You provided him with a safe space, a loving space, and a compassionate space. You stood by the truth and have been our rock.

Reverend Pat Blythe, Father John Wilton and the St. George's On-The-Hill community. Thank you for your generous outpouring of support both financially and spiritually. You never forgot us, always had faith and always answered our call for prayer. A truer collection of God-serving folk does not exist.

Gavin Ashley. You are my chosen brother. The energy was undeniable and the Universe knew it! You fill our home with the essence of unconditional love and you have always taught me that through forgiveness, you gain freedom. You never gave up on me and have been a constant source of support and laughter.

Paul and Melanie Shuebrook. Thank you for your serendipitous friendship that came from the most unlikely source and for sharing your wisdom, time and Divine light.

Louie Manzo. Thank you for answering the call and for being a true life Santa Claus in so many ways.

James Desroches, I thank you for sharing your wisdom and compassion and most importantly, the five words that have guided me to the other side.

Beverley Charchalis. Thank you for every late night phone call, every bedside visit and absolutely everything in between.

Gus Larnaudie. Thank you for the hours and hours of conversation and comradeship and for teaching me to always do my due diligence.

Anatoli Guelfgat. Thank you for always being there for my son. You were a constant and solid support at a most critical time.

Noel Martin. Thank you for believing in me and encouraging this project of love. You inspired me through the writing of your own memoir which gave me the courage to put pen to paper. The reason I hold my book in my hands today is largely because of the bravery you showed by writing yours. Not only did you offer your mentorship, but you blessed me with your talent by being a content editor. I couldn't be happier that you were the first to read my story.

Joanne Windh. Thank you for believing in me and this project from the very start. Thank you for graciously and generously stepping into the technical role seamlessly with your attention to detail and commitment. More than 35 years later, you just keep getting better.

Robert James Martin. Editor Extraordinaire! Where do I even begin...You serendipitously took on the role of editor and gave freely from your heart everyday. You have taught me more about the English language than any classroom ever did but, more importantly, you made me realize that I am indeed a fellow wordsmith. I am so grateful that you always respected my work and allowed me to keep it my own, never compromising the integrity or spirit that it was written in. You have dedicated hundreds of hours of your time, wisdom and knowledge but, what I am most grateful for, is your friendship and laughter that you brought to the project everyday. I could not imagine doing this with anyone but you!

Michael Hankus, Genifer Jameson, Leanne Lepore, Letizia DiComo, Carol-Ann Martin, Mooney Masarat Khan, John Patrick Courtney, Tony Hunt, Lena and Joe Pusateri, Dina Mastrofrancesco, Anne Marie Sawicki, Rosemary Green Clarke, Anne Marie and Nancy Marie Formusa and Neha Patel for your collective support and love for me and this project.

To all of you that visited, called, messaged, sent cards, prayers and thoughts of encouragement, I thank you deeply and most sincerely. It is because of this beautiful village of love, that something beautiful bloomed. I love you all.

JoJo Marie Schillaci

Prologue

This is my personal memoir. My life story from my earliest memory at three years old to the age of fifty-one. As the eternal optimist, I'd like to think I'm just halfway through this life on earth and that the best years are yet to come. Undoubtedly, there will be more stories to tell and more wisdom to share in another book that waits in the wings. The impetus for writing my story now, is my deep need to share the wisdom that was gifted to me. I trust that by sharing the most intimate and vulnerable part of myself, it will empower, motivate and inspire at least one person to not give up. My wish is to show people that there is life beyond fear and that absolutely anything is possible when we beat the drum of our desires and operate from a place of peace and love.

Writing my life story has enabled me to give a voice to what has been laying in silence within me. It has afforded me the opportunity to cleanse, renew and close the past of my life, enabling me to walk freely and peacefully into my future. A future that is no longer based on fear but solidified by love.

My grandmother told me, time and time again, her dream of writing her life story. Unfortunately, she would die before realizing that dream. Within my story lies a portion of hers. A small way of giving my deepest thanks to her for keeping the spirit of so many alive through her love.

JoJo Marie Schillaci

Chapter One

My earliest childhood memory is, what I now know to be, the wake following my father's funeral. It was August 6, 1971. Time magazine named Nixon man of the year, the Montreal Canadiens won the Stanley Cup and the microprocessor was invented. The number one song was Joy to the World and the Etch-A-Sketch made its way to the top of all Christmas wish lists. I would have been three years old, my sister nine and my brother eleven.

    I vividly recall sitting on my Auntie Rea's (her given name was Maria) lap, in the hall of our family home in Mississauga, Ontario, which at that time, was a small suburb of Toronto. My Auntie Rea was my mother's baby sister and they were extremely close. Auntie Rea was twenty-one years old at the time of my father's death and had been on a trip to Florida with friends when she received the news. We sat on a 1960's style metal chair that had a thick vinyl cover where I was perched upon her lap with my legs straddling both sides of her. I remember her crying profusely as she held me tight. I was oblivious and continued to play with her beautiful, long dark hair that cascaded down her back like a horse's tail. To a little girl, it was irresistible. My aunt was the kind of woman that when she walked into a room, everyone's head would turn. She was a stunning beauty that could make a clock stop ticking with her energy and smile. As I sat with her, I didn't know exactly what was transpiring. It was happening around me like white noise. I couldn't tell you what people were upset about but, even to a child of three, the energy and emotion of sadness, profound sadness was obvious. When I recall that moment, it's as if the adults were speaking through long tubes of Christmas wrap, their voices distorted to a muffled, inaudible sound. I don't recall being concerned. I was too busy admiring my aunt and tinkering with her jewelry that always adorned her like a Christmas tree. The only thing I clearly remember someone saying was: "Maria flew all the way back from Florida." This sentence remained with me my entire childhood, until I grew old enough to question it and know better. Though I don't recall what age that was, perhaps, far older than I care to admit. I kept picturing her flying through the air with two white suitcases, one in each hand, flapping like a giant bird through the blue sky and passing through the most beautiful marshmallow clouds. Even at that young age, I had watched the sitcom The Flying Nun with Sally Field and it made sense to me that if she could do it, so could my aunt! My Auntie Rea had flown home from Florida to be part of this gathering of sadness, but I had no idea why. This was the event that would forever change our family and the trajectory of all our lives.

At five years old I was clearly aware of the fact that I did not have a father. He was gone, but I have no idea how or why this came to be. I had overheard some family scuttlebutt, but I never did get the entire story. It was more like a thousand piece jigsaw puzzle in my mind. I began attempting to put it together bit by bit, but I felt like I was in a pitch black room groping blindly, trying to find the *missing piece* that would complete the picture. My mind was a fearful place full of darkness, a terrifying place that made no sense and gave no comfort. I was riddled with fear and anxiety that never seemed to stop. As I attempted to piece together the puzzle, I recalled hearing someone telling me in the days that followed his death, "Your daddy is at work." I don't remember who said it. Maybe it was just another story I told myself in those early days, but this statement began the absolute catastrophic, apocalyptic fear that propelled me into a state of crippling emotions for the next forty-three years of my life.

As a young child, I desperately needed facts. I needed some form of reality to make sense of the fragmented memories, and to diminish my active imagination. What really happened on that August day? What was it about the day that would sequester everyone to such silence? I would never ask a living soul such a question. No one ever spoke of him or of the event that took his life. It was like he was simply swallowed up into a dark hole, never to be seen or heard from again, as if he never existed. As a child, you need something to enable you to understand and process the loss. You need something to help make sense of it, and as I learned many years later in therapy, if it's not given to you, your subconscious will create a scenario of its own. The subconscious is always craving closure and completion, so I created a story in my mind, my story which I believed to be the absolute truth. This is how my subconscious completed the "incompletion" of the event, void of any facts, but it was clear in my mind.

"The day was dark and gloomy, looking like a storm was going to come through at any time. The phone rang and as my mother answered it her face turned pale with a look of shock. It was my fathers' boss calling to say there had been an accident. I can see her standing in our tiny kitchen with the receiver in one hand, as she held the kitchen counter tightly with the other. My father had been in an accident at work. She dropped the receiver and as it swung back and forth from the wall mount, she began crying hysterically. Frantically, she picked me up in her arms as she ran out to the car, a 1968 green Pontiac Parisssiene. It was the size of a small boat with a huge bench seat where I laid down close beside her. Off we raced to PrimoArgo where my father worked as a truck driver.

As we approach the accident scene, I can see an ambulance with its lights flashing and sirens screaming to a deafening tone. I recall complaining to my mom about the noise hurting my ears. I am in awe of all the policemen running about, trying to calm the chaotic scene of traffic and emergency vehicles. Our car came to an abrupt stop as my mother jammed it into park and pulled me out into her arms. She began running towards the ambulance and I can clearly see my father lying on a stretcher with an orange blanket wrapped tightly around his entire body. I can hear him calling out to her in a loud and frightened voice, begging her to meet him at the hospital. With that, the doors closed and away the ambulance went at light speed, until all I can hear is the distant echo of its siren. When we arrived at the hospital my mother gathered me into her arms, and we made our way to the nurse's station where we were told *that he had not survived. He was dead. Not even a chance to say good-bye."* End of memory.

My childhood home, Mississauga, Ontario.

When I was twenty-one years old, I shared my story, the one that I deeply believed to be true, with my Uncle Joey. He was my father's youngest brother and of all my relatives, he is the solid one. He's the guy you can go to with any question and he'll tell it to you straight. He never took being an uncle lightly, showing up to birthdays, visiting regularly and always being there whenever we needed and/or wanted him. When I was a little girl Uncle Joey was larger than life to me. A giant! He was a big teddy bear with a bushy beard, a soft voice when needed and a boisterous belly laugh the majority of the time. He could tell a story like no one else. Many times, he would pick up my sister and I in his little green MG sports car. We would grab a pizza and then spend the evening with him and his then-wife Catherine. I never felt cooler than driving down the road with the top down and my hair blowing in the wind, secretly hoping friends would be out biking and catch a glimpse of me. His home was such fun to visit. He was a collector of so many odd and truly different treasures. He taught me to buy things that have a story behind them and to collect those that I loved. I always remembered those lessons as I grew older and I most definitely inherited his keen eye for a unique find. He always made me feel incredibly special and that my voice mattered. Even as a little girl, he valued my opinion. My uncle was the one in the family who strived for higher learning and thrived in the world of academia. He received his undergrad degree at university and then went back later in life to get his PhD. Two things he always told me were that I could be anything I wanted to be and to never, ever, be reliant on a man. After my father died, Uncle Joey never stopped being an important and active part of my family's life and he remains an integral part of my life today. He was, and is, someone I trust with every ounce of my being and someone for whom I have deep, deep respect.

It was a Sunday afternoon in 1990 and Uncle Joey invited my fiancé and I over for tea. Uncle Joey lives on a beautiful man-made lake where you can hear the birds and geese and enjoy the view of the water from his living room. His home has an incredible peacefulness to it and the most calming energy. As we began discussing my uncle giving me away at my upcoming wedding, the unusual topic of my father came up. Uncle Joey asked if I remembered anything at all about him. It was then, for the very first time ever, that I would share my story. I told of going with my mother and seeing my father in the ambulance, as well as when we received the tragic news at the hospital. He looked perplexed. I would even say gobsmacked. He softly said, "Dear, that's not what happened." He proceeded to tell me that my father did not die in front of PrimoArgo Brick. Not myself, nor my mother had been to the accident scene or the hospital. He then explained my father had been in a multi-vehicle crash on highway 401, a major Toronto highway, where he was thrown from his vehicle. I don't know what my face looked like as he spoke to me, but I can only presume that I resembled a deer in headlights. My body felt like it had been hit by those same glaring lights. I felt my stomach clench as all my muscles went weak and an overwhelming sense of fear cursed through me. Had I really made this whole scenario up? Had I put together the puzzle pieces incorrectly? In short, yes. I had in fact fabricated a story that made sense of the events and gave my mind some semblance of peace. It was in that moment, that I realized where fact ended, fiction began.

My siblings and I, 1975.

JoJo Marie Schillaci

Chapter Two

My entire childhood was spent with ongoing stomach issues and extreme anxiety. I constantly "did not feel good." From the moment I woke up in the morning, my stomach would begin to churn and turn over a hundred times while my mind started racing on a never ending track of fear. If you asked me what exactly I was afraid of, I don't think I could have articulated what it was in that moment. It wasn't one particular thing. It was life. Life in its entirety was one big giant monster in my eyes. Not the sweet cuddly ones I found comfort watching on Sesame Street, but the dark creepy kind without a face; the kind I never saw, but could feel in every breath I took and every move I made. It lurked around every corner, waiting to get me. I never wanted to be alone and constantly ached to be by my mother's side. Even from a very young age I recall never being able to just be in the moment and enjoy it. I always had a record of fear playing on a continuous loop in the background of my mind. In an attempt to self-soothe the fear away, I used a pacifier. This was my go-to until I was five years old. Secretly of course, my friends never knew. Kindergarten was pure Hell for me. Looking back, I don't remember a fun or lighthearted memory from this time of my life. Each moment in the classroom was riddled with anxiety and I ached for my mommy to come through the doors and take me home. I desperately wanted the soothing comfort of my pacifier and the safety I felt when I walked through the door. I could feel the beating of my heart and the flopping of my tummy like a fish trying to take a breath out of water. Quickly I would snatch my pacifier from its hiding place between the cushions of the orange recliner in our living room, and then slip behind the piece of furniture or tuck myself behind the curtains. There I would self-soothe until the anxiety, or that "I don't feel good" feeling passed. It never completely went away. I was constantly made fun of by my siblings and adults who knew of my secret vice. No one took the time to really think about the deeper issues going on. In those days, the connection between a child with stomach issues and anxiety after a parent's death and needing to self-soothe was not as glaringly obvious as it is to people today.

Me, age 4.

My Missing Peace

I spent the majority of the first ten years of my life in and out of countless doctors, pediatricians, and specialist's offices. I was as skinny as a rake and an extremely picky eater and this, coupled with my ongoing complaint of "I don't feel good," caused my mother to constantly look for answers. Each time, the same diagnosis would be given...a nervous stomach. Unfortunately, there never seemed to be a solution to the problem; heaven forbid a doctor should search for the root cause. Coping mechanisms, such as gripe water were the standard recommendations, which never did much other than provide a mild placebo effect.

My entire elementary school career was spent constantly being in the sick room of the school office. Most days, I had an overwhelming feeling of unwellness. Sometimes I could push through but, more often than not, I would succumb to the fear and overwhelming sense of "I don't feel good." As I sat at my desk, the feelings of panic would hit me with the force of a tsunami right in the centre of my stomach. Each time the waves of panic hit, I felt an immediate need to run, but from what and to where I didn't know. I was a scared little girl who needed and wanted her mommy. Everything would be ok if I could just be with my mom. Each time, I would take the long walk down the hallway to the school office more embarrassed than the last. Mrs. Murray, the office secretary, barely lifted her head from the typewriter to peer over her horn-rimmed glasses, acknowledging that I was back yet again. She would motion her head in the direction of the sick room as if to say: "Go ahead, take your bed and I'll call your mom," with a less than compassionate or concerned tone. It was more a sense of indifference than anything else. Who could blame her? Seeing me walk through her door was as predictable as the sun coming up each day.

The anxiety always worsened in the sick room. Now, embarrassment and isolation layered themselves like sheets of concrete on my already heavy little mind. I was always cold in that room and shook uncontrollably. As I lay there, the anxiety grew with each minute feeling like an hour. I just wanted my mom. I needed my mom. I was alone, I was scared and "I didn't feel good." Nobody checks on you in the sick room when you're there as much as I was. You begin to resemble furniture, an inanimate object that's just always there. The room itself was no bigger than a 10ft x 10ft space. Just one mid-century modern, hard leather and wood chair in the corner and a leather covered chaise type bed. I remember it was dark burgundy in colour and had the smell of an old school or church office, a sort of stale smell. If old did indeed have a smell, this was it. I wouldn't feel relief until I heard my mother's voice as she arrived in the office to pick me up yet again. I felt like a human pressure cooker that had just been taken off the stove. An immediate decompression and releasing of stress and anxiety. Decades later, I pieced together the logic behind the emotions I was feeling in those early years. If daddy could go to work and not come home, so could mommy. In my very young mind, every time my mother left for work, I thought it may be the last time I would ever see her. The next paralyzing thought naturally surfaced. Without parents, I would be an orphan. Who would take care of me? I repeated the question over and over throughout my days and long into my nights.

My mother always treated me to the most wonderful little day trips and theatre that she could manage on her budget. Some days we would go to Casa Loma, another day Black Creek Pioneer Village. Always someplace special, just her and I. I looked forward to these times with her and could enjoy myself knowing she was safely with me, as I was with her. I remember one very special day in particular. She brought me all the way into downtown Toronto to the then O'keefe Centre (currently The Hummingbird Centre), to take in the musical Annie, the story of Little Orphan Annie. I immediately fell in love with the music and performance but, as much as I was enjoying the play, I couldn't help but picture myself starring in the lead role in real life. Every night I thought, "could tomorrow be the day? Would it be the day my mommy would die and leave me?" The constant terrifying question played over and over in my mind. After finally falling asleep, inevitably I awoke partway through the night with the, "I don't feel good" feeling stirring inside me and I would end up sleeping with my mother in her bed. It got to the point where I didn't have to say a thing. She just opened one eye, looked at me, rolled over and I got in. No words needed to be said, we knew the drill. Many nights, I never closed my eyes. I lay there wondering what would happen to me not if, but when my mommy would die.

When I was five, my Mom began working at my grandmother's florist and garden center as a secretary and accounts receivable clerk. My grandparents started the business together in 1951. The nursery was an old country cottage on a busy street corner in west Toronto. There was a storefront and florist as you entered and a private kitchen/family room to the left of the entrance way. In the private room stood the most beautiful stone fireplace taking up the entire south wall. It had a stone mantle that measured the entire length of the room and it held many of my grandfather's hunting achievements: mainly pheasants. I'm sure to him, they were beautiful, something to admire and be proud of. To me, a little girl and lover of all creatures big and small, they scared the heck out of me and made me very sad. A huge velvet Mexican sombrero also hung above the mantle to the right. It was a souvenir from a trip my grandmother had taken years earlier. What I recall most of all, was my grandmother's "dream book." It was a 5x6 soft covered book wrapped in manila paper and probably an inch thick. It had come back with grandma from one of her many trips home to Sicily and it purported to tell the meanings of your dreams. Many times, relatives and Italian ladies from the neighbourhood would ask her to look up their dreams in the infamous dream book. Grandma always communicated to them in Italian and though I didn't understand each word I always knew from her facial expressions and hand gestures if it was good news or bad. I recall one day in particular, when an older lady spoke of a dream that all her teeth had fallen out. Quickly, the words: "Oh Dio, oh Dio" came out of my grandmother and were followed by a lot of shaking of her head and "Mi despiace." "Oh God, oh God, I'm sorry", was not good news for sure. Grandma later told me when you dream all your teeth fall out, it means you are going to lose everything. For some strange reason, I never forgot this, and it would only make sense to me many years later.

During the wintertime, the fireplace was always blazing as we used it to burn boxes and crates from deliveries. We would also roast chestnuts in a pan on the open flames. My great grandmother (Nonna) would sit right beside it all day long, doing her rosary beads and she couldn't have been happier. For a woman in her nineties, she always welcomed the warmth that the fire provided her.

The most delicious meals were made and enjoyed in that kitchen. On Saturdays, you could always smell my grandmother's infamous meatballs and sauce boiling on the stove. The aroma of sweet basil mixed with ripe tomatoes and Romano cheese permeated not only the building, but the nasal cavities of every customer that walked through the door. She would put it to cook early in the morning and by lunch time fresh pasta and meatballs were ready to serve up to all the employees and the odd customer. Even Pepper (our German Shorthair Pointer), would get his fair share of carbs!

Most Saturdays, holidays and PD days, I would go to work with my mom. We arrived early in the morning and stayed until five in the evening. It was a long day for a child to amuse themselves, but the garden centre made it easier. The entire business was founded on nature, and nature of any sort was a source of comfort that helped to alleviate the constant fear and anxiety within me. There was something calming about it. I felt safe with a feeling of belonging to something which I never felt in any other place in my life. Also, knowing I was with my mom, allowed me to breathe just a little easier.

Me, Halloween, 1977

As a child, I loved to read. It was another coping mechanism and it allowed me to escape from my mind into another place, a safer place. My mom regularly brought me to the library and bookstore to choose another adventure for me to dive into. She always encouraged my love of reading though she never enjoyed it herself. I would take my book and a little snack out to the far end of the property under the tall pear trees and I'd read for hours on end. I loved hearing the birds and having butterflies land on me while I turned the pages and escaped a little deeper into the adventure of the day and vacationed from my thoughts. When I wasn't reading, I could be found in the dirt pile, my other favourite place. As a child, the topsoil pile at the front gates seemed as high as the Himalayans but in reality, it only reached five or six feet at its highest point. I was always happy to get a shovel and go knee deep in it, filling my fair share of customer's wooden bushels. We received weekly soil deliveries which, to a little kid, was a big and exciting deal. I loved it when the old man would jump out of the cab of his enormous dump truck and hand me the shovel to scrape the truck bed clean. 'Up to my knees in shit' seems to be an ominous foreshadowing of what was waiting for me years later. My grandmother gave me different little tasks to do during the day which, for the most part, I enjoyed. Picking the dead heads off flowers was the job I liked the least, but it seemed to be the one I got stuck doing the most, especially in the springtime during busy season. Come springtime, at the north side of the building there were rows and rows of annuals with every colour of the rainbow in mass clusters that covered the knee-high wooden racks. The smell of spring was unforgettable. The sweet scent of the flowers mixed with the aromatics of manure was a combination that would be etched in my memory forever. The showcase of colour and beauty, was one that adorned the street for nearly 50 years. It was a staple image in the community and a forever landmark for many.

    The garden centre wasn't just a place for me to do time and daydream, it was where I learned a disciplined work ethic and where I also learned that no one ever perished from a hard day's work. It also set the stage for every true-to-life course that you couldn't get in a classroom. I watched my mother merchandise and market product, learned the importance of customer service and the best math lessons came from working the cash with a line up around the corner. In the spring and summer months, the cash register was kept outside. It was an old, wooden register with heavy metal keys. There was no relying on technology to do the work for you and you had to learn quickly as the line grew long, and customers' patience grew short. In the cold winter months, mom let me pound the keys of her typewriter in the office and taught me the basics of shorthand, which was already obsolete, but fun to learn anyway. Another job I would be given in the winter months, which never thrilled me much, was to organize and dust the chemicals. It was approximately a twenty-foot long wall which housed all the pesticides, herbicides and insecticides we carried. Not knowing the risks back in the 70's, I would be covered in their dust, which posed a long term threat to my health. The connection would take years to realize.

My grandfather purchased the land that he built the garden centre on in 1951 from an older couple, the Nortimes, who lived in the home right next door. They stayed on as employees until their deaths well into their 80s. Mr. Nortime was a farmer at heart. A sweet, older man with a rough exterior. He always wore the same green work pants and a white small, checkered, short sleeve, button-down cotton shirt. He had a green and white straw hat, that he never took off unless he was in the comfort of his own home. Mr. Nortime had a distinct smell. It was an earthy smell, like dirt mixed with rainwater. He was a staple around the place, and I liked that. I followed him around like a shadow, learning how to water the plants properly and helping (or hindering, if you asked him) with the odd jobs he would do around the grounds. I was his constant side

My Missing Peace

kick. He wasn't a man of many words and he could get quite surly when things weren't going just right, but I always felt comforted when he was around. He would teach me how to plant floral containers to sell with geraniums and dracena in the middle and petunias around the rim. I would give it a try on my own and each time, his response was the same: "Not bad for a greenhorn." I knew that was his way of saying good job and I was ok with that. The garden centre had an old stand up Coke machine from the fifties outside, and one of my jobs was to keep it stocked. In those days, it would be filled with Coke, 7Up and Country Time Lemonade (that was Mr. Nortime's favourite). I can still picture him today, as if it were yesterday, standing by the garden hose and taking out his handkerchief to wipe down the sweat from his head and face while slugging back his ice cold lemonade. The image was straight out of a television advertisement. His wife was a sweet, mild-mannered lady, reminiscent of Edith Bunker (from the 70's sitcom All In The Family) in almost every way. She always wore a floral house dress and apron. Her horn-rimmed glasses and never-ending smile are what I remember most. She repeated herself incessantly and was forever smiling and willing to lend a kind hand. My favourite time of the day was "tea time" which happened every single day, without fail, at 3pm. It was my duty to walk around the garden centre and announce to everyone that tea was ready, and they should come inside. Though it was called tea time, we never drank tea. Coffee was always served and never a day passed that there weren't plenty of sweets to enjoy. To this day, when 3pm comes around its snack time for me, no matter where I am or what I'm doing. Old habits die hard and this is one I'm quite comfortable keeping. The garden centre was my second home and it's where I spent the better part of my childhood and I adored it. I never felt like I fit in anywhere except with nature and it provided me so much of that. It was absolutely one of my very few happy places.

Chapter Three

Since I spent so much time at the garden centre, I was blessed to also spend a lot of time with my grandmother. She was born Antonina Schillaci in February 1919, in Termini, Sicily and was the youngest of three children. At just sixteen years old, she had two men that were in love with her, but it was my Grandfather Giuseppe (Joe) Badali that would win her heart forever. He sent his soon to be bride to the big city of Palermo to get her hair done for their wedding and spared no expense on the festivities that would follow. They were deeply in love and soon after the nuptials, they were sponsored by a family friend and immigrated to Toronto. Though they had little money and no knowledge of the language, they did have each other and, in their eyes, that's all they needed. They travelled by ship and arrived in Canada in March 1934, through Halifax Harbour.

My grandparents settled in Toronto and moved into a building at 624 Bloor Street (in an area now known as The Annex), owned by their sponsor. Grandpa Joe was an entrepreneur at heart and soon opened up a fruit store in the commercial space below. The apartment was large enough to welcome their growing family with three spacious bedrooms on the third floor and a large kitchen and living room on the second. They were thrilled by the arrival of their first child, a boy, in December 1936, followed by my mother in November 1938 and a second girl in April 1942. Picking up the rear would be Maria, who was born in April 1950. The first three babies were all delivered in the upstairs apartment and weighed on the fruit scales in the store below, amongst the apples and bananas. It seemed the natural and logical thing to do at the time, though we always giggled when my grandmother would retell the story.

Grandma was constantly by the side of her beloved husband. They were committed to each other and to working together with the hope of realizing their dream of creating a better life for their children. This meant bringing the babies into the store while they worked hard hustling the business and trying to save every penny in an effort to gain their independence. The babies would lay in their prams behind the counter while my grandmother tended the cash and served customers. She was a master at multitasking, and never looked at this as a burden, but as a blessing. Grandma would tell stories of their long days in the store and then up until all hours washing cloth diapers in the toilet, only to begin the whole process all over again at the crack of dawn. This was, in fact, the life she dreamed of. Beginning a new exciting life with my grandfather and starting a family was all she ever truly wanted. This was exactly where she wanted to be, doing exactly what she wanted to do, and she was doing it alongside the man she adored. She was happy, very happy!

Money was tight in the early years and she recalled that most days, breakfast would consist of stale bread soaked in heated milk with sugar, but she seldom spoke of the hardships. She always focused more of her attention to sharing their love story. She spoke of her life with my grandfather like it was something of which fairytales were made. Each time she spoke of him, her eyes lit up and she would grin from ear to ear, as she recalled their love affair with the excitement of a young schoolgirl. When she referred to him in conversation, she always called him "My Joe." They were madly and passionately in love and were never afraid to show it. When watching old home movies, you can see the love and affection they shared. He could never keep his hands off her. Sneaking a kiss, pinching her cheek and always an arm around her.

Life was difficult during these years and not just for the adults. My mom remembers back to when she and her brother were assigned the chore of cleaning their sponsor's apartment every Saturday morning. She would have been ten at the time and her brother twelve. Cleaning included polishing the wood floors to a gleaming high shine. Unfortunately, there was not an electric polisher to be had, only a manual buffing brush on a stick. To use it as is, would never produce the shine that was demanded so the two young minds became inventive. Determined they needed more weight, my mother would sit on top of the brush, holding tightly to the stick as her big brother pushed the broom back and forth with vigor. As they say, "necessity is the mother of invention!"

Their sponsor was not the kindest of men and although he had helped my grandparents to immigrate to Canada, he continually held it over their heads and did all he could to ensure they stayed needing him. This, of course, did not sit well with a man as proud as my Grandpa Joe. In 1948, they had saved enough money to purchase their own piece of land in the west end of Toronto at Bloor and Royal York Road. My grandfather soon began construction of the building at 3071 Bloor Street, which remains there, in its original form to this day. Though not professionally trained in the field of construction, he never let that stop him. He became proficient at it and constructed several buildings and numerous houses in the same area.

Soon after they moved into the Bloor Street building, he came across a potential property close by for a business he had in mind. He had grown restless with the fruit store and had his sights on something different. He dreamed of opening a garden centre and as a keen businessman he could see its potential in the community. In an effort not to act in haste, he decided some "Sicilian style" market research was needed. Grandpa rented a small piece of land close by on Islington Avenue, just north of The Queensway and erected a tiny greenhouse. It was there, that he would set my then twelve-year-old mother up with several flats of flowers for sale perched on top of milk crates. After school and on Saturdays, she would walk to the greenhouse and sell until her small inventory was sold out, and then return back home for more. It was soon confirmed that people did indeed want what they had to sell, and that was the beginning of the now infamous, Islington Nurseries. With nothing more than a handshake, he purchased the land that the garden centre called home for over 55 years. Husband and wife together again, began a business into which they would pour their heart and souls. There are pictures of my grandmother shoveling bushels of topsoil right alongside her husband. When asked why on earth she would want to shovel manure, she almost answered with disgust at such a question. It wouldn't matter to her if she was shoveling diamonds or manure, as long as they were side by side, she was more than happy.

My grandfather was always smiling, laughing and happiest when he was with his family. A hardworking, respectful, family man who knew not to take life too seriously; this was the Grandpa Joe I understood him to be. Grandma would tell the story of their niece coming to visit them at the garden centre as a little girl. Her mother was always very fussy, obsessed with cleanliness and keeping her daughter like a little china doll. A day never passed that she wasn't outfitted in frilly dresses, lace socks and patent shoes. Without her mother knowing, Grandpa Joe would lift her high up on his shoulders and place her on top of the manure pile, frilly white socks and all! That was Grandpa Joe!

My grandparents were never particularly concerned about the less than glamorous business they were in. In fact, they both believed in the saying: "You had to eat a peck of dirt before you die." Although this is how they made their living, you would never know it if you met them on the street. Grandma took pride in her appearance, always in a lovely, detailed dress with a frilly apron and her neck adorned with pearls. If it wasn't for the shovel in her hand and the bushel at her feet, you would have thought she had donned her Sunday best for church. My grandfather also always showed himself at his best in a crisp white shirt and pleated trousers with the waist up as high as his chest.

Grandpa was a businessman through-and-through and was known as a man of integrity. My grandma would tell the story of when they first opened the business and he was in desperate need of a truck and despite funds being low, he never let that stop him. Grandpa Joe approached the local car dealership and pleaded his case and explained that all he had to put down was his word of honour. My grandfather already had a stellar reputation in the area and with that as his only deposit, he drove a brand new truck off the lot. He made good on his word with weekly payments and had it paid off in full, in no time. A young immigrant couple who came to this country with nothing and with no knowledge of the language, managed to raise a family and contributed to the building of their community. This is something that continues to leave me in awe.

My grandfather soon saw an opportunity for a new twist to the fruit business. In addition to having the garden centre, he opened up a stand on Toronto's Centre Island. It is the largest of the fifteen islands off the shore of the downtown core. Centre Island was and remains, a popular seasonal attraction for tourists and locals alike. Grandpa saw it as a golden opportunity and opened a mini putt along with a fruit stand which offered soft ice cream and hot buttered corn on the cob. This was not a venture for the lazy or weak. Going to the wholesaler in the early hours of the morning and loading the family and supplies on the boat was only the beginning. Their days were nonstop as hordes of people poured onto the island from the ferry to enjoy the beaches and they all had to pass by the family business along the way. My mother ran the mini-putt and cared for baby Maria while her mother and father ran the ice cream stand. They stayed over at the old Manitoulin Hotel, located on the island, in order to make the best use of selling time during the short summer season. My mother recalls this as one of her favourite times of her childhood.

Grandpa Joe also started the only fruit concession stands at the Canadian National Exhibition (CNE), Canada's largest and oldest annual fair. If you visited the CNE and bought a piece of fruit, I can guarantee it was from my grandpa! They sold everything from apples to pomegranates, with ice cold cider and lemonade always on tap. They had multiple stands and enlisted the help of friends during the three-week exhibition and although it was hard work, the enjoyment always outweighed the labour!

Grandpa Joe at one of his CNE fruit stands, circa 1956.

Unfortunately, Grandpa Joe passed away far too soon in July 1965 at just fifty-five years old, three years before I was born. He fought a brief, but courageous battle with cirrhosis of the liver. Grandpa never drank, so I often wonder if it was exposure to the fertilizer and pesticides, that were possibly to blame. My mother and her brother helped grandma continue to run both the garden centre and CNE stands for years to come, but nothing was ever quite the same. She never got over losing her one true love as a piece of her died along with him. Although I was never given the chance to meet him, I feel like I know him well. Grandma made sure that we all knew him as she kept his spirit alive. When grandma spoke of him, she always looked up to the sky with her hands clasped together as if in prayer, repeating over and over "Joe, where is my Joe?" You could feel the deep, visceral loss when she spoke, like an echo of emptiness in her heart.

My grandparents at their 25th wedding anniversary, March 1959

My grandmother was a proud woman and you would never see her without lipstick and of course, her signature dark burgundy nail polish. By far, what she was best known for, was her jewelry. Every finger had at least one ring, perhaps, even two or three, a watch gilded with rhinestones and half a dozen bracelets jingling on each wrist. Her eyeglasses were bedazzled and even the likes of Elton John would feel inferior standing along side. Her clothing was just as flashy, with heavily beaded tops and skirts in a rainbow of colours. If she had a motto for dressing it would be: "Go big or go home!" or "If a little is good, more is better." Every Saturday morning, she had her hair done at the local salon. Forever styled in the big, backcombed bouffant of the '70s and '80s.

The loss of Grandpa hardened my grandmother and she developed a bitterness about her. It was a frustration that was obvious to most, especially those of us that were closest to her. She wasn't the type of woman who was warm and fuzzy and she was never going to be the one to cuddle and say she loved you or smother you with kisses. It just wasn't her style. She was more the type that would pound her fist on the kitchen table and tell you in no uncertain terms, to suck it up. Or her famous saying: "Put up and shut up!" She was a determined and hardheaded woman and once she had something in her head, there was no way you were going to change it. You didn't dare try. It was that determination and hard-headedness that allowed her to continue for forty-nine years without her beloved Joe. She had artificial knees due to arthritis and walked begrudgingly with a cane. Every chance she could, she would shake that cane to instill the wrath of God into you. There was no mistake when the cane got raised, she meant business! If you were really testing her patience, she'd bang it on the kitchen table or anything else that happened to be within reach. To say the very least, my grandmother was not for the faint of heart. Her stubbornness and rough exterior came from hardship and heartbreak. Underneath, she was a pussy cat; a scared, lonely woman, who ached for her beloved that was taken away from her far too soon. She showed that softer, more vulnerable side many years later when she had great-grandchildren, showering them with love and kisses and spoiling them with gifts. I remember many relatives, nieces, and nephews coming to sit at her kitchen table asking for advice as they valued her opinion; it mattered. She was a woman of character and great integrity and people held her in deep regard.

Chapter Four

My great grandmother Giueseppina Schillaci, or Nonna as we called her, was born in January 1887, in Termini, Sicily. Nonna gave birth to four children. Her third child was a little girl who had the most beautiful curly blond hair. Sadly, a young relative was holding the baby when the unthinkable happened and the child slipped from her arms causing a fatal head injury. Despite a broken heart, her deep faith allowed her to carry on and have a fourth child, who is my grandmother. Unfortunately, tragedy would strike again, leaving her widowed at a very young age.

Nonna was another example of a strong and fiercely independent woman in my life. When she was a young girl, her dream was to become a nun, but her father wouldn't hear of it. Although she never joined the sisterhood formally, I believe that in her heart, she committed herself to her Lord. Many people believed that she lived the life of a saint. Never did you hear her curse or speak ill of anyone or anything. My mother always said, "Nonna wouldn't say shit if her mouth was full of it!" Her strength was paired with a significantly softer side, not found in the other women of our family. Where the rest were loud and boisterous, she was always quiet, with a reserved demeanour. She would never be one to engage in idle chit chat or gossip of any sort. If she was speaking, everyone listened because you knew she had something important to say. She immigrated to Toronto, Canada in 1963, and lived with my grandparents in the Bloor Street apartment. She spent her days at the garden centre in the same chair at the end of the table, beside the fireplace. Inside her oversized apron pockets, you were sure to find her rosary. It was a simple, black beaded rosary that she used to repeat her prayers over and over throughout the day. She would sit quietly for hours, staring straight ahead, rubbing each bead between her fingers and whispering Hail Mary's to herself. Along with her beads, she also carried her black prayer book, which was constantly by her side. She always wore a simple house dress with a full length apron and her white hair reached all the way down the middle of her back and was set in a tight conservative bun, held together with long metal bobby pins. On the days I was at the garden centre, it was my duty to ensure her hair was neat and tidy. Nonna was so grateful when people took the time to help her in any way. Nonna was passive and extremely tolerant. One day, I recall getting into some mischief. Having just read the adventures of Pippi Long Stocking, I became inspired to recreate Pippi's iconic hairstyle on my great grandma. I made the perfect braids on either side of her head and then began feeding long pieces of wire I snatched from the florist through each one. Perfect, now to bend them up! There she sat, looking as cute as could be, at least in my eyes. Unfortunately, when my grandmother saw what I had done to Nonna's hair, I got an ear full! Out came the wire and down came the braids, which were never to be seen again. Needless to say, that was the last of my experimenting with hairstyles for Nonna.

My Missing Peace

Nonna beside her beloved fig tree at the garden centre, circa 1979.

Nonna moved very slowly and had more of a shuffle to her walk than a stride. She was always incredibly healthy, never taking medication or going to the doctor. Her way of exercising was climbing the 20 stairs of the apartment, each and every day whether she was going out or not. It took her some time, but she made sure to do it and never made an excuse not to complete her task. She was an incredibly disciplined woman in so many ways.

The only time you wouldn't see her in prayer, was while she was eating and of course, when watching the soap opera All My Children. Although, she didn't speak English, make no mistake, she knew exactly what was happening during every episode. When she would turn around and chastise us for making too much noise, we couldn't help but giggle at how out of character it was for her.

Dancing with my Nonna at her 95th birthday party, circa 1982.

Nonna was ninety-six years old when she asked my grandmother to take her back to her hometown of Termini, one last time. Of course, my grandmother was more than happy to oblige her and did so that fall. They had gone back several times through the years but somehow, I think we all knew this trip was going to be different. She had a slight sniffle when she left Toronto, which was unlike her. She had always enjoyed perfect health and I believe it was the good karma coming back to her for being such a kind and gentle human being. Whenever my Nonna went to Italy, it was like a celebrity coming to town. Everyone was thrilled to see her and had such admiration for her. It was November 21, 1983, when we received the news that Nonna's sniffles had not gotten better. She had gone to sleep and ever so peacefully and true to her character, gracefully slipped away into her eternal rest. I can remember my grandmother speaking of her death when she returned home some months later. The entire town could not believe their eyes when they saw her laid out to rest in the family's living room. Her skin had pulled back and her face looked like that of a woman half her age with pink blushed cheeks. They said this was a sure sign that she was indeed, una Santa! A saint. In my mind and eyes, she always was and forever would be.

JoJo Marie Schillaci

Chapter Five

My mother was born Antoinette Badali in November 1938. She was a spitfire as a child, always full of energy and constantly getting into mischief. She was a little girl who chose to bounce, jump and leap instead of simply walking. I remember a story from when she was eight years old and seeing her father walking down busy Bloor Street with his back to her. She thought it would be fun to surprise him. Running as fast as she could down the busy sidewalk, she took a running leap and attached herself to his back with her arms wrapped in a choke hold around his neck. My grandfather would have welcomed the jovial childhood surprise if it had indeed been him. Unfortunately for her, it was another man with the same camel hair coat and fedora, and he was less than impressed with her antics. Upon realizing this, she slowly released her grip and slithered down his body like a snake to a most embarrassed puddle on the sidewalk. This was typical of her shenanigans.

In 1953, the family travelled to Sicily on the SS Andrea Doria to attend a family wedding. The ship was an ocean liner, most famous for her sinking in 1956, killing forty-six people. It was during their return trip home, that my mother's youngest sibling, little Maria contracted chickenpox. She was put in quarantine along with my grandmother, forcing Grandpa Joe to tend to the other three children alone. During this time, they began sailing through a vicious storm which left most on board extremely ill. Ropes were installed down the long hallways to help passengers keep their balance as the ship rocked violently back and forth on the huge ocean waves. My grandfather gave strict orders for the children to stay in the cabin while he checked on grandma and the baby but true to my mother's character, her mischievous side won. She opened the door and followed along the ropes, swaying back and forth with unsteady steps, finally making her way to the upper deck. A door clearly marked DANGER HIGH WAVES DO NOT OPEN was just too enticing to pass by. Her curious side took over and in no time at all, she was standing on the deck in awe of the storm. An enormous wave began curling over the side of the ship and it wasn't long before fear outweighed curiosity. Grabbing hold of the door handle and with all the strength she could muster, mom was able to pull herself to safety. I'm convinced she had a guardian angel watching over her. This event would trigger in my mother, a paralyzing fear of water for the rest of her life. As a child, I can remember my siblings attending swimming lessons and my mom and I watching from the observation deck above. She would grab me so tight while watching them that it hurt, and I could hear her gasp each time they dove into the water. It was at this point, that her fear of water was passed down to me.

She attended Our Lady of Sorrows Catholic elementary school, just down the street from the Bloor street apartment. She then moved on to St. Joseph's Catholic high school for girls. My mom never liked studies and despised mathematics more than anything. After struggling through grade nine, she opted to leave traditional secondary education and enrolled in the nearby Shaw Business School. It was there that she found her groove and excelled. With shorthand at 130 words per minute and typing at over 70, it was obvious this was where she was meant to be. Shaw was a co-ed learning environment and although there were plenty of boys enrolled, she never found one that piqued her interest. After graduating, she began working as a secretary at Montgomery Elevators and shortly thereafter, secured a position as secretary to the president of Seiberling Rubber in downtown Toronto.

My mom working the CNE fruit stand, 1956.

In 1955, she began dating Vincent Amodeo. They married on November 21, 1958, at Our Lady of Sorrows Catholic Church, right across from the Bloor Street building. My grandfather spared no expense in celebrating the marriage of his first daughter. I think Grandpa Joe invited everyone he had ever bumped into since arriving in Canada as the wedding list grew to an incredible 1,500 people in size. The huge celebration was held at the Columbus Hall in downtown Toronto. The cost of such an affair was unimaginable and, in those days, a wedding was an all-day event with both lunch and dinner being served. They hired a remarkable full orchestra which provided dance music, long into the evening. From the pictures you would think it was an MGM movie set! A memorable image shows a five year old Maria standing by the stage dressed as a precious little flower girl and as she gazed up at her big sister, you could see the special connection between the two.

My parents at their wedding reception with little Maria looking on. Columbus Hall, Toronto, 1958.

My mother was the only person I knew of who came back early from her honeymoon because she was home sick. The newlyweds had driven to Florida for their romantic getaway but, from the few pictures I've seen, she looked more like someone being held against their will rather than someone in love on their honeymoon. She ached to be back with her parents and after a few days, my father succumbed to her tears and began the long drive home.

My parents purchased their first and only home a short while later in 1959. It was small three-bedroom bungalow with an enormous yard which backed on to beautiful park land. Mom continued working for Seiberling until giving birth to a boy in March 1960. She was now a full-time stay at home housewife and mother. She welcomed her first daughter in May 1962, and I made my entrance in June 1968.

If you were to ask my mother how I was as a baby, I'm sure her first word would be "Hell." I suffered from colic and as the story goes, I cried the entire first year of my life. Growing up, I remember her wishing that I would have a child just like me. Mom admitted to not always having the patience for babies and was glad when we were all old enough to tell her where it hurt.

My father, being a very old-fashioned man, left all the daily parental duties to his wife, along with the housekeeping and shopping. She was given a weekly allowance and the rest of the finances were my father's concern. After he passed away, she was left with no income, leaving her in an unfavourable financial state; a single mom with three kids and absolutely zero financial experience running a household. My father had purchased a triplex not far from where I live today in southwest Toronto, which would have been extremely lucrative, had she been able to hang on to it. Unfortunately, the estate lawyer in charge of the Will convinced her it was impossible to keep, so she ended up selling it for a song, to of all people, the lawyer. She had been taken advantage of during her weakest moment by someone that was supposed to be on her side. Being widowed with three children and left in financial strife created years of struggle for her. I would never forget that story, nor the regret my mother lived with for having listened to the lies of a deceitful lawyer.

My mother is a fiercely proud woman and was not going to accept handouts from anybody, although, I don't think there were many being offered. She went into task mode and I believe she has remained there ever since.

Determined to find a way to make it, she used the resources available to her at the time - her secretarial skills. With no money for a babysitter and me being only three years old, she had to think outside of the box. My mother answered an ad for a typing job she could do from home. I can still hear the Underwood typewriter with its hard box case that she dragged out from the front hall closet and placed upon a metal desk. I can clearly see a businessman dropping off boxes of yellow cards similar to index cards and she would pound those keys from morning until dinner each day. The sound of each key striking the paper made a constant rhythmic echo that was comforting to me. Hearing her typing meant she was home, and I was with her. All was good.

My mother was hard working and resourceful, and somehow, she always managed to pay the bills and provide us with all we needed, including the best food we could have asked for. When I was five years old, she began working as a secretary and accounts receivable clerk at her mother's garden centre. As the years passed, her duties expanded to everything from floral designer, buyer, chief merchandiser and general store manager; most times working six or seven days a week and all holidays without ever uttering a complaint. As the buyer of all the inventory, this meant that she was required to go to the Ontario Food Terminal and search out product and negotiate the best prices, another way of saying "wheeling and dealing." The terminal was, and still is, a male-dominated environment and is not for the weak at heart. It is notorious for misogynistic attitudes and language that would curl the toes of a streetwalker. In my mother's mind, she was there to do a job, and no one was going to take advantage of or intimidate her. Mom proved through the years she was a force to be reckoned with and one to be respected first and foremost. After almost fifty years of showing them what she is made of, my mother can go to that market without a dime in her pocket and have her car packed to the roof. Her word is as honourable as her father's was so many years earlier.

In addition to her usual duties at work, she also managed one of the many family fruitstands at the CNE. For years of my childhood, she would be up at the crack of dawn and work straight through until midnight for the twenty-one-day fair. Weeks before, she cooked up a storm, making meals that would then be frozen, ensuring we never went without a warm home cooked meal. I always found this time stressful as a little girl. Sometimes, a couple of days would pass without ever seeing her, but I was left in the care of the most incredible babysitter. Doris was a young woman who lived across the street and I couldn't have wished for a kinder, sweeter and more incredible caregiver. Doris did everything possible to keep my days filled with fun and distraction, but I still felt the "I don't feel good" feeling constantly. Sometimes, the only proof that my mom had ever returned was a bag of my favourite Tiny Tom doughnuts on the counter with a note or perhaps a carnival toy.

Despite the grueling hours she worked each day and the never-ending double role she played at home, there was never a school trip or event she didn't attend. Part of the reason mom never missed a trip was because she didn't trust anyone else with her kids and wanted to keep us safe. By todays standard, she would definitely fall into the category of helicopter mom. Whether it was control or not, I was always grateful to have her with me and there was never a classmate that didn't want to be in her parent group. She was fun to be with, kind to the kids and always went out of her way to get a treat for each child from wherever we were visiting. I was recently connected to an elementary classmate who recalled when mom accompanied us on a school trip to Black Creek Pioneer Village. He remembered her buying each child a piece of candy from the general store. My mother is kind, almost to a fault. She will go without if it means making someone else happy.

No matter how tight her budget, she always made sure we had the best food. We had a seemingly bottomless bowl of fresh fruit that adorned our kitchen table and on Saturday mornings, it was not uncommon to wake up to a box of yummy chocolate doughnuts as a special treat. Fast food or take out were not staples in our house. Somehow, she would step through the door at 5:30 each night and with the most amazing organizational and time management skills, put a hot meal on the table by 6:00.

My mom and I have always shared a special bond. We were always together. It was obvious how protective she was of all three of us but, particularly me, the youngest. It was also obvious to everyone the comfort that I felt when I was with her and the constant anxiety I endured when I wasn't. She continuously worried about her kids and never liked it when we were doing something out of the normal routine. She liked to keep things as predictable as possible, limiting any chance of something bad happening. In my mind, I began believing that different meant unsafe and it induced terrible fear within me.

As a little girl, I was shy and didn't talk much, but was always listening. Quite often, due to my severe anxiety, I preferred to fall asleep on the sofa in the living room. The kitchen and living room were joined which enabled me to see mom, thus helping me to relax and eventually drift off to sleep. It was during these times when she thought I was sleeping, that I overheard her many conversations with Auntie Rea sharing her concerns of money and not knowing how she was going to pay for this or that. Those worries about money stayed with me and I began being preoccupied with trying to find a solution. On weekends, my grandmother would give me five dollars for the little jobs I would do around the garden centre. Without my mother being any the wiser, I slipped the money into her coat pockets, purse or wallet. I'd put it anywhere she may look and think she had misplaced it and actually put it there herself believing these little gestures would fix all our worries. Money quickly became another one of my fears.

Friday nights were baking nights with The Love Boat television show playing in the background as my mother and I decided what treat to bake. By far, the family favourite was her infamous apple pie. Absolutely nobody can make an apple pie like my mom. By the age of eight she had taught me to peel an entire apple in one piece while not splitting the skin at all! This was quite a feat and a skill of which I was very proud. I loved watching her cut the Crisco into the flour and slice the apples in a huge mound for the awaiting pie plates. I sat by the stove watching them bake and bubble until finally the timer would ring. The buzzer was a signal to my brother to come running from whatever room he happened to be in. Many times, I clearly remember sitting with him at the kitchen table, eating warm apple pie and ice cream. The aroma of apple and cinnamon will always be reminiscent of those times spent baking alongside my mom.

Even to this day, I think baking is what takes her mind off her stresses, her anxiety and her own fears. Just as I turn to nature, she turns to baking. Baking takes her to another place that keeps her hands busy and her mind occupied.

No matter how tight money was, I can't recall our mother telling us that we couldn't have friends over or that someone couldn't stay for dinner. Somehow, she always made sure there was more than plenty, although I still don't know how she managed this. Our home was the gathering place for friends and family alike, everyone was always welcomed, and our friends respected and enjoyed having mom around. Many of my brother's friends, who became more like family, never called her by her surname. It was always Mama and they all loved Mama.

My brother is a bassist and was a part of many garage bands during his teen years. Somehow, they always ended up practicing at our house. With mom working weekends, it allowed them to play as loud as their amplifiers would go, never having to worry about parents complaining. My mother was happy to have them, and not because of her love for AC/DC, Alice Cooper or Black Sabbath, but because she loved that they were at home and not getting into any trouble. Perhaps, another fear-based choice, but everybody was happy. It worked. The Rolling Stones' Brown Sugar echoed out of the basement windows so loud that the glasses on the bar would actually vibrate, and eventually, fall to the ground one by one. Another one gone and another one gone, another one bites the dust. She never once closed down the jam sessions, she just shrugged it off and carried on.

When I was six my mother began dating Ron. She had met him through a neighbour and in a very short time, we all couldn't be happier. He wasn't a man of wealth, but he was a kind and gentle man who treated us extremely well. Looking back now, I have a whole new respect for the way he treated me in particular. I was the forever tagalong with the two of them. Wherever they went, I went too. Never once did he make me feel less than truly wanted. His family quickly became our family and we enjoyed years of laughter and great times together. I loved being with them. I can never recall them saying a bad word about anyone. It was always about sharing food, good times and plenty of laughter. We spent countless Sundays at his brother's pool and the most memorable Christmases I can recall.

Ron and I, Christmas, 1980.

    I always felt safe and at ease with them, never judged or teased for my attachment to my mom that I constantly felt from so many others. Ron asked my mother to marry him several times, but she refused. She was committed to being a mom and her children always came first. Each Father's Day at school, I would make him a gift and be so proud to present it to him and he was equally grateful to receive it. When I was thirteen years old, Ron was diagnosed with pulmonary fibrosis, a disease that had taken his mother and years later, his sister and brother. He succumbed to the illness in September 1981. Though heartbroken, mom didn't skip a beat after the funeral, again, she went into task mode. Unfortunately, the families would soon lose their close contact with each other. I missed Ron terribly and his death left a tremendous hole in my heart.

Mom spent the majority of her time with her mother, grandmother, baby sister and me in tow. We went everywhere together. Summer vacations in Niagara Falls were by far the most memorable. Every June we went for a four day getaway which included touring through the little-known town of Niagara-on-the-Lake. It was in its infancy in terms of being a hot tourist destination, just a small, quiet town off the beaten path from the hustle and bustle of Clifton Hill. We would enjoy an old-time country meal at Louisa's Restaurant and tour the quaint shops along the main strip including our favourite, Pauline's mini department store. Nonna looked forward all year to these trips and my grandmother especially loved stopping at the farmers' roadside fruit stands. Fresh cherries were a must as well as sweet juicy peaches. Sitting by the pool playing scrabble was the usual daily scene for the ladies, while my cousins and I would be either in the pool or strolling along Clifton Hill. We took in the cheesy haunted houses and wax museums that resembled a carnival sideshow while my grandmothers sat in the shade under a tree. Watching the two younger generations gave them such joy; this was their happy place.

Mom is a confident driver with a deep mistrust for others on the road. My father's accident instilled a fear in her that has remained since his death. Growing up, I recall driving at night on the highway to be the worst for her. She avoided it any chance she could. As kids, each time we left the house with the car, we were met with the phrase, "be careful." Always with the undertone that something terrible could happen out there. She would have preferred us to stay at home where we were "safe." "Don't go on the highway" was another term she often used. This was also another fear that was transferred to me. I began believing that people I loved were going to die on the highway, because that's where bad things happened.

After thirty years of widowhood, my mom remarried at the age of sixty-three to my godfather. They had known each other since she was a young teen and as much as I wanted to be happy that she had found companionship after so very long, it was an incredibly difficult time for me. Up to this point in my life, I had always had mom to myself and I wasn't enjoying sharing her. A feeling of abandonment overcame me, and I felt like I was losing her. My childhood stresses and irrational fears were coming back to haunt me, and many nights I lay awake thinking "I don't feel good." Unfortunately, after ten years of being together, he was diagnosed with lung cancer and lived approximately one year before it took his life. She was alone again.

My mother is a most amazing woman. In spite of the many tremendous losses she has endured, she continues to epitomize the word strength and carry on regardless of what obstacles lay in her way. She has found a way to smile despite what life has thrown at her. A true-life Wonder Woman in so many ways, forever my hero.

Chapter Six

This section of my book is going to seem vague in comparison to previous ones, but for good reason. Being only three years old when my father passed, I have no real memories or recollection of him at all. What follows are mostly anecdotes shared by my brother Anthony, who seems to have an endless supply of stories up his sleeve which he is always happy to share.

My father was born Vincent Amodeo in August 1936. At first glance, he was a tall, intimidating man. From what I'm told, he had a heart of gold, a slightly twisted sense of humour and a temper you wouldn't want to tangle with, especially if it had to do with protecting his family. He ran his home and family with old fashioned thinking, where the husband was the man of the house and he set the rules. He was a jokester, a ball breaker, the life of every gathering and by all accounts, he was a character through and through.

My father, a true entrepreneur at heart, was a hardworking man who always had multiple side hustles that kept him busy. Trucking was his main gig and he worked for local companies like Carling Breweries and Inter City Cartage until eventually beginning his own small trucking company called Amodeo Cartage. His side hustles led him to some unconventional business endeavours. Raising chinchillas was just one of those oddities and though I was never told what they were raised for, I'm sure it led to an undesirable demise for them. He housed them in old wood and wire cages in the basement, which one can only assume, created a most unpleasant odour causing my mother to very quickly put an end to that particular business venture. My brother recalls going out with him the night before garbage day and scavenging for copper wire, then bringing it back to burn off the plastic and sell the copper. Selling wholesale wine was another way to make a few bucks on the side. He also managed to find time to own a gas station across from the Ontario Food Terminal, as well as a used car dealership in downtown Toronto. He even began selling motor oil out of the garage, something with which my brother always enjoyed helping. After his death, my mother carried on the oil business for years and was the only female selling agent the oil company had. Before his death, he was also successful at purchasing the triplex close to my home. He would be furious to know that it was swindled out from under my mother by the dubious likes of a crooked lawyer. There didn't seem to be anything he was afraid to try in order to make a little money; it was always to better the life of his family.

  Our father was as unconventional in his parenting as he was with his money-making. He was a true outdoorsman and would often go deer and moose hunting with his father and father-in-law, bringing my brother along any chance he could. At eight years old, Anthony joined him bear hunting, which I'm sure, was both exhilarating and terrifying for a young boy. They hunted during the day and slept on the floor of the front seat of the car at night. This was no ordinary childhood experience to say the least. When they were fortunate enough to come within range of a bear, my father managed to take the shot! My brother was in awe and so proud of his dad. Once again, true to his unconventional form, he strapped the animal to the roof of the car and drove the four and a half hours back home from Sudbury. After arriving, they unloaded the days catch into the garage to await the taxidermist. Anthony, being young and extremely proud, was quick to call his neighbourhood buddies to come and see the bear hanging in the garage. The boys didn't even give it a second thought to consider if he was telling the truth or not, because they knew with my father, anything was possible.

    Our father never hesitated to volunteer for school trips. He enjoyed taking the kids to the police station, firehouse and local newspaper. He even volunteered to take twenty-five kids on his own to go fishing. Anthony recounted the story of a young boy (who was unknown to them) who fell into Lake Ontario and it was our father that didn't think twice and jumped in the water to save him from drowning.

    Firearms were a big part of my father's life, never for violence, but for his adored hobby of hunting, which he enjoyed sharing with my brother. After purchasing a new gun, he decided to give Anthony his first lesson on firearms which did not involve a shooting range. As horrifying as it is to retell, they went to the basement with a mattress and two phone books in hand. Clearly, this was not going to be any regular Saturday afternoon playtime and quite frankly, it never was. After setting up the mattress against the wall and placing the phone books in front, Anthony took his first shot. BANG! Within seconds, my mother was flying down the stairs screaming, "Vince what the Hell are you doing now?" A phrase I am sure she said over, and over again. Though exciting for a child, I can only imagine what all these antics did to the nerves of my mother who waited in angst for what was next to come on any given day.

When it came time to teaching Anthony how to swim, our father cut to the chase and tossed him into the water. In my father's eyes, pony rides were also a good test of a young man's courage. He would pick the pony with the most fire, Anthony would climb up, and when no one was watching, our father gave the horse a good slap on the ass. My brother held on for dear life as the pony took off at what seemed to him to be light speed! Unkind by today's standards for sure but, back then, it was considered providing your kid with a thick skin for life.

My only memory of my father is of him taking the family to Pinecrest Speedway to see the smash up derby and powder puff car races. It was an Amodeo family tradition. Though my memory is vague, I can picture myself sitting upon my mother's lap, watching the cars smash together and hearing them race around the track.

When my brother tells stories of his childhood, you can hear the pure joy he felt back then. Anthony would be the first to tell you that he had the best childhood ever, one that little boy's dreams were made of. In comparison to my memory and thoughts of my own childhood, you would think that we grew up in two different families. In a sense, we did. His childhood was fun, adventurous and full of great memories. Mine was riddled with anxiety and fear in every single moment.

For many years, every Sunday in the summertime I went with my grandmother to visit my father's grave, as well as our other departed relatives. Mr. Nortime would drive us to the cemetery and he and I would water the flowers and pull the weeds. Each time I would look at the headstone and gaze at his picture, hoping to feel or remember something about him. Sadly, nothing ever came to my mind.

JoJo Marie Schillaci

Chapter Seven

In April 1950, my aunt Maria Badali was born. My grandmother always said that from the time she was born, Maria had fire inside her, she was different. Twelve years separated Maria and her eldest sister Antoinette (my mom). By the time Maria was born, Grandpa Joe had already begun construction on the Bloor street apartment and soon after, started the garden centre along with the Centre Island business. As a businesswoman, Grandma's hands were always full, so she passed the caring of Maria down to my mother. The baby would sleep in her big sister's room and along with my mom's daily chores and schoolwork, it was also her job to feed the baby during the night. Mom wouldn't have had it any other way. She adored the baby and cared for Maria as if she were her own.

  Maria was a particularly beautiful baby. She had a round face with big rosie cheeks and angel soft black hair, but it was her eyes that attracted you. Auntie Rea had the most spectacular pitch black eyes. You couldn't see the pupils for the darkness encircling them; like shining onyx gemstones that sparkled as the light hit them just right. I don't know if it was their physical beauty, or her soul that poured through that was so captivating. Either way, it was undeniable. Maria began walking when she was just seven months old and never stopped since taking that first step.

She was constantly on the go and seemed to have endless amounts of energy.

She was fiercely devoted to her family and was the glue that held everyone together. Maria was a social butterfly who organized every gathering and was passionate about everything she did. If my aunt liked you, she loved you. If she didn't, she let you know.

You couldn't help but want to be in Maria's company. She had a zest for life and her energy was contagious. What was truly remarkable about Auntie Rea, amongst a plethora of other things, was her amazing ability to appreciate absolutely everything in life. So many of us have to go through tremendous adversity and lose so much before we begin to appreciate the little things that are the real blessings in life. Not Maria. My aunt could be mid-sentence and if she saw a bird at her birdbath or, perhaps, a squirrel that had come to seek a treat, everything stopped and was admired in the moment. She took nothing and no one for granted. Not people. Not nature. Not wellness. She lived every day like it was her last, being kind, making people laugh and enjoying absolutely all that life had to offer.

Like her father, she knew not to take life too seriously. It was meant to be savoured and she enjoyed every day to the fullest. When she was around, there was never a dull moment and food fights were a common theme at most family gatherings. Sometimes it was eggs being tossed across the kitchen over Nonna's head to my screaming mother on the other side or, full-on cakes in the face! You just never knew what hijinx she would be up to.

Dressing up for Halloween and being the life of every party were her norm.

She was a master entertainer who loved to cook gourmet dinners for family and friends. They were never complete until she served one of her infamous booze-laced desserts; not even Jello could escape her bottle of rum!

Auntie Rea, Halloween, 1989.

Auntie Rea never called me by my given name unless she was in a stern mood because of something I had either said or done. Otherwise, it was always Sho Sho. I was blessed to spend much of my childhood with my aunt and she often picked me up from the garden centre to spend the day at her apartment in my grandmother's building. I loved those days when it was just her and I, and I would help her clean. Not because she demanded that I help, but because my aunt always made it fun. Like my mother when she was a child, it was my job to polish her kitchen floor but, unlike mom's task of drudgery, I adored doing it. Auntie Rea had a nifty electric polisher that was so powerful it pulled me in every direction like a tiny carnival ride. I loved how it banged into the walls like a mini bumper car. Little things amused my young mind.

Auntie Rea posing in a traditional "carretto siciliano" during a trip to Siciliy, 1975.

I remember helping her do laundry in the basement of the building, using the old wringer washer. It was a novelty to feed the clothes through the rollers and watch them come out the other side flat like a pancake. My aunt was fastidious about cleaning and I can still picture her ironing everything, from underwear to kitchen towels. When it came to folding sheets, sweet Lord, that was an art form unto itself. When the weather allowed, she brought her laundry to the garden centre and would hang it on the Nortime's clothesline that ran the length of their yard. Every fitted sheet was folded like a Christmas gift with perfect crisp corners, a feat I have not yet, at fifty-one, been able to replicate. Each time I attempt to fold a fitted sheet, I'm sure she is looking down and shaking her head in disappointment, but smiling at the fact that at least I'm still trying.

She was as meticulous about her appearance as she was about her surroundings. She was always beautifully dressed and though she looked sexy, Maria always respected herself. My aunt never wore clothing that would make her look anything less than the classy lady she was. Auntie Rea was petite and often wore her beautiful hair in a tussle on top of her head and her pillowcases were always made of satin so as to not mess or crumple her hair. Maria always slept on her back to avoid getting wrinkles but, sadly, she would never be given the time to get any. When away together, we always shared a bed and I would stare at her in awe as she slept, always looking so beautiful and graceful even in slumber. She would lay with her arms above her head cascading over each other, as if posed for a photoshoot. That was Maria, a natural beauty in form and spirit, carrying herself with nothing but class.

JoJo Marie Schillaci

Auntie Rea on her wedding day February 14, 1968.

Maria was fifteen when her father passed away. She was incredibly close to him and took the loss hard. From what I was told, she was never quite the same after. Auntie Rea took on a little bit of a wilder side and perhaps, some would say, a preoccupation with boys, a stark comparison to the teen years of her older siblings. On February 14, 1968, she married at the age of eighteen. Everyone had their concerns but, just like all the other women in my family, once they made up their minds, there was no changing it. My mother was five months pregnant with me at the time of their wedding and the only picture in existence of my parents and I was taken on that day. Even though you can't see me, I know I'm there.

The marriage, as predicted by so many, was short-lived. He was an officer with the Toronto Police force, and he abused her both verbally and emotionally. Though he tried to physically, she was far too quick on her feet and always a few steps ahead of him.

There was never a shortage of men surrounding Maria but, in reality, I think men found her intimidating. She never meant to be, I think men and women alike found her to be larger than life. When I was eight, Maria began dating an older man that she had met through friends, but I was never crazy about him. It just didn't seem like a natural match, though I believe he enjoyed having her on his arm immensely. I think she looked to him as a stable, secure male, perhaps a father figure to take the place vacated at such an impressionable time. He was kind enough, pleasant enough and just enough for her to settle down with. In my eyes, it was more like settling than settling down.

Regardless, they remained together for more than fifteen years until her death.

Together, Auntie Rea and my grandmother ran one of the fruit stands at the CNE and on the days that I was fortunate enough to go along with my mom, I stayed with them. Their stand was situated in a much quieter area of the fair than my mother's midway concession. My aunt made a bed for me out of foam and placed it under the centre fruit display, which was encircled with a decorative curtain. The foam would be placed on top of a bed of watermelons and this is where I would nap or have my quiet time each day. Even though I was just a wee one, I was still given little jobs to do like sweeping, mopping, and stacking fruit for display. It was here with my aunt that I was instilled with the most disciplined work ethic. Never lean against the display! Never stand with your hands in your pockets! And never, ever say that there's nothing to do!

Auntie Rea was a Godsend after my father's passing. Since she never had children of her own, she looked to my siblings and I as an extension of herself. She was a staple in our home and loved giving haircuts, dressing us for Halloween and helping with birthday parties. Maria made everything better but, make no mistake, if you crossed her or a family member in any way, you would feel Maria's wrath. She had a temper that sometimes reared its ugly head and you didn't want to be in her line of fire.

It was 1989 when I began working an office job at Yonge and Eglinton in uptown Toronto. It was during this time, my Aunt and I traveled the subway together each day. On one of our morning rides, Auntie Rea told me of a small bump she felt on her lower abdomen. We both surmised it was probably a cyst as she'd had them before. Unfortunately, this did not turn out to be the case when a biopsy determined she had uterine cancer and was immediately booked for surgery. After the operation, she then had a run of radiation that put the cancer in remission, allowing us all to breathe a heavy sigh of relief for a little while. It returned with a vengeance and sadly, spread to her lymph nodes. In 1991, without us knowing, she was given a bleak prognosis. I was to be married in June of that year and I knew nothing, nor did anyone else, except that they were keeping an eye on it. You can see from my wedding pictures she was not at all well, no longer that same captivating energy or possessing the exuberant joy for which she was known; instead Maria looked preoccupied. Little did any of us know what she was truly facing and facing alone. Maria never wanted anyone to worry and above all else, did not want my grandmother to know. Like her big sister, she was selfless to a fault.

By May 1992, it was obvious that she was in a battle for her life. She confided in a select few of us and refused outside company from that point on. She was getting extremely frail and losing weight quickly. My mother and her best childhood friend would be her primary care team, and I was also there every day doing all I could to support her. A daily task was to put on her support hose, which were used to treat the extreme edema that was now setting in. This was an arduous task taking more than half an hour to get them from her toes to the top of her thighs. From the waist up she looked like a starving child and from the waist down, a morbidly obese woman. I recall her look of horror as she stared at her image in the long chevel mirror in the bedroom. She looked down at me as I sat on the floor by her feet and said: "Sho Sho, never grow old." I will never forget those words, or her face in that moment.

She had begun working with a Traditional Chinese Medicine Doctor, but the help had come far too late. Her body was ravaged by the cancer and she was soon hospitalized. My mother received a call asking the family to summon a priest to come to her side as she wasn't expected to make it through the night. Mom gathered with her siblings and their mother, sitting vigil for hours as she was given the last rights and prayers were said at her bedside. Surprisingly, she began to stabilize and when my mother returned after briefly going home to rest, she was dumbfounded by what welcomed her. There was Maria sitting up in bed, hair up in its usual tussle on the top of her head, lipstick on and in the process of applying her eye makeup! My mother stood in shock beside her neatly made hospital bed and asked her what she was doing, she simply replied, "Putting on my makeup." My mother then asked if she knew what had happened the night before, and she replied, "Yes." When she was questioned further, Auntie Rea seemed a little perplexed about exactly what had transpired and said she had to work really hard to come back, and with that, she continued applying her baby blue eyeshadow.

Eventually, a tube ended up being inserted in her nose and down her throat to pump out the poison gathering in her stomach. It was at this point, that she insisted on going home. As much as my mom was never good with illness and caring for the sick, she showed up for Maria. My mother cared for her as she always had from the time Maria was born.

Her decline was agonizingly slow, but never once did she complain or feel sorry for herself. Maria's concern was for the people she was leaving behind; always wanting to spare them the pain. Even in dying, she remained graceful. Auntie Rea fought hard to stay on this earth, never conceding to the enemy of death. When she finally slipped into her forever sleep, it was unfathomable. It just couldn't be. She couldn't be gone. Not our Maria.

My aunt's funeral was as surreal as her passing. Hers was the very first funeral I had ever attended as it was always thought better to spare children the reality of life and shelter them from the inevitability of death. The cavalcade of vehicles was more than a hundred cars long and the visitation saw literally hundreds and hundreds of people pass through the doors. Floral arrangements were stacked on bleachers at least four high from wall to wall, eventually overflowing to the hallways. They gave off the most overpowering scent that made you dizzy and even a bit nauseated.

The church was packed with an overflowing crowd of mourners, whose lives were somehow touched by our Maria. I will never forget sitting in the church pew next to her steel blue casket with its' floral spray of orchids draped down the sides. It didn't feel real. Everything seemed to be in slow motion. As the mass was said, it was reminiscent of that somber day when I sat on her lap during my father's wake, that indistinct sound as if people were speaking through tubes of Christmas wrap. I couldn't tell you one word the priest said, it was just indistinguishable noise. My emotions made it impossible to focus or listen. The feeling of loss was immeasurable. Everything felt empty. I was empty.

As the priest made his way down from the alter, he encircled the casket with the brass thurible held high as he swung it by its heavy metal chain. The smoke billowed out of its opening at a choking rate and the smell of frankincense saturated the room with an overpowering smell of sadness. To this day, its scent brings me back to that moment in time.

The graveside was like something out of a Hollywood starlet's funeral. People gathered in droves to say a final farewell and cars were jammed in double rows throughout the cemetery and down the street. I can still hear my grandmother's shrieks of grief as she made her way to the grave, screaming over and over, telling her Joe that the baby was coming. She repeated: "Gioia Mia, Gioia Mia." My Joy, my joy, with screams of disbelief in between. Hearing and witnessing my grandmother in such pain ripped through the hearts of all who were there as we watched Maria carefully lowered into the ground to rest next to her father.

The passing of my Auntie Rea had an immediate impact on our family and left a massive void in all our lives. You could feel the glue disintegrating as each one began to pull away and we were no longer a cohesive unit. My grandmother was devastated by the loss that no parent should have to endure. None of us believed she would survive losing her baby, but she proved us wrong. Her incredible inner strength and determination allowed grandma to keep going without the two people to whom she was closest, though I'm not sure if she ever truly wanted to.

The only picture in existence of my parents and I, taken at Auntie Rea's wedding. My mother was 5 months pregnant with me.

JoJo Marie Schillaci

Chapter Eight

I was thirteen when it happened, nobody knew. I didn't dare tell a soul. I felt like it was my fault. Somehow, I must have asked for it. One of my relatives got engaged to a man in his mid-twenties and since I was close to my relative, I naturally became close to her fiancé. He was a sweet and charming guy, always paying a little more attention, listening to what you had to say, lending a helping hand and kind ear. He was a short, stocky young man who had been a high school wrestler. Teen years can be difficult and the early ones even more so. I was very tall for my age, extremely thin and I felt awkward, unattractive and was still riddled with my childhood anxiety. As with most thirteen-year-old girls, I had incredibly low self-esteem and was constantly doubting myself. Somehow, he made me feel less awkward, less unattractive, and more comfortable. To me, the attention began innocently. He would often give me a hug or reach for my hand when the three of us were out together. In my eyes, he was protecting me, keeping me safe and I liked that. Never before had I felt so protected. To me, this was a good thing, or so I thought. I never had a crush on him. I never found him particularly attractive, but I did feel a male nurturing bond; something that I had lacked my entire life. All seemed well, until it wasn't.

It wasn't long before my relative left him, and the marriage ended, and he began coming to our house more than usual. Maybe, he found comfort in being close to some of her relatives. It was then that his hugs became different. They became longer…lingering. He began spending time with both my male and female friends who all loved him as he joked around, took us for ice cream, or a movie. One day, he was teaching us some of his high school wrestling moves and it was during one of his demonstrations that he first took advantage of me, grabbing and groping me in the most inconspicuous ways so no one else could see or question his actions. I was stunned and in shock. He then decided we should watch a movie together, an innocent act that would quickly uncover his true motives. He complained it was cold, reached for a blanket and within minutes it was done. He had molested me. I felt sick to my stomach. I was an innocent thirteen-year-old girl that had yet to experience her first kiss. I immediately blamed myself and felt dirty, unclean and bad. No one would believe me. Everybody loved him and thought he was a great guy. Somehow, I felt I must have done something to ask for it and now I got it. It continued for more than a year, each time he would visit the nausea would hit, the shaking and the "I don't feel good" feeling would return. I would be in my room and hear his voice out in the kitchen and it felt like all the blood was draining out from me. Each and every time, he found a way to deepen the wound that sliced me to my core. If I resisted and stood up for myself, I was afraid he would tell, and I would be horrified. I would take it each time, feeling like another part of me was dying. My daily anxiety grew exponentially, and I had even less ability to concentrate on my schoolwork. When the teachers asked me what was wrong, I chalked it up to not understanding the work, headaches or not feeling well. No one ever delved deeper and I wasn't prepared to give up the dirty secret. Thankfully, and I'm not sure why, the visits finally came to an end. They became more and more infrequent until finally stopping altogether and I couldn't have been more relieved. Many years later as an adult I would come to realize that I had done nothing wrong. Despite this realization, I carried shame throughout my life. He knew me well and preyed on my insecurities and vulnerabilities. He was the adult. I was the child. He was the wolf. I was the lamb.

*****

In grade eleven, a small group of friends and I attended career counseling sessions. After reading from the infamous book *What Color Is Your Parachute?* we were asked to fill in a long questionnaire about our likes, dislikes, strengths and weaknesses. When completed, they were entered into an offsite main frame computer and within a couple of weeks, we would have our perfect career suggestions revealed to us! It felt a little like a carnival fortune telling machine.

The results were finally in and we all gathered around a table to hear the exciting news. Each of us were handed an envelope containing our career prospects. I quickly opened mine and instantly wanted to die. There had to be a mistake! It had to be a joke! Was I on Candid Camera? Where was Allan Funt? Each person was required to stand up and share their results with the group. The first person stood up and proudly said: "accountant", followed by a dental hygienist and a librarian and so on until it became my turn. I'd rather have walked the cafeteria catwalk naked as a jay bird singing O'Canada, than share what was on that piece of paper. I was overcome with anxiety and sweating profusely. I took a deep breath and with a shaky voice I said it… "CLOWN!" The great and all-powerful computer had determined that what I was best suited to be, of all things possible in this life, was a clown. Maybe I filled in a few circles wrong, maybe the computer read it wrong, maybe the names got mixed up. This couldn't be what I was really destined for. Everyone broke out laughing. How could they not? They tried to reassure me that it was a good thing because I always made people smile and laugh, but their kind intentions didn't help. I felt like I was a joke, my life was a joke and now my future was a joke. I didn't dare tell my family, I couldn't bare the humiliation and I absolutely could not tell my Uncle Joey. Not because he would judge me, but because of the pressure I was putting on myself. I wanted to make him proud but, yet again, here I was not feeling good enough and that I was coming up short again.

My high school years were not ones that I look back on with the same fondness as most. I was still riddled with anxiety about every little thing and I was constantly worried about my mom and my ongoing concern about finances. Ron had recently passed away and the comfort of his family was no longer part of our life. I missed them more than I ever let on. There was a comfort in being with them, in being accepted for who I was.

I struggled with schoolwork constantly. Just as in elementary school, my mind was never wholly present during class; always wandering to the land of what-ifs and what might be going wrong next. This put me in a vicious cycle, worrying about life and the schoolwork I either didn't understand or never completed due to the stress and anxiety I was feeling. My stomach was constantly churning and nauseated and headaches were the daily norm. Looking back, I can easily see why I couldn't grasp the days lessons. My mind was in overdrive, filled with catastrophic thoughts, and it didn't have room for anything else. I was always too scared to ask for help, always feeling like I was going to be judged and misunderstood as lazy or stupid. I desperately wanted to learn, but I had absolutely zero focus. At the time, I didn't see it this way. At the time, I just thought I wasn't smart enough and not good enough. That was pretty much my ongoing opinion of myself for my entire high school career.

I was friends with every clique in school, but never really felt like I fit in anywhere, never feeling like I truly belonged. I wasn't smart enough to fit in with the academic group. I wasn't sporty or skilled enough to fit in with the athletic group. I wasn't pretty enough, or popular enough to fit in with the cool group. I always felt like I was on the outside looking in. It wasn't that I necessarily wanted to fit in, I just didn't. I felt different from everyone else, not better by any means, just different. Despite being the proverbial black sheep, I was well-liked, friends with everyone and had my fair share of boys admiring me, even a few boyfriends.

One boyfriend in particular was very special. His name was Gus and he was two years older and in his senior year. He was tall, very cute and had a great sense of humour. After being introduced, we immediately clicked, and the young romance blossomed. I don't know where I found the confidence for that relationship, it just somehow showed up. Those months I spent with him were the happiest I could remember. My anxiety seemed to have diminished and I wasn't constantly thinking the stressful catastrophic thoughts, something pleasant had taken its place. His parents lived in Uruguay, South America and had gifted us a trip to visit them at the end of the school year. It was a once in a lifetime opportunity, but the farthest I had been on a plane was to Florida to visit my grandmother and I had never been away without my mom. To this day, I still have no idea how I got the nerve to go. The only thing I can surmise, is that I felt a deep trust with him. I knew he could take care of anything that came up and I knew he would take care of me. He made me feel safe. I also don't have a clue how we ever convinced my mother to let me go. She never liked it when I went downtown, never mind the other side of the equator with a boy and a twenty-three hour flight! I was two weeks short of my seventeenth birthday and there I was, flying over the Andes Mountains! What was I thinking? But I did it and was never once homesick. I took in and experienced all that was offered to me and I loved every minute of it.

His family treated me with kindness and immediately put me at ease. Uruguay would prove to be an experience of a lifetime and one that I would never forget. His mother made me feel very comfortable and by Uruguayan standards, they lived like royalty. Unfortunately, that is not the case for the vast majority. I had never witnessed such extreme poverty in my life. It resembled the pictures I had only seen on television of children in third world countries living on the street. I distinctly recall driving down a busy street in town and seeing a little boy who couldn't be more than five years old. A small, skinny boy with shoulder length black hair that was dirty and matted to his head. He was begging at the side of the road and was covered in filthy rags he wore as clothing. When he wasn't begging from people, he was huffing what we presumed to be, glue from a paper bag. The profound sadness and despair on his face would never leave me. We took a scenic drive into the countryside to the family farm for an afternoon of food and celebration with friends. Driving along the country roads, I remember palm trees lining either side like the entrance to a magical forest. The colourful landscape was captivating but, looking back, what is most vivid in my memory of that day is an image far less magical and more tragic. The city's garbage was hauled off to the outskirts where it was piled high like mountains. From afar, it looked like a quaint village high above the landscape but, as you drove closer, the sad reality came into focus. Scattered amongst the mountains of garbage were tin shacks no bigger than large outhouses. This is where entire families would dwell and live off the heaps of rubbish and festering rotting trash. There were so many children running and playing in the filth that it gave a feeling of disbelief and dismay. Another image forever etched in my mind.

I spent my seventeenth birthday in the air, flying back home from Uruguay. I was quite literally on cloud nine. It was the most incredible adventure I had ever been on and certainly not one that I would ever forget. Upon arriving back home I received the tragic news that a dear high school friend had perished in the Air India bombing. On June 23, 1985, Air India flight 182 was traveling from Toronto to Delhi through Montreal and London. During the flight over the Atlantic Ocean, the plane was taken down by a terrorist bomb. It killed all 329 people onboard, including my dear friend Anita, her younger brother and mother. It is the largest mass killing in Canadian history, the deadliest aviation accident in the history of Air India and was the deadliest act of aviation terrorism until 911. Their bodies were never recovered. I was in shock. Anita was the kindest, most gentle soul you could ever be blessed enough to meet. Always a sweet smile and never an unkind word. She not only appreciated life, but she added to all of ours purely by her existence in it. She was an incredibly intelligent and disciplined young girl, who was most certainly destined for success, and now she was gone. After the shock wore off, it wasn't long before my thoughts turned inward. I began thinking of what could have happened to me on my trip that took me so far from home, and it was in that moment that my paralyzing fear of flying began.

During that same summer, I had an accident while riding my bike. The cable of my ten-speed broke off, became entangled in the front wheel and I came to a screeching halt, but not before my jaw smashed down with force onto the handlebars and propelled me ass over tea kettle. I lay on the road with blood seemingly coming from everywhere but, in reality, it was my mouth and chin that took the brunt of it. Upon impact, my teeth bit down off centre, causing several of them to break. As I moved my tongue along the top and bottom of my mouth to give a quick inspection of the damage, I could feel the sharp edges. I could also feel a huge gash under my chin. I ended up at the hospital getting stitches and then to the dentist for extractions and root canal appointments that lasted months before being completed. As a result of all the damage and pre-existing issues, I now needed braces. Not good news for my mother, a single mom without dental coverage. I worked two jobs to help make the monthly dental payments and this played right into my financial worries.

In August of that year, the young romance ended. He was scheduled to go out of town to university in the fall and our paths were no longer aligned. It was my first heart break.

Back at school in September, there was never a shortage of smiles and hugs to be had and given when walking down the hallways. But, regardless of how I was on the outside, I always felt lost. I was incredibly self-conscious about my appearance, struggling for years with acne and was constantly on prescription medication (tetracycline) in an attempt to control it. It never helped, but they kept prescribing it and I kept taking it for reasons that to this day, I can't explain. I tried every prescription drug on the market, as well as everything from natural supplements to creams. I even saw a dermatologist whose answer was to dig into each lesion with a scalpel and remove the root. Not to worry, he was kind enough to give you a tennis ball to squeeze through the pain. As luck would have it, he was certifiably deaf and he couldn't hear the screams of anguish from his patients that he slowly marred over time, both physically and emotionally. Though I'm sure his intentions were good, the end result was not, and the procedure would leave scars forever.

I tended to spend more time with the teachers than I did in the cafeteria with students my age. The cafeteria was its own trauma-inducing shit storm for me. You had the cool party group, the jocks, the athletic group, the awkward group, the brainiacs, the goth, headbangers and druggies etc. It was a true-to-life Breakfast Club. Walking in there was like walking a catwalk that ended at a feline slaughterhouse. All eyes would turn as the doors opened; sometimes there were catcalls, but mostly just uncomfortable stares. Perhaps, it was all in my imagination. Maybe I made it out worse in my mind then it was in reality, but I know what I felt and it was sheer dread.

Me at High Park, Toronto, 1985.

I wasn't the type to go to parties. I never drank, I never smoked and would never, ever have tried a drug. I was unshakable and never succumbed to peer pressure. My nicknames throughout high school were Holly Hobbie (after a 1970's pioneer doll) and Mom. Both were pretty much reflective of my personality: a protective mother hen who constantly worried about everyone and everything and a shy, simple old-fashioned girl, who was more comfortable talking to butterflies than people. Everyone knew where I stood and what I stood for. They also knew that pressuring me was futile. I was solid and would never cave under pressure of any kind. True to the women in my family, once I had something in my head there was no changing it. I think people respected me for it. Nonetheless, I was still feeling like a square peg in a round hole. I did go to a few parties, but never understood the enjoyment behind getting drunk and throwing up. You would find the same scenario at school dances. That's one thing I never missed was a school dance. I never felt like I needed alcohol or drugs to have a good time; just put on some good tunes and away I went into my very own self-induced high. Years later, I reconnected with a schoolmate who has struggled his entire life with alcohol. When he asked me how I went through high school without ever trying a sip of alcohol or drugs of any sort, my answer was simple: "I was afraid of everything." When I asked why he succumbed to his vices, his response was equally simple. He was afraid of nothing. This was the one time fear worked in my favour.

My close friend Genifer belonged to a local church youth group and brought me along to their dances and functions. This is where I felt far more comfortable and at ease with the innocence of the surroundings.

I didn't have a lot of free time as a teenager, always working at least two jobs at any given time. I was always working at the garden centre in the spring and summer, as well as odd jobs like cashier at the local grocery store, babysitting etc. By far, the best job of all, was the annual three week family gig at the Canadian National Exhibition (CNE). It was there when I was just fifteen, I met the man I would marry seven years later. He was Italian, good looking with the physique of a bodybuilder. He was kind and always polite, coming to say hello and buy his daily dose of strawberry ice cream. The young people that worked the CNE were generally people you saw over, and over again, year after year. We all looked forward to seeing each other. It wasn't like now with Snapchat, Instagram and Facebook, where you can keep in touch and find each other in an instant. Back then, you exchanged phone numbers and maybe, you would connect once throughout the year. One day, when shopping at the local mall close to home, I bumped into him working in a popular record store. We were surprised to see each other considering I lived in the suburbs and he resided in the heart of downtown. We often met at the food court to catch up, share a laugh and give a hug. In June 1986, we decided to go to the movies to celebrate our birthdays, which were just two weeks apart. Though I don't recall the movie, I certainly remember when he put his hand on my knee. I melted, that is, after the shock wore off. "Was he really interested in me? He couldn't be." My immediate thought in the moment was: "I'm not good enough for him." After a romantic kiss good night, I got in my car and to this day, I have no clue how I drove back home. All I remember thinking over and over again was: "what just happened?" We continued to see each other more and more often. There was chemistry between us, we enjoyed each other and always had a great time when we were together. Despite all that was positive in front of me, I could not get over constantly feeling "I'm not good enough."

JoJo Marie Schillaci

Chapter Nine

After high school, I was accepted into college. My Uncle Joey was pleased to hear the news and kept reiterating the importance of being self-sufficient and continuing my education. I enrolled in the business administration course but, after the first day, I was completely overwhelmed; I was ill-prepared for college studies. I had managed to pull through high school, but this was a totally different animal. Personal computers were coming into mainstream studies and I was lost, not to mention my ongoing struggles with mathematics. I didn't want to tell my family and most certainly not Uncle Joey, although ironically, he would have been the one person that could have helped me the most. I was far too embarrassed and already feeling like a failure, again "not good enough." The anxiety grew more each day and my stress was beginning to be unmanageable. Since the bicycle injury, I began suffering from extremely debilitating headaches which compounded everything. I attempted to get help from student services, but to no avail. It seemed to be a lot of surface talk and shuffling from counselor to counselor without solid assistance in any way. The more stress and anxiety that built up, the more behind I was becoming in my studies. Finally, after numerous appointments with the guidance team, they believed I had a learning disability called dyslexia. This was a hot new buzz word in the 80's and though it gave me comfort that there was a reason for my struggle, I was never provided a clear solution. I painfully and shamefully decided to leave college to enter the workforce full time. Deep down, I knew I was making a big mistake because it went against everything Uncle Joey had instilled in me about the importance of education and being self-sufficient. Be that as it may, I felt that I had no choice. I didn't feel smart enough, or good enough and absolutely, I felt in my heart that I would be a big disappointment to my uncle.

Fortunately, during high school, a teacher approached me and suggested I enroll in a co-operative education program and I was soon placed at General Electric Canada. It was a phenomenal company that provided both real work experience and incredible people to mentor me. They were thrilled with my work and I was equally thrilled to be a part of such an amazing organization. They treated me extremely well and I never once felt anxious or nervous. My boss was the Vice President of Sales and when my term was up, he gave me a stellar letter of recommendation. After leaving college, his recommendation helped me land the position of Canadian Coordinator for Arby's Canada. I was the liaison between franchisees for both the American and Canadian headquarters. I excelled in the position and my superiors were suitably impressed. I loved problem-solving and supporting the franchisees, along with learning about national marketing and purchasing.

Our US parent company made a major staff reorganization and I decided it wasn't in my best interest to stay; a decision I would immediately regret. I worked at different companies in various positions, but never quite found my groove. Unfortunately, I never felt passionate about any of these positions. I definitely did not inherit my mom's natural secretarial skills, but I managed to muddle my way through. Eventually, a major North American oil company hired me as an administrative assistant to the President of Sales and his three District Managers. I should never have gotten that job and was in way over my head. I always gave one hundred percent, but my lack of typing speed put me behind each and every day. I went into the office at 6 am, hours before anyone else arrived to catch up on my work and get ahead before another day began. My nerves were shot as my anxiety was maxing out, the headaches were worsening, and I was continually nauseous. The oil industry in the 80's was a misogynistic man's world, where secretaries were objectified and deemed subservient. When it came time for performance reviews, in order to obtain a raise each year, it was quite clear that you had to conform to what the men were looking for and it had very little to do with secretarial skills and everything to do with physical attributes and attitude. One day, I was called into a salesman's office to have what he called "a chat." He was a short, small-framed man who lacked any sort of class and was the furthest thing from a gentleman. I sat nervously across the desk as he said in a most serious tone, "Why are you dressing like that?" I was puzzled and didn't understand what he was referring to as he gestured up and down at my blazer, blouse, pants and heels with disapproval. I always dressed very professionally; there was nothing sexy about the way I dressed for work, I dressed for the job and the job alone. A co-worker of mine knew how to play the game and she played it well. As a result, she received the maximum increase every year for her "performance." Though she had good secretarial skills, we all knew those weren't the ones being reviewed. It was nauseating to watch. Her daily routine included sitting on desks and leaning over to tease the hungry hounds with her voluptuous curves. The sexual innuendos and off-colour jokes that she not only tolerated but played along with, were vile and degrading to women. On Secretary's Day, while she was being taken out to the finest restaurant in town and given gifts and flowers, I was given a container of bug wash from the warehouse. You read that right...bug wash! As a young woman of twenty, and with my self-esteem already on shaky ground, this reinforced my ongoing mantra of "I'm not good enough." I recall being asked to retrieve a file from one of their desks only to find a centerfold from Hustler magazine. Should any of this happen in today's world, they would have been called out in the #Metoo movement. Unfortunately, in the 80's it would have been my word against four senior sitting men as well as a team of corporate lawyers. I decided to instill my grandmother's philosophy: "Put up and shut up."

Each day, the stress increased and the thought of going to work literally made me feel sick to my stomach as my nerves felt like frayed wires ready to short out. I never knew what degrading, abusive behaviour I was going to have to endure when I entered the office. I didn't know it at the time, but I was beginning to suffer from panic attacks. I experienced my first while touring the historic site of Casa Loma with my future fiancé. Casa Loma is a beautiful, gothic, revival style castle built in 1911 in midtown Toronto. We had decided to take the long, steep and very narrow climb up a winding iron staircase which brought us to one of the many turrets on top of the castle. It was an extremely busy day and the staircase was crowded with people. I felt myself getting warmer as I climbed the circular trail, stair by stair with people in front and behind me. I was sweating profusely as a surge of fear and panic began setting in. My hands were shaking, and my body felt weak. At the same time, I felt like I could move a cement wall with one blow if I had to, in order to get out. I needed to get out. NOW! MOVE! I kept pleading as I pushed my way down the steps and over anyone that was in my path. With tears pouring down my face, I stumbled past them like a bull in a china shop, stepping on feet and elbowing people out of the way. My fiancé didn't know what was happening and I didn't know myself, I didn't have an explanation. I felt the exact same thing from when I was a little girl in school, only now, it had grown exponentially. These episodes were getting more frequent and growing in intensity. "I don't feel good."

JoJo Marie Schillaci

Chapter Ten

Prior to my boyfriend (future husband) and I dating, he was dating his high school sweetheart. They were, from what I've been told, quite happy together. That is, until her parents relocated to Australia, at which time the two parted ways, for no other reason than logistics and circumstances. After approximately one year of us dating, he called me up and sounded different, beating around the bush and talking in circles. I immediately knew in my gut she was back. Even as a young girl, I could sense it. I finally mustered the courage and asked him: "Is she back?" The response was a quiet, almost hushed "yes." My heart sank over a thousand feet until it hit bottom. I took a deep breath and can remember my words as if I spoke them yesterday and not decades ago,"You know what I'm all about, I'm not going to fight anyone for you." He told me that he understood and was going to meet her for lunch the next day and would give me a call right after. It felt like an eternity, but he would eventually show up at my door. Nothing needed to be said, he made his decision. I was happy although I was never told what he based his decision on. It was from that moment on, until our last moments together more than 25 years later, that in my mind, there would always be three people in our relationship. I lived with her ghost-like image every day, not feeling good enough and always wondering if he had doubts about his decision.

* * * * *

On Christmas Eve 1989, after three years of dating, my boyfriend asked me to marry him and everyone was very happy for us.

* * * * *

On May 13, 1990, I agreed to take part in a co-ed volleyball tournament with my fiancé's company. It was early into the tournament when I set up a return and a teammate tripped over my extended leg. He was a gentle giant but built like a linebacker weighing in at over 240 pounds. SNAP! Both my tibia and fibula had broken. Instinctively, I grabbed hold of my leg with both hands to keep it together. I remember looking at my fiancé and saying, "something's wrong" as I melted into the gymnasium floor.

I was taken by ambulance to the nearest hospital and was told I required surgery. One bone could be reset, but the other was going to be tricky. They insisted I couldn't possibly endure the pain of resetting it, but I quickly responded to their doubts with: "I can do it. I can take the pain." My fiancé reassured them that I could, and they reluctantly began the process of dangling my leg off the gurney, jamming it up and then yanking it down. I would best describe this process as barbaric, as I could feel the bones grinding with each thrust. It was a violent and stomach-turning pain. Through screams of anguish, I persevered without ever asking them to stop. The doctors, though amazed by my courage and pain tolerance, were disappointed with the results. Apparently, a tendon had gotten wrapped around the bone and despite their efforts and my bravery, operating was inevitable. I was prepped for surgery and laid on a gurney alone in the hallway, waiting to be brought into the operating room. I was in excruciating pain, unable to move the slightest without causing the bones to grind together. It was then that I felt it begin, that feeling of anxiety which was building to a mounting crescendo inside of me. Here it comes! An incredible wave of panic was starting to come over me and I couldn't escape and even worse, I couldn't run away from this one! It built like a storm within me, as each nerve ending vibrated and every part of my body began sweating profusely. The trembling started with my feet and escalated through my body until it reached every cell in my brain. I had constant looming thoughts of, "I'm going to die! I have to get out!" I began to scream for help, but it fell on both deaf and hardened ears. I felt a flashback to the school secretary looking over her glasses and never coming in to check on me as I laid shaking in the sick room. The more intensely I shook, the more my leg moved increasing the pain. The episode was reaching critical mass and as it hit the tipping point, it felt like enormous brass symbols being clashed together over my entire being and then just as suddenly, it was done. The feeling of life or death is all you can comprehend in the moment of an attack and in my mind, I had barely come out of this one alive.

JoJo Marie Schillaci

Chapter Eleven

While my fiancé and I believed we had a good relationship, it was constantly challenged by stress, brought on by other family members. In the year that followed, the stress was mounting, and the panic attacks were happening more frequently and stressful situations became increasingly difficult. The ongoing family stress had not improved but worsened with the planning of the upcoming wedding. On January 21, 1991, I scheduled my weekly shiatsu treatment which was recommended to help combat the anxiety and headaches that were increasing in frequency. It was during this treatment that I had a massive panic attack. I felt the increasing uneasiness and my heart began pounding as if it were going to come through my chest! When my therapist asked what was wrong, my proverbial "I don't feel good" was all I could manage. It escalated so fast and with such intensity that barely clothed, I leaped from the massage table, ran out of the room and down the hall with no clear destination. I had to get out and save myself from the impending doom that was biting at my heels. My therapist was a kind and gentle soul, who came to my side as I lay in a shaking heap at the end of the long hallway. Holding my hand and with his arms around me, he reassured me that I was safe, all was good, I was not alone. What made this episode different, was that someone was there for me and I wasn't left to battle it by myself. He arranged a drive home for me and when I arrived my mother asked: "What is wrong?" I simply answered, "I don't feel good." It was a mantra that had come to fall upon deaf ears. People had heard it my entire life and it had simply become white noise.

From that day onward, I could not be left alone. I was terrified of another attack and not having anyone to help get me through to the other side. The very next day, my mother took me to our family doctor who immediately prescribed Ativan. It is used to treat anxiety and belongs to a class of drugs known as benzodiazepines. They act on the brain and nerves (central nervous system) to produce a calming effect. They are highly addictive, but also highly effective. As well as putting me on meds, he referred me to the top psychiatrist working in Mississauga at that time. Disappointingly, my first appointment wouldn't be until February 14th (more than three weeks away), which seemed like a lifetime. It was exactly 128 days until the wedding and I was feeling the stress to get well and to get well fast. The pressure I was putting on myself was already bad enough but, add to it, the insensitive comments of a few telling me "I better not be garbage for the wedding", added more weight to an almost unbearable load.

My fiancé and I loved each other, but there were many issues around family boundaries that were not getting resolved. This caused the dynamic between us to be strained and was becoming more difficult to manage. I never felt supported, always feeling left alone to conquer the conflict and criticisms that seemed to be around every corner. Nothing was ever "good enough." My openness and natural characteristic of wanting to please was, slowly over time, eroding into bitterness, resentfulness and frustration. I'm sure he was equally frustrated in his own way and for his own reasons. An entire book could be written on our relationship and our families alone but, to be fair, that would take two people writing it together. It would not be fair or respectful to either of us to hash out personal details here. He didn't understand me and my actions, and I didn't understand him and his. We were constantly going through treacherous peaks and valleys with incredibly great times followed by inevitable lows from the ongoing issues that were no closer to being resolved. This is my journey, my story, my feelings and my interpretation of my life.

As I waited for my first appointment with the psychiatrist, the stress became more unmanageable. I was now experiencing trouble swallowing food and each time I took a bite, it felt like I was attempting to swallow a watermelon. It just wouldn't go down, as if I had something lodged in my esophagus. In a desperate attempt to get food into me, I resorted to jarred baby food, swallowing one small spoonful at a time; sometimes taking hours to finish the tiniest jar. The migraines were also becoming intolerable and the fatigue debilitating.

My mother was trying her best to understand and be supportive of me. Like so many years earlier, I would end up going to work with her, only this time as a grown woman and the humiliation was unbearable. Each day I arrived and wanted to hide. My thoughts would flash back to the same embarrassment I experienced as a small child behind the recliner or curtains using my pacifier. I carried such shame and wanted to hide from the world but instead, I felt like a spectacle on display for all to see and judge. And judge they did.

February 14th finally arrived, and my fiancé accompanied me to my first appointment. From the moment I met Dr. M., I instantly felt at ease. He had the most compassionate eyes and smile that made me trust that things were going to get better. Our first session lasted three hours and I recall the first thing he said when looking at my medication was, "This has to go." That alone, would have sent me into a tailspin as the pills helped minimized the panic attacks, but there was something about Dr. M. that induced a sense of safety, calm and trust. I felt supported and more importantly I felt understood like I never had before. I explained that I had to be well for the wedding that was just 107 days away and his response was, "We have a lot of work to do." I attended weekly appointments with each one lasting at least two hours. Before beginning with Dr. M, the anxiety was so bad that I could not walk to the end of the driveway by myself without it inducing paralyzing fear. I was now constantly in the state of "I don't feel good." After many hours of therapy, the unprocessed pain of my father's death came to the surface and the fear of following in my mother's footsteps of widowhood became a certainty. The fear of abandonment coupled with the inherent fear of his trucking accident began to cripple my thinking, taking over every conscious and subconscious thought. The upcoming nuptials seemed to be a natural catalyst for what I like to call "my breakthrough."

As a society, we have coined the term breakdown, but I don't believe that's accurate. Over time, I've discovered that the holding, denial and sometimes neglect of our pain slowly breaks us down. When it comes to the surface unexpectedly and unsolicited, we begin the process of healing and experience the breakthrough. I had overwhelming feelings of fear, fear of loss, of being left alone and of being a widow before I was even a bride. The lump I was feeling in my throat was indeed psychological and eventually, I would learn breathing techniques that would allow the muscles to relax. This, along with the processing of emotions, allowed me to eat normally again and I was on my way to reaching my goal.

Looking back, the planning of the wedding felt more like planning a party than the start of our new life together. It always felt like he and I, but never us. The big day came and thanks to the most gut-wrenching hard work and the most amazing doctor, I made it. I was feeling better and stronger than I ever had, but I knew there was still much work to be done. Although I was there in body, I felt like I was a million miles away. It was as if I was high above, looking down on the entire event as an observer and not feeling at all present.

A year earlier, my mother, Auntie Rea and I went to a warehouse sale for bridal dresses. We walked into what looked to be a war zone, invaded by a few hundred bridezillas foaming at the mouth. This was not going to be a task for the faint of heart and my immediate response was, "yeah, I don't think there's anything here for me. I'm good, let's go", to which my Aunt sternly replied, "Get in there and grab something, anything!" At that point, I knew there was no getting away from the chaos ahead. Maria had it in her head that this was going to happen so into the jungle I went, elbows up, head down, grabbing the first armload I could get my hands on, all the while avoiding getting clawed raw by the veil draped psychopaths. The only one that was remotely decent was a size twelve and at the time, I was a whopping size one! It would never work, but my Aunt had a different opinion as she pulled, tucked and rolled the fabric in an attempt to make me see that anything was possible. It was $250.00, a mere fraction of what the going prices were and I could see that my mother was happy at the thought of being able to purchase the dress for me. In the end, I would say yes to the dress. However, when I put it on the day of the wedding, I looked in the mirror and felt indifference. I wasn't in love with the dress or, was it that I wasn't in love…period.

Chapter Twelve

The reception was off the charts and a resounding success! Everything from the food to the venue and music were amazing, a traditional Italian affair by all accounts with an entourage of bridesmaids, a seemingly never-ending stream of food and a DJ that had the dance floor hopping all night. The entire day was wonderful, but not magical on any level for me. Looking at the photos, one can see we played our parts well but upon looking deeper, the disconnect was obvious. When I gazed into his eyes, I did not see our future, more like going through the motions of what I was, "supposed to be doing." I decided to replace the traditional father-bride dance with a mother-bride dance. Everyone who witnessed it could see the level of attachment my mother and I shared and the underlying feeling of sadness between us. My new husband would also share a dance with his mom and again, it was clear to all the undeniable emotional storm inside both of them. Looking back, these dances spoke volumes about the issues we both had going on outside of us as a couple.

To me, the wedding night felt more like a wake. I felt a piece of me had been torn away. The umbilical cord that was never really cut twenty-three years ago, had now been ripped from what felt like my solar plexus, forcing my mother and I to now live free of one another. Looking back, it's clear to me that my husband was going through his own emotional Hell being away from his family, coupled with the fact that his bride was far from amorous and more to the point, aloof.

Uncle Joey walking me down the aisle. June 22, 1991.

As a result of my intense fear of flying we decided on the historic and beautiful Quebec City as our honeymoon destination. This allowed us a little taste of Europe close to home. I was made to feel by many that this was yet again, "not good enough" and of course, that energy permeated the entire trip. Add to that my anxiety about life without mom and my husband's own emotional issues, and you have a recipe for disaster. I kept repeating to him over and over "I don't feel good, I don't feel good, I don't feel good." In turn, I could feel his less then content energy. At this point, you will recall the story of my mom coming home early from her honeymoon. Well, guess who followed in her footsteps? Yes, soon after arriving and being physically ill, I begged to be brought back home again. As my father had acquiesced to my mother, my husband eventually and reluctantly obliged me. I'm sure he wished he could drop me off on my mother's doorstep, just as I was secretly wanting to bring him back to his. I don't think we spoke more than a dozen words the entire eight-hour drive back to Toronto. My stomach was inside-out and you could see the anger, frustration and sheer exhaustion on his face. He parked the car, leaving everything in it and silently climbed the stairs to our new home. We had rented a beautiful two-bedroom corner unit in my grandmother's building on Bloor Street. He went directly to bed and I laid my head down on the sofa and within seconds I fell into a deep sleep from both the physical and emotional exhaustion.

For years I felt a tug-of-war with his mother over the man I loved, but I wanted to believe it was going to be different when we were married. A week before the wedding, my aunt shared with me her concerns regarding the glaringly obvious issue. She looked me square in the eye and said "Sho Sho, there will always be three people in your marriage. I of course, in all my youth and naiveté, told her she didn't understand, and that it was going to be different. When it came to our marriage, I felt like my husband never truly arrived. On my end, I was continually mourning my mom and was wrestling with my many fears brought forward from childhood. The battles within ourselves intensified, and naturally spilled out to each other and into our marriage from day one.

The first year of marriage was horrible. Married life was far from what I dreamed it was going to be and I continually felt "not good enough" at practically every domestic task I attempted; constantly feeling like I was being judged as inadequate. Though he never said it out loud, I felt the comparison between his mother and myself. My cooking was that of a new young bride and though I had spent years in the kitchen alongside the women in my life, I suddenly lost all confidence. I recall attempting to make my husband a romantic dinner only to end up with it being dry and over cooked. Frustrated and stressed, I heaved the entire thing at the kitchen wall, not one of my finer moments. Expectation can lead to disappointment and eventually, resentment.

As difficult as it was, I tried my best to adjust to living away from my mom and into my new married life. One day, after a Sunday dinner at my mother's house, we drove back to our apartment with my grandmother. I was unsettled when we left, and grandma knew exactly why. She wasn't going to have any part of it and quickly put me in my place and reminded me of when she left her mother back in Sicily at just sixteen. My grandmother told me the story (one I had heard many times before) of the letters she wrote to her mother. She then gave the letters to soldiers (her version of the Sicilian pony express), who would in turn deliver them, sometimes months later. The process then began of the return letter from another solider, taking many months to eventually make it back to Grandma's waiting hands. She made it clear that I was to, "Put up and shut up." I had a new life with my husband. End of story. As a couple, neither one of us were putting the family nucleus first. There was no way she was going to understand the connection of abandonment regarding my father and now, the feeling of losing my mother. Best to do as she said and just suck it up, at least when she was around.

* * * * *

Due to many circumstances, I hadn't flown in six years. Anita's death in the Air India tragedy prompted a traumatizing fear within me when it came to flying. I also had a deep mistrust of my husband's ability to calm me down while in a state of panic, never feeling comforted or supported; more like isolated and ostracized. I felt guilty more than anything else and was constantly reminded by others that I was holding my husband back.

It was 1992 and I was working as an executive assistant to the Vice President of a mining company. He was a lovely elderly gentleman who was coming up to retirement. He nicknamed me Radar in reference to the "M*A*S*H" character, as I always seemed to know what he wanted long before he asked. The position eventually required that I do some minor traveling within Canada. I was upfront with them and shared my issue with flying and that I would prefer to take the train. Instead, they decided to send me to a "fear of flying" weekend course offered by a major Canadian airline. Saturday would be in-class and Sunday would be the graduation flight. It seemed like a "crash course" to me, pun intended. I arrived that Saturday full of both hope and anxiety; wanting to believe this was going to work and trusting they would provide the tools necessary to kick this fear once and for all. Immediately upon arriving, I had the distinct feeling that this was not going to be the case. In comparison to the work I had done with Dr M., these counsellors were Mickey Mouse at best and appeared to be ill-equipped to help anyone experiencing major issues up in the sky. In order to break the cycle of our fearful thoughts they had us snap elastic bands around our wrists. In my head I was thinking, "you're kidding me, right?" I'm absolutely sure my facial expression shared the same sentiment. In my mind, there was nothing real or tangible being taught. Though I stayed committed to Saturday, on Sunday I took a hard pass going 35,000 feet in the air with this questionable crew.

I decided to go back to Dr M. whom I trusted and believed in, to help get me back on a plane. During the next year, we worked extensively with imagery and hypnosis, as well as delving deeper into self-discovery and facing the fears. It was now time for me to either shit or get off the pot! Feeling as ready as I was ever going to be, I booked a flight to Ottawa with a friend who would accompany me for the ride. We notified the flight crew that I was a fearful flyer and that this was my graduating flight. They were marvelous! I could not have asked for a more understanding and compassionate group of people. My anxiety began to grow as I walked through the jetway and approached the massive metal bird that would carry me into the sky, well beyond my fears. I walked down the aisle, found my seat and respectfully declined the window. My hands had gone from clammy to dripping wet and my entire body felt like

Jello. I began implementing the relaxation exercises taught to me by Dr. M., as I closed my eyes and reflected back to our imagery sessions, tapping into the memory of his calm and peaceful voice.

Coincidentally, our stewardess shared my mother's name of Antoinette and for some juvenile reason, this gave me familiar comfort. The engine began to roar, and the plane started to taxi down the runway. I began to feel panic, terror, exhilaration and freedom all at the same time. As we picked up speed and our wheels lifted from the ground, I knew I was at the point of no return and in that moment I realized I had already achieved my goal of flying. My nervousness presented itself as laughter with a plethora of jovial profanities that would make a trucker blush! Luckily, the other passengers found it all quite amusing, laughing along with me and sharing encouraging smiles and a friendly sea of thumbs up. As we ascended into the beautiful blue sky, I couldn't contain my joy. The fearful thoughts that had tethered me to the ground loosened enough for me to escape and soar far beyond my wildest dreams…I was flying! Did I like it? No. Regardless, I was doing it.

In an attempt to settle my nerves, I was asked if I would like to join the pilots in the cockpit. Obviously, in a post-911 world, an invitation such as this would never be extended. I reluctantly accepted. They showed me the controls and procedures, explaining much more then my scattered mind could comprehend. What little I did take in was fascinating and a brilliant distraction. The thirty-five minute flight quickly came to an end and when the wheels finally touched the runway, I claimed victory! We hastily made our way through the airport and purchased a postcard at a newspaper stand. I quickly scribbled three words, I DID IT and popped it in the mailbox to Dr. M. In no time, we were on our return flight with the same amazing crew and again I was invited into the cockpit only this time for the entire return flight. I jumped at the opportunity. The cockpit was incredibly small to the point of being cramped. I was relaxed and dare I say, almost enjoying it until we began banking over Toronto. With water on one side and sky on the other, I was quickly getting neurologically disoriented and feeling like my brain was in a blender and immediately sensed my anxiety building. I felt like I was on a rollercoaster, hanging upside down with my stomach in my mouth. I kept saying to myself, "just keep breathing" and when our wheels finally touched, I felt emotionally relieved, but still suffering from the neurological upset. My husband was there to welcome us back and his smile said it all, he was incredibly proud of me.

We immediately booked our first trip. A week-long stay in beautiful Barbados would be the honeymoon we never had. I was very excited, but still apprehensive. Flying was definitely not something I enjoyed or jumped at the chance to do, but I was willing in order to arrive at my desired destination.

Barbados was magical! I had never been to the Caribbean and was taken aback by all its natural beauty. Growing up at the garden centre, I saw so many glorious flowers, but never in their indigenous habitat. The lobster claws were magnificent, and the hibiscus were breathtaking. By far, the most captivating were the mango trees, weighed down heavily with their bounty of fruit. The beach was spectacular, the water so blue and clear just like the pictures I had always admired in magazines. My husband immediately wanted to book a catamaran tour and I immediately wanted to pass, but I was willing to try. I pleaded with the tour guide to kindly stay as close to shore as possible but, inevitably, we ended up much farther than my comfort zone. It was a never-ending sail from Hell as a storm began to set in and the waves grew higher putting us just about on our side. I attempted to stay in the boat by grasping, or more accurately put, clawing the leg of our tour guide in an effort to not fall overboard! The motion of the waves made my brain feel jumbled and disoriented, causing the anxiety and fear to increase. I was drenched by a combination of the waves that swept over the boat and the fear that was sweeping over me. My inherent childhood fear of water was being tested like never before. After what seemed like an eternity, we finally hit shore. Stick a fork in me, I was done!

The next reluctant adventure was a glass-bottom boat which I had as much interest and excitement in as the last. Nevertheless, onward I went from the frying pan and into the fire. Ironically, it was my husband, who had the less then desirable experience on this one. While he was above deck green with nausea, I remained downstairs captivated by the beauty submerged below.

I knew my husband would have loved to have taken in many more of the experiences the island had to offer, but I had no interest. I had never been a thrill seeker and was likely never going to be one. It wasn't just the fear at play, I had absolutely no interest. This is one of the many ways in which we were profoundly different from each other. Even in my marriage, I constantly felt like a square peg trying to fit into a round hole. Conversely, things I felt passionately about, he had no interest in. I wouldn't learn for many years that my passions were neither small, nor insignificant. My likes, desires and comforts made me not less, just different. Not everyone had to skydive in order to soar.

* * * * *

On a positive note, I found great joy living next to grandma. We were renting Auntie Rea's old apartment that I had spent so much of my childhood enjoying, and this gave me great comfort. In the evenings, we shared espresso and she regaled us with stories of her past. They all seemed to have the theme of love, each one reminiscing about "her Joe." With all her wisdom I'm sure she could see that we were struggling in our new life and she wanted to support and guide us through. Although she showed a tough exterior, my grandmother at her core felt emotions deeply and believed in the united front of a married couple. Grandma always encouraged us to live with love, not to take each other for granted and to never go to bed angry. I tried with all my heart to follow her example, hoping my husband felt the same way. We constantly fell short.

Our first anniversary arrived, and I looked at it as an act of survival. We made it, by the skin of our teeth, but we made it. I chalked it up to being an adjustment year and had my fingers crossed that better days were ahead. On my twenty-fourth birthday we took possession of our first home, located in south Etobicoke, just five minutes from my grandmother. It was a tiny, nine hundred square foot bungalow with two bedrooms and a beautiful huge backyard. We had a very small deposit to put down but did it on our own without anyone's assistance. My family was thrilled about the news with Auntie Rea being by far the most excited. Unfortunately, some would not share our joy and we were made to feel like the house was inadequate, the usual "not good enough." Looking back, it was sad. A newlywed couple trying hard to begin their life independently and not being supported. I could feel my husband's embarrassment of not measuring up to expectations and of course, this cast a negative vibe during a time that should have been exciting for us.

By now, Auntie Rea was terribly unwell. She was barely able to stand, vomited constantly and was merely skin and bones as the cancer ravaged her body. Our beautiful Italian Goddess was a mere shadow of her former self. The day we took possession of our house and despite everything Maria was going through, she was sitting on the front stoop with veal sandwiches and a bottle of champagne. The first thing out of her mouth was: "Ok, come on let's get to work!" She wouldn't take no for an answer and was Hell bent on helping us prepare our home in any way, shape or form that she could. Her frail body now moved slowly and gingerly. Gone were the days of her endless energy and mischief. Her movements were now painful and draining, but she was determined to help me strip the brutally unattractive 1980's wallpaper in the master bedroom. Out of ear shot I called my mom quietly from outside asking, "what should I do?" I couldn't possibly put her through so much pain. My mom replied, "Let her do it, it will make her happy." We piled pillows high for her to sit upon and as I used the industrial steamer, Maria painstakingly tugged at the loosened paper in a frail attempt to strip it off. Slowly, bit by bit we would get a tiny section complete. The smile on her face was the brightest I had seen in months. She was thrilled to be helping us and we were equally thrilled to have the help which came from her heart.

That little house became her refuge. Through the illness, her partner was less than loving and supportive, so she turned to us for love and comfort. Despite my aunt's reservations about my marrying into a difficult family dynamic, she loved and adored my husband and he loved and adored her as well. Anything she wanted or needed he was more than happy to get for her. Auntie Rea and I shared an extremely close bond my entire life and she turned to me for support and understanding. Whenever Maria wasn't feeling well she would come over to lay on the couch sometimes closing her eyes and resting, other times conversing with us.

There was no denying it, Maria was getting progressively worse. Not long after we moved into our home, she was hospitalized but, upon her insistence, she was discharged, returning home to fight her painful battle in her own way. It was agonizing to see her in such a state. It had been weeks since she had eaten food and was being sustained through a feeding tube.

During this time, it was my mother who was truly her hero and mine in so many ways. My aunt was insistent on sparing my grandmother the pain of the doctor's grim prognosis and hid much of her suffering for as long as possible. It was mom who bore the burden of breaking the news to Grandma that her baby girl was not going to make it. Maybe not eloquently, but she certainly said it bravely. I don't know how she summoned such courage while she was going through so much of her own pain, after all, this was her baby too. She faced every bit of fear courageously as she loved, cared and supported her baby sister to the very end.

Maria passed quietly at her home on September 19, 1992. My mother held her while they awaited the coroner and it was my mother who closed her little sister's eyelids shut one final time. The incredible strength that she showed that day is something I reflect upon often. The day Maria passed, I was reluctantly representing the family at a wedding and it would be the one day I wasn't by her side. I had spent the entire journey with her from that first ride on the subway when she discovered the bump until now. I missed my chance to say goodbye, I felt robbed, just as with my father.

Maria's death took a terrible toll on the entire family as we were all truly gutted. The world lost a living, breathing, earth walking angel that day and the void that was left behind was immeasurable. The empty chair at the dinner table was ghost-like and haunted every occasion. To me and I'm sure everyone else, holidays became uneventful and something I dreaded. Christmas lacked its luster and each holiday felt empty and meaningless.

*****

I continued on with therapy, working hard to better understand myself and was thoroughly enjoying the process. I remember Dr. M saying he liked working with me because I was, "ripe, ready and did the work." Some days, I sat in his office with pure dread, not wanting to face what the session had in store. But each time I left, I felt better for doing the work and for showing up, open and somewhat ready to explore the darkness. I was learning about the impact of my father's death and the subsequent false stories that my mind had conjured up. Feelings of insecurity and loss, along with the mistrust of the natural process of life were all aftereffects of that early childhood trauma. Looking back, I remember a book on the shelf in his office and the title always screamed out to me. The spine read *I'm OK, You're OK*. It was like a little friend that would quietly whisper to me when the pressure of the session was getting to be too much. Some days, I wanted to bolt from that room, other days, I felt like I was going to projectile vomit into the garbage can. Some days, I shed tears and some days were about finding joy. I loved the exploration of the mind and the connecting of life experiences along with the mystery of the subconscious. I had begun my journey of self-discovery and authenticating that would span decades.

* * * * *

As time went on, I felt more and more like I was supposed to pick up where Auntie Rea had left off. I not only felt that it was what I needed to do, but also what she would have wanted and expected. Particularly, when it came to caring for my grandmother and watching out for mom. Though my mother had grown up caring for her,

Maria definitely became her sister's keeper. My aunt was fiercely protective of her, having no trouble speaking up when necessary. She was as bold as she was beautiful. Looking back now, I know I definitely inherited so much of her personality but, I think perhaps, it was because I missed her so much that I attempted to take on her role as protector in the family. I ached to keep her feisty spirit alive and to carry on where she left off.

By not being able to say goodbye to Maria, I never experienced closure. It always felt open ended, unfinished. It was at this time, that a friend suggested I see a psychic. Maybe some insight would give me the closure I was looking for. He was a well-known and respected man who worked with police forces in Ontario and after doing my research and despite being skeptical, I decided through desperation to give him a try.

I kept second guessing my decision the entire way to the appointment. I would not normally seek out such a person for help, but a part of me was desperate for answers. When I arrived at his office, all appeared safe enough. No oracle ball or tarot cards to be seen, just a simple desk and chairs in a space that looked as unassuming as any other. He was a man of few pleasantries and more about getting down to the business at hand.

Placing a picture of Auntie Rea on his desk and without giving him an ounce of information about her, I said, "tell me something about this woman." What followed would haunt me for years to come. He immediately said: "She didn't want to die; she wasn't ready to die and is extremely angry about dying." He continued, "the moment she died, I see blood in her throat like something was being either forced up or down." Maria had been pulling the tube out of her throat several times that week and it was during one of these episodes that she passed. He said, "She is passing the weight of the family on to you. There are two women that are coming up that she is most concerned about. I think one may be her mother and the other, I'm not sure the relation, but the name sounds like something with Ann in it, but I cannot make out the full name." I was frozen at this moment as my mother's name is Antoinette. He went on to say more things about Maria and her past, personal things that were far from generalizations and hit the bullseye each and every time. I thanked him and was about to get up when he said he wasn't done, there was something about me he needed to share. Before I could interject and say, "no thank you", he blurted out "You are going to fall deeply in love in your late forties." I stammered, "ummmm...NO!" I just got married to the man I love, you are wrong, but thanks anyway. "You may love this man, but he's not the one that will be with you forever. You will see later in life." I felt all the blood leave my body. He was wrong, plain and simple, he was wrong…he just had to be.

Chapter Thirteen

I had begun shopping alternatively during my college days out of necessity and discovered I had taken a genuine liking to thrifting, which consisted of shopping at church sales, garage sales and consignment shops. Now, it was a way of life for me and I love it! When I picked up my first evening dress for an upcoming wedding that had a whopping price tag of $1.50, I was hooked! For me, retail was a thing of the past, I could never go back and why would I want to?

When one of the retail spaces in my grandmother's building came up for rent, I saw it as the perfect place to open my dream consignment shop! Without anyone knowing, I called the real estate agent and rented the space. I didn't want anyone to think I was taking advantage of my grandmother or assume that I was trying to get something for nothing. So, on July 11, 1993, I opened the doors to my business.

Growing up at the garden centre served me well in running my own business. Customer service, merchandising and procuring product were all things that my mother taught me well. The community loved us, and people would come to talk about the great stuff and not so great stuff in their lives, purchase a little something to make their day and they always made ours. I was so blessed that my grandmother would come in after working at the nursery to answer the phones and critique my displays. I absolutely loved her being there with me and everyone who came in adored her. I had the best staff and once they came, they pretty much never left, with my longest serving employee Joanie, staying with me for over 18 years. My girls were the best and a source of so much joy to me, as was the store.

I had purchased some metal racks to use for displays which required a bit of cleaning up and painting. I used TREMCLAD metal paint, which is highly toxic, and lead based. Normally, I would have used this paint in an open and well-ventilated area but, for some unknown reason, I decided to paint them in the basement without a hint of ventilation. Not my brightest moment. That decision resulted in me suffering from paint poisoning which, moving forward, would have a significant impact on my already challenged health, and was the beginning of a severe chemical allergy that would worsen over time. I also discovered that the interaction I had with the chemicals at the garden centre as a young girl, may have actually been the catalyst for this allergy.

Chapter Fourteen

Since Maria's funeral, something had been stirring inside of me. My first funeral had left me both intrigued and terrified. There was something about the industry that drew me near, calling me closer. I was curious about the entire process of helping people find their final resting place and after spending my entire life sheltered from death, my curiosity had now been peaked. It felt like a call to action for yet another stage of my healing. It was time to face the natural process of death head on, so I made the choice to be brave and/or stupid, I wasn't sure which one. Even though I had my store, I decided to submit my resume to a local funeral home for a part-time position as a front office greeter and was promptly hired.

Imagine my family's reaction upon telling them I had gotten a job at a funeral home. People couldn't understand why I would want to do something so morbid and I wasn't about to get into the depths and reasoning with everyone, but I did share my thoughts with a select few, one being my mother. Mom could not wrap her head around why I felt the need to do such a thing. I think her exact words were: "Are you crazy?" Crazy or not, I was going to feel the fear and do it anyway. I threw myself into the midst of it, not unlike my father tossing Anthony into the water or slapping the pony on the ass. It was time to grow my own tough skin, my way.

Approaching the front doors to begin my first shift, I was thinking the exact same thing as my mom, and probably with as much conviction. What WAS I doing? Was I out of my mind? Was I doing this by choice? Well, it's now or never so I took a deep breath, and in I went.

The funeral home was an old red brick building built in the 1930's which resembled a residence more than a place of "final" business. I pushed the old wooden double-entry doors open and immediately smelled the unique and eerie contrast of both life and death. The heavy floral scent was reminiscent of my years spent at the garden centre, but the undertone was quite opposite, a heavy and foreboding smell that lingered and made me uncomfortable. The interior was tastefully decorated in tones of rose and blue with comfortable furniture that made you feel welcomed, but not too welcomed if you know what I mean. From the centre foyer I could see into a visitation room and was brave or nosey enough to strain my neck to look inside. At one end of the room, a somewhat comfortable distance from me, a body was laid out in a wooden casket. I felt uneasy and could feel the anxiety growing inside as the sound of footsteps startled me from behind. I turned around and walking towards me came a most memorable character, the owner's brother Morley. I use his name freely because I know he wouldn't want it any other way. He would want full credit in the spotlight, putting himself centre stage as he was as vain as he was unique.

He and I would be working together on this, my debut into the life of death, and as he looked me up and down, I could tell he was less than impressed. Morley was in his early sixties, average size, walked with a bit of a limp and wore a particularly horrid toupee. He had a remarkably inappropriate and cringe worthy sense of humour that was definitely socially unacceptable. Despite his colourful jokes and lack of any sort of filter, everyone loved him.

Before my shift officially began, he gave me the five-cent tour which he conducted while sitting in an oversized wing chair in the front foyer. He would lift his arms just high enough to point in each direction, not giving any real clear information or guidance, just a general overview from his easy chair. Not knowing where the bodies were kept, I experienced growing fear with each newly opened door. I felt like I was on, "Let's Make a Deal" and had to somehow avoid the zonks!

The rest of the evening my duties consisted of greeting guests, ushering them into visitations, assisting with donations, answering phones and monitoring the lounge. As my first shift wound down, I was relieved to have had no major mishaps or discoveries and to come out of the whole experience fairly unscathed. That is, until I went into the garage to retrieve a late floral delivery. I knew the morgue was somewhere within the garage but, where exactly, I wasn't sure. Kneeling to pick up the flowers and turning to leave, I spotted what I assumed to be the 'gut sucking machine'. It was a blue box-like machine on wheels, approximately two feet square in size with a long hose attached to the side and appeared to be dripping some kind of liquid. Next to the 'gut sucker' was a gurney with a red velvet body bag on top. I quickly grabbed the arrangement of flowers and made a beeline for the main foyer as gracefully as I could manage. I was far too embarrassed and shy to ask Morley what I just saw, and part of me didn't want to know. I simply carried on that night avoiding the garage and the 'gut sucking machine' at all costs.

My first shift came to an end and I was glad to get out of there. My husband was working that night, which meant I was coming home to an empty house. I sat in the dark on the living room sofa waiting for what seemed like hours for him to return. In the meantime, my mother called to see how it went. I told her it scared me to death and I was going back tomorrow. She was losing her mind and exclaimed: "Why do you need to do that again? Quit and be done with it!" I knew I couldn't quit now. I had to face it all in order to get over the fear, otherwise, I was just compounding it.

The next day I went in to begin my shift and explained to my boss what had transpired the night before. He was horrified to find out that I had not been given a thorough tour of the building and an explanation of "things." He gave me an extensive tour and made sure to fill in all the gaps from the previous evening. He made me feel much more at ease and I felt I could ask him about the horrifying 'gut sucking machine'. He looked confused, as if he had absolutely no idea what I was talking about. Following his lead into the garage, I pointed to the big blue box with its dripping hose attached, at which point he broke out into hysterical laughter. My boss stepped forward and slowly turned the box around to reveal the other side which had a label that read: "Easy-off Carpet Steamer!" I wanted to crawl under a rock. How could I be so stupid? Again, when faced with the unknown and lack of information and where fear resides, the mind will create its own far less accurate reality in order to make sense of things.

Morley, the odd character with no filter from that first evening, ended up becoming one of my dearest friends. Over time, I began to understand him and his big heart that he guarded so well. When he passed away from cancer, the funeral home was never the same. Everyone in the community missed his brutal honesty and ghastly inappropriate humour that always made us gasp and laugh out loud. He is forever in my heart.

Over the ten years I worked there part-time, they always treated me like family, taking the time to teach me about the industry and allowing me to observe and be a part of as much as I was comfortable. They were very supportive of my reasons for joining their team and my deep need to conquer and overcome my fear. They gave me every opportunity to face my fear and so much more. I had not only faced it, but I learned to embrace death as a natural and beautiful part of each of our existence. Oddly enough, I had begun to find my strength through something that left the vast majority of society uncomfortable. For once, I wasn't the one afraid. Unfortunately, the empathic side of me took a beating during my time at the funeral home. My big throbbing heart felt everyone's pain and loss as if it were my own. It's no wonder that there is such burn-out in the funeral industry as day after day, you are exposed to an incredibly low vibration of energy, both from the dead and the loved ones that are left behind. Not long after the birth of my child, I would resign from my position. As a new mom, every time I observed a body lying on a gurney, I saw someone's child. I found it difficult to avoid transference, I felt everything. During the time I spent there, I felt like I made a difference and if I made one person's experience a little easier, then I did my job. It served its purpose well and it was time to move on.

Chapter Fifteen

I was twenty-seven years old and had completed my time with the psychiatrist. I gained the skills necessary to bring myself to a relative place of calm, not having had a panic attack since six years previous in the shiatsu clinic. At this point in time, I felt like I had dealt with my demons, or at the very least, knew who they were and what they looked like. Little did I realize that this was just the surface layer peeling off the onion. Though I didn't see any progress with the extended family dynamic, I was still holding on and believing it would change. We trudged along through the mundanity of life, that was about it. After five years of marriage, we decided it was time to begin our own family. It was truly a terrifying thought for me, someone who had developed an aversion to hospitals and was constantly playing the never ending "what if" game in my mind. Regardless, I took a breath, faced the fear and did it anyway. Within the first month of trying I began feeling unwell. I was extremely weak, out of sorts and had never felt like this before. It couldn't have happened already. I decided to take the pregnancy test before work. My fingers fumbled with the packaging as I removed the test stick and placed it on the sink. I walked to the other room nervously awaiting the results and I could feel my knees were weak and a pounding headache had begun. I jumped as I heard the timer go off indicating the test was ready and I stood paralyzed in fear. Oh my God! What if it was positive? There was no going back! So many fearful scenarios played at lightning speed through my mind. Sure enough, it was positive, and I was pregnant...I was more terrified than excited.

I stopped on the way home from work and picked up a card and of all things, a pacifier to announce the news to my husband. In hindsight, maybe my subconscious was at work, attempting to self-soothe away the fear, just like I had as a child. As my husband sat on the sofa next to me, I could feel the butterflies in my stomach. My hands were clammy and shaking as I handed him the card with both excitement and apprehension. He opened it and with tears in his eyes, leaned over and kissed me. He was incredibly happy to hear that we were expecting.

In the days that followed, he was very supportive, recognizing that I was overwhelmed and not feeling well. I scheduled an appointment with my GP, and he confirmed that I was in the early stages of pregnancy. I was taking each day one at a time, not lifting anything at work and really trying to conserve what little energy I had. Each step I took felt like a mile, and the weakness was unlike anything I had ever felt. We shared the news with our families right away and everyone was thrilled beyond words.

My body didn't feel right. I had never been pregnant before and did not know if this was normal. Some days, the lethargy and weakness was so intense I couldn't go into work and could barely make it out of bed. My husband would accompany me to my first appointment with the obstetrician who was a very soft-spoken, kind and compassionate man. He was not concerned with my symptoms, although he did reiterate what the family doctor had said, that it was very early and his advice was to take it easy and relax.

The next morning, I began feeling lower back pain. I went to the washroom and discovered I was bleeding, clearly, there was something wrong. We immediately left for the hospital with my sister accompanying us. They put me on a bed in the emergency ward to await an ultrasound. I was terrified of the unknown, not knowing how my baby was or if I was losing it. As the technician performed the ultrasound, I asked repeatedly: "What do you see? Is everything ok?", only to be told I'd have to wait for the doctor. It would be hours before the doctor arrived and when he did, I almost wished he hadn't. He was completely lacking compassion, empathy, or sensitivity as to what I was enduring. When I asked him about the health of my baby, he coldly replied: "I have no idea." He performed the exam with no discretion. He donned his rubber gloves and I endured the most horrific, borderline violent internal examination that I could never have imagined! I repeatedly screamed out in pain and when the ordeal was finally over, there was blood everywhere. Without even glancing in my direction, he said: "You've lost the baby, you're not pregnant anymore. It all came out. No procedure is required." And with that, he turned and left the room. The nurse and I looked at each other, both equally horrified by what had just happened. She was a compassionate, kind woman who put her arm around me as I began sobbing. She encouraged me to be patient and trusting and to try again. She advised that I go home and rest and to return to the hospital if I had any more pain. And just like that…it was over.

My immediate feeling was that I was a failure, followed by emptiness, fear and disappointment. It wasn't long before the all too familiar feelings of "not good enough" came flooding back. I felt like I had let everybody down. Although I was in the very early stages of pregnancy, it was still my baby and the little life that was in me was now gone.

Mom and grandma came over, neither one saying much. I do remember my mother saying what she had always told me, "Put some lipstick on, you'll feel better." You could be on death's door and mom would still give you this same advice, always believing that no matter the obstacle, lipstick would always make it better and I had to admit she was usually right, but not this time. Neither one really knew what to say. I was just happy to have them close, that was all that mattered to me. I can never quite put into words the depths of emptiness and inadequacy I felt that day as a woman. We put such pressure on ourselves to be perfect in every way. Even when things are out of our control, somehow the self-induced guilt takes over and begins running on auto pilot. It wasn't long before the fear started to set in, and the catastrophic thinking began. What if I don't get pregnant again? What if I have another miscarriage? What if the cord gets wrapped around the baby's head? What if I have a stillbirth? My mind was a myriad of "what ifs." It would be more than a year before I would be ready to feel the fear and try again anyway.

My Missing Peace

My grandmother, my mother and I.

JoJo Marie Schillaci

Chapter Sixteen

It had been a year since the miscarriage, and we were ready to try again. I became pregnant very quickly but, this time, stayed quiet until the three-month mark. I was cautiously excited but didn't want to disappoint people again. This time around, I suffered extreme nausea that lasted all day long. My only relief came every day at midnight like clockwork. Three months almost to the day the nausea subsided, and I never felt better in my life.

     Physically, I was doing great, but spent the majority of my pregnancy preoccupied with the never-ending thoughts of "What if?" I ran so many scenarios over and over again in my mind, everything from losing the pregnancy, stillbirth and crib death etc. Added to that, were the usual concerns women have regarding labour and delivery. The fear throughout the entire pregnancy overshadowed the joy I should have been allowing myself to feel. Ultrasounds were always stressful until finally, the technician would give the all-clear and let me know my baby was on track. From the first time I saw and heard the beating heart, I had no doubt it was that of my baby boy. My due date was June 27, 1998, two days before my thirtieth birthday, but the baby had other plans.

On May 26th, I awoke at 5am and something felt different. My back was aching, and I was suffering from terrible cramps. I had been experiencing Braxton Hicks pre-labour pains for a few weeks, but this was much more intense. Realizing we needed to go to the hospital, I woke my husband immediately and asked him to call my mom. My unusual calmness could be attributed to a state of shock and disbelief, as it was still four weeks until my due date. As we pulled up to the hospital's maternity ward, my calmness quickly turned to anxiety as I began thinking of all the unknown that lay ahead. Shortly after being admitted, it was decided that they were going to break my water and that's when the real panic set in. Once they did, I knew my baby was transitioning from the safety of my body and into the scary outside world. I was literally, already resisting the natural flow of life.

Labour was relatively easy for me. I spent as much time out of the bed as possible, walking up and down the halls with my husband and squatting at the bedside. A few hours into the process, I was sequestered in the bed with a fetal monitor inserted and attached to the baby's head. Determined to give birth naturally without the intervention of medication and in order to push through the pain, I summoned all the techniques I had learned from Dr. M. The contractions were coming one after another with barely a minute to recoup before the next one hit causing me to scream out in pain. When I became pregnant, I had asked my mother to be at the birth. She both reluctantly and excitedly agreed. I knew in her heart she wanted to be there, but I knew full well another part of her would rather have had bamboo shoved under each fingernail than to see me suffer. She would do anything not to see or hear anyone cry out in pain. After hours of labour, the baby still wasn't coming and as hard as I was pushing, I knew there was another force within me pulling and resisting. It was the natural process of letting go and trusting the next phase of life and naturally, I was fighting it every step of the way. During the most intense part of labour my mom turned to me and said, "I'm going to go to the food terminal (which, coincidentally, was located on the same street as the hospital) to check on some geraniums." To which I answered, "no damn way are you leaving me now!" She was desperate for a way out and an escape from the pain she was witnessing me go through and in turn, feeling herself. Florence Nightingale she isn't and when I screamed out in pain eleven hours into the birthing journey and yelled: "Mom I can't do it, I just can't do it.", she replied with a stern and raised voice, "You can and you will!" There was no hand-holding or mushy talk, sugar coating was not my mom's style. Straight and to the point, void of bullshit is the only way she knows how to be. Now that I am a mother, I can only imagine how difficult it was for her to see me in such a state. For someone who avoided seeing people in pain and uncomfortable situations, she was sure thrown into the fire this time. She helped me gain my second wind and eventually, after almost twelve hours of labour, my baby entered his new world at 4:31 pm, weighing in at six pounds one ounce and given the name Joseph.

Our son had arrived four weeks premature and was immediately whisked to the care of the neonatal specialists. My mother was the first to hold him as she stood by the specialists and watched them care for her tiny grandson. It was in that moment, that precious moment, that the most incredible bond began between grandmother and grandchild. After being examined by the doctors, Joseph was finally brought to my arms and I remember his smell most of all. He laid on my chest and we opened up the receiving blanket to display and examine his little body, ten fingers, ten toes and the sweetest, tiniest little ears I had ever seen. He was perfect in every way.

As a premature baby, Joseph had developed jaundice and was kept at the nursing station in an incubator. I spent most of my time by his side, with my hands pushed through the holes, touching and caressing his tiny body, holding his hands and massaging his little feet. I was terrified something would happen to my baby. After four days we were given the 'all clear' and Joseph and I were released from the hospital. As relieved as I was, the thought of parenting this little human being was completely overwhelming. I remember looking at Joseph like a lump of clay and it was up to my husband and I to mold him. How on earth do we not screw him up?

One month after giving birth, I celebrated my thirtieth birthday. I could not have received a more perfect gift than my beautiful, healthy baby boy. Joseph was thriving, sleeping very well and eating around the clock. All was settling nicely until he turned six weeks old. It was like a switch was flipped and my quiet, calm baby did a 180-degree turn. Do you recall the baby my mother wished upon me? Well, I got him! Along with having colic, he was also diagnosed with an umbilical hernia that caused both mother and baby great distress. A hernia is when the intestine pushes through a weak spot in the stomach muscle. They would most likely need to operate. We had to wait six months before deciding, hoping that his tummy muscles would have enough time to develop and rectify the hernia on their own. I was now on a mission and asked the doctor for exercises to develop his little six pack and I did them constantly throughout the day. The colic and crying continued, causing him to strain, which was the worst thing for his hernia. Trying to keep him from crying was a next to impossible task and at this point every one of my nerves were shot. He cried constantly. The only time Joseph didn't cry was when he was napping, which took him hours to fall asleep and if I was lucky, would last a whole twenty minutes. I had zero rest during the day and almost no sleep at night for months, all the while nursing him every two hours. I was spent both emotionally and physically. I constantly felt that everything I did was "not good enough", whether it was cooking, cleaning or the baby. I felt like a failure, again.

Joseph at 5 months old.

With Joseph a little over six months old, I let out a sigh of relief after receiving the most wonderful news that the hernia had corrected itself and surgery was not necessary. The exercises had done their job!

Life progressed and so did the colic, it seemed like it would never end. When Joseph was eight months old, I caught a flu that lasted more than two months and I just couldn't shake it. After complaining to my family doctor about not getting better, he weighed the baby and said, "Here's your problem." Joseph was now ten months old and topped the scale at a whopping THIRTY-TWO POUNDS! He was as solid as solid could be and had roll after roll on his chubby thighs and arms and was still breastfeeding every two hours. The doctor looked at me and said: "He's thirty-two pounds! He's good. You've done great, but he's sucking the life out of you! You have to stop breastfeeding." I couldn't disagree with him but felt like a failure for not achieving the goal I set of breast feeding him for one year.

As Joseph's first birthday approached, physically and emotionally I was feeling worse than ever. Despite stopping breastfeeding, I was still exhausted from sleep deprivation. I had a major issue with my husband's incessant loud snoring and in an attempt to gain a couple of hours sleep, I headed to the basement and slept on the futon. Sometimes, the snoring was so loud that it travelled through the venting system keeping me awake downstairs as well. I would then resort to the downstairs shower stall and on more than one occasion, would end up sleeping in the car. I was desperate for rest...for sleep...for peace.

Joseph still barely napped and although the colic was slightly better, it was still a daily challenge. My headaches were back with a vengeance and my nerves were frayed from the physical and emotional exhaustion. My husband helped out when he could, but his hours at work were long and I was alone the majority of the time. Feeling burnt out, I decided to see Dr. M., who diagnosed me with postpartum depression and immediately prescribed medication.

Many women don't talk about the emotional roller coaster they experience after childbirth. New moms can begin feeling inadequate, overwhelmed, and frustrated. Before long, depression and anxiety can set in and just as in the fairy tale stories related to us about marriage, we are also told about the wonderful life of being a new mom. The image of perfectly dressed, fresh faced new moms pushing prams with their peaceful bundles of joy and couples being brought beautifully together by their "plus one", can create unrealistic expectations. I'm here to tell you that in my case, nothing could be farther from the truth. The self-judgment is relentless, and the stigma associated with mental illness, though much better, is still a heavy burden to bear and the shame is compounded by feelings of failure, depression and anxiety. Postpartum depression generally rears its ugly head the first three weeks after giving birth but, may present itself at any time during the first year. It is similar to the baby blues, but with much more intense and long-lasting symptoms.

The Mayo Clinic has listed the following as symptoms to watch out for:

- Depressed mood or severe mood swings
- Excessive crying
- Difficulty bonding with your baby
- Withdrawing from family and friends
- Loss of appetite or eating much more than usual
- Inability to sleep (insomnia) or sleeping too much
- Overwhelming fatigue or loss of energy
- Reduced interest and pleasure in activities you used to enjoy
- Intense irritability and anger
- Fear that you're not a good mother
- Hopelessness
- Feelings of worthlessness, shame, guilt or inadequacy
- Diminished ability to think clearly, concentrate or make decisions
- Restlessness
- Severe anxiety and panic attacks
- Thoughts of harming yourself or your baby
- Recurrent thoughts of death or suicide

If you have recently given birth, or know someone who has, be aware of these symptoms and either get, or offer help. Although postpartum depression is most often associated with women, men can also suffer from it. New fathers have their own pressures and stresses requiring understanding and support.

My son's first birthday arrived, and the entire day was a blur. The medication made me extremely ill and I constantly felt in a fog. I did my best to host the party but, again, "not good enough" to some. Year one was done and so was I.

Chapter Seventeen

I remained on the postpartum medication for exactly one year. My hormones seemed to be stabilizing, the depression was diminishing, and things had somewhat settled with the baby. Despite the challenges of that first year, I very much enjoyed being a mom. Joseph and I had developed a beautiful bond and I felt a depth of love for another human I never knew imaginable.

From the moment he arrived, I knew there was something different about Joseph. He entered this world as an old soul, I could feel it and others could too. Joseph said his first word Mama at seven months, soon followed by Dada, Nana, dirt and car. He was late in taking his first steps at fourteen months but, once he started, there was no stopping those chubby little legs. We had decided long before getting pregnant that I would be a stay at home mom. This was something my husband and I were both fiercely adamant about. Though I had multiple jobs throughout my life, many of them challenging, nothing compared to that of motherhood. It was twenty-four hours, seven days a week non-stop demanding and exhausting work and I wouldn't have had it any other way. I felt incredibly blessed.

Relations with my husband continued to be strained and dysfunctional. Since the baby came, the extended family dynamic was worsening, and in turn, it was driving an even deeper wedge between us. The issues we both struggled with individually were ever-present. My husband and I never lived as a couple, it was always he and I, never us. We never became the nucleus that my grandmother wished we would become but, when it came to Joseph, we provided him with a loving, happy family environment. We were simply friends raising a child together, but with totally different personal goals and aspirations. We played to each other's weaknesses instead of building on our individual strengths. It was a continual tug-of-war which always landed us both in the mud. Not to mention the constant presence of the other two ghosts (his mother and high school sweetheart) that, in my mind, haunted our marriage every day.

My formal work with Dr. M was complete, but I was hooked on self-discovery. I loved self-exploration, delving deeper into myself, my past, triggers and what made me tick in general. I loved the process of uncovering and peeling back the layers of the mind. It was at this point, we decided to see Dr. M as a couple. He spoke to us at length about the importance of being a united front and God knows how I ached for that.

Unfortunately, I was still very challenged physically. Joseph learned at an early age to use the little stool and reach up to the freezer to get ice packs for mommy's head. The headaches were completely debilitating with blinding migraines, that time and time again, would be dismissed by the doctors as stress and hormones. Joseph was three years old when I began sleeping full-time in the basement. As I laid on the downstairs futon, I recall thinking over and over, that peace was all I craved for. Never in my life did I feel like I could just breathe. I was always fearing the next issue, knowing I had to deal with it alone. The stomach issues were back causing me to wake from my usual half sleep with an overwhelming sense of "I don't feel good." I kept praying for peace...*my missing peace*.

* * * * *

My neighbourhood was always a comfort for me. We were blessed to be living on an amazing street with the most wonderful people, everybody lending a helping hand, exchanging the bounty from their gardens and enjoying socializing together. I loved organizing Canada Day BBQs, movie nights in the backyard and fireworks on the street. By far, the best events were the annual Easter egg hunts and our renowned water gun battles. We were all very close, but my next door neighbour, Rizwana, soon became my dearest friend and her family became our chosen family. We participated in each other's achievements and celebrations along with challenges and struggles. We shared food, fears and everything in between. Her youngest son Arman, was five years older than Joseph and in my heart, will always be my second son. From the day Joseph came home from the hospital, they instantly became, "brudders from different mudders!" Arman was the first on the street to see Joseph, running up to the car wanting to sneak a peek at the newly arrived bundle of joy. The boys had a beautiful, simple childhood together. Summer mornings began early with each one running out the front door to meet the other and playing from sunrise to sundown. They amused themselves with the simplest things found around the house and everything nature had to offer. Outdoor forts, bug collecting, rockets made of baking soda and Alka Seltzer were some of their favourite things to do. But what they were most passionate about was LEGO. It was the only toy we bought without hesitation and I found enough LEGO at garage sales to fill numerous huge storage bins. They would put their blanket out under a tree in the backyard and build all day long stopping only long enough to quickly eat and get right back at it. Taking it a step further, they would film stop-motion movies with the sets created the day before. They built an incredible, beautiful bond, that would last a lifetime.

Joseph and Arman sitting on our front stoop, 2002.

Despite mom's grueling work schedule, she always made time for me, but I longed for her to be at home. Growing up watching shows like Leave it to Beaver and Happy Days, I wanted to have my mom in the kitchen or hanging laundry on the line. I'm sure that my mother desired the same. My brother and sister had a taste of what circumstances had robbed me of. I wanted Joseph to have what I never got the chance to experience, so I became that mom. We provided Joseph with a simple childhood where he was supported and shown love every single day, complete with clothes hanging on the line and cookies baking in the oven.

 Joseph attended kindergarten at the same Catholic elementary school my mother attended fifty-two years earlier. It was located on a beautiful, picture-perfect post card street, just a short walk from my grandmother's building. I had been reluctant to send him to a school in such a prestigious neighbourhood as the Kingsway because we didn't fit the usual demographic. We came from the "blue collar," other side of the tracks. This fed into my constant "not good enough" and "square peg, round hole" mindset. I was concerned that Joseph might feel inferior to his classmates' jet setting lifestyle and mansion homes, in comparison to our simple understated life. My husband was the one that insisted we take the opportunity presented before us and enroll Joseph, a decision for which I am forever grateful. The school had one of the best reputations in the area for both their caring staff, as well as a thorough and intense curriculum. Though through the years I spent an incredible amount of time at the school volunteering and attending every event, I never felt like I belonged.

 Joseph invited a little girl from his kindergarten class over for a play date. For those of you that have been spared the pain of this new age social construct, I'll explain.

Children no longer spontaneously play outside together. Parents are now secretaries, taking bookings for their little ones, checking their social calendars against a plethora of extra-curricular activities and penciling them in as openings become available. I despised play dates, nonetheless, I conformed in order to not have my son feel left out. The two kids sat in the van excitedly jabbering away until I pulled into our driveway and the little girl went silent, the look on her face said it all. She turned to Joseph and said in disgust "Is THAT your house?" My heart sank for my son and I'm embarrassed to say, a little for me as well. I wanted to turn around and give her what for, but the rational side of me took over and I just waited for Joseph's response. As always, he did not disappoint. He calmly and peacefully turned to her and replied "Yes, it's got a lot of love AND two bathrooms!" And with that, I smiled and laughed out loud. Best response ever! Children can bring the most complex emotional situations down to the simplest form. Joseph, summoning his old wisdom, had figured out that he was a child of riches in the simplest form and more than comfortable in his own skin, even at five years old. Oh, how I wish I could say the same for myself.

Our little house with "a lot of love and two bathrooms."

It was June 27, 2003, the last day of school for the kids and I think I was more excited than they were. Summers were about enjoying every day and all that the weather had to offer. Summer was about simple living. Movie nights in the backyard, BBQ's at nanas, water balloons and playing LEGO on the grass. I couldn't wait for it! First thing every morning, we would pack a cooler, load the van and we were off! Pioneer Village, High Park and Centre Island were some of our regular favourites. Toronto offered an abundance of buildings and historic sites for us to explore. Biking, hiking and fishing were also regular outings that we enjoyed. "Transportation Day" was by far, one of our most memorable excursions. We decided to go downtown using as many methods of transportation as possible and taking pictures of each along the way. Our adventure began with us driving to the Go Train station. Joseph was so excited to be on the big green and white double decker commuter train. He sat by the window and did a running commentary the entire way to Union Station. From there, we took the subway uptown to visit his father at work, which was always a treat for both of them. Joseph enjoyed sitting up front by the driver which allowed him a clear view through the dark tunnels from station to station. We then decided to board a bus taking us into the heart of Chinatown where we wandered the shops and got a bite to eat. We then hopped on a streetcar which took us to the waterfront. The day was beautiful, so we decided to enjoy a ferry ride to the islands. The 600 tonne Trillium ferry began operating in 1910 and wouldn't be retired until 1956. When my grandparents had their small business on Centre Island, they would take this same ferry. The Trillium came out of retirement in 1976 and is still operating today at over a hundred years old. I felt a sense of comfort knowing that we were sitting on the same seats my family sat on generations earlier. Looking back, some of my greatest memories were of Joseph and I sitting on the ferry's gleaming wooden bench seats and looking out on to Lake Ontario, his big brown eyes were as wide as could be, taking in the smell of the lake air and counting all the ducks along the way. We heard seagulls calling out and finally, the sound of the ferry's horn blasting hello signaling our arrival. To me, there was no better place to be. We took the ferry back to Toronto harbour, followed by a bus to Union Station for our final Go Train ride home.

Joseph had helped his dad build an awesome treehouse in the backyard, complete with a secret trap door, small deck and big blue slide. On the last day of school, Joseph and Arman decided to kick off summer vacation by playing with LEGO in the treehouse. After venturing up to bring snacks and get them settled, I chose to take the easy way down and use the slide. Walking through the doorway to the deck, I had forgotten it was child size and hit my head on the wooden frame. The impact made an audible whack and I was almost knocked out cold. I can still remember the boys coming to my side and asking if I was ok. I felt like the cartoon coyote that had just been hit with a falling anvil, complete with a halo of stars encircling my head. I gently put my hand to my head and was relieved to find that there was no blood. With the help of the boys, I eventually managed to make my way down the slide and immediately needed to sleep which I now know to be exactly the wrong thing to do after a head injury. I laid on the sofa and was out for an hour, waking with intense fatigue and a horrible headache.

The next day while at work, I was soon overcome with vertigo, nausea and a terrible headache. I went to the hospital and the doctor confirmed I had suffered a mild concussion. When I inquired about a CAT scan or MRI, I was told that it was only a minor concussion and I should be fine with a couple days of rest. A few days went by and then a few more, with no relief in sight. I then went to my family doctor who concurred with the hospital's diagnosis: "Give it a week and all will settle down." It had now been three weeks and I was not better and infact, I felt worse. I felt like I needed to lay down all day, but it exacerbated the dizziness. Back to the hospital I went again, only be told the same as before, it was a minor concussion and the symptoms would eventually pass.

It had now been almost six weeks since the head injury and my summer was a bust. Our usual daily adventures turned into Joseph and Arman playing LEGO on the blanket in the backyard day after day. Thankfully, they were more than thrilled to spend their days like this. Me...not so much. I was terribly depressed and saddened about each day of summer that passed me by. Every day, I struggled to walk, to cook, to do the simplest of daily tasks. I didn't feel supported or understood and it was obviously my problem to figure out, a job that I was failing miserably at. I could barely move without violent dizziness, nausea, and headaches that never went away. Every step I attempted to take left me with never-ending motion sickness and I was barely eating. My entire menu consisted of dry toast, rice and maybe, on a good day, a banana. At my wits end, I recalled a medical doctor who practiced alternative therapies. I had seen him many times previously with great results and decided to give him a call. Dr. Ravi was an incredibly gifted Western Medical physician who was decades ahead of his time. He immediately booked me in for a Cranial Sacral treatment. I had never heard of such a procedure, let alone had one done. Wikipedia defines it as "a form of bodywork or alternative therapy that uses gentle touch to palpate the synarthrodial joints of the cranium." It is an incredibly subtle, but intense and effective treatment.

To say that I was nervous would be an understatement. Laying down on the treatment table immediately induced major dizziness and vertigo, my brain felt like a boat fighting a stormy sea. The nausea intensified and before long, the panic set in. The doctor reassured me I was safe and it would improve shortly. Dr. Ravi asked me to stay trusting and to breathe deeply through it as he placed his hands on either side of my head with a most gentle, but energetically solid touch. After a few short minutes, he diagnosed that my frontal and sphenoid bones of my skull were misaligned, as well as structural issues in my neck. Add to that, the rhythm of the cerebral spinal fluid was also off. This would create a sloshing feeling in my brain and would certainly cause the symptoms I had described. Very quickly, the symptoms began to lessen, and I could feel a shift for the better. Reluctantly and fearfully, I sat up at the edge of the table and slowly opened my eyes. I was shocked to find that for the first time in more than six weeks, the room wasn't spinning, the boat had stopped rocking and the never-ending headache was gone! Even my appetite returned! I was so very grateful for the skilled hands and wisdom of this man. I was finally cured...at least temporarily.

JoJo Marie Schillaci

Chapter Eighteen

I spent my thirties experiencing extreme debilitating stress. My nerves took a beating the first few years as a new mom. Joseph's hernia and colic wore me down terribly and the continual sleep deprivation from the snoring was taking a toll on my health. Headaches were a constant and as the years past my sensitivity to chemicals had begun to worsen. Where previously I would react primarily to paints and solvents, it had now spread to cleaning products and perfumes. Once exposed, I would become dizzy and nauseated which was always followed by extreme fatigue and debilitating headaches. Sometimes, I would be down for an hour, sometimes a few days and many times it would take me a week to get back on my feet. Back then, the vast majority of people had not yet heard about what we now know to be MCS (Multiple Chemical Sensitivity) or did not believe in its validity. Throughout my life, I have learned that in most cases, ignorance breeds disrespect. I would explain to friends, family, and strangers alike the horrible consequences I endured when exposed. I begged them to refrain from using perfume and harsh cleaning products in order to give me a safe place, a reprieve from the poison and its effects on me. My requests were met with rolling eyes and the dismissal of my feelings. I was in constant defensive mode, dodging the chemical invasion that seemed to be around every corner of my life. Public transit was next to impossible with each bus and streetcar containing enough perfumes and colognes to supply a small brothel. My store was becoming a constant hazard. People were bringing in their clothing to sell drenched in heavily fragranced laundry products and customers would come in soaked to the skin in the latest high fashion fragrances. Visiting friends and family presented a whole other level of stress, embarrassment and judgement. Upon receiving an invitation, I would have to call ahead and find out exactly what I would be walking in to. Do they allow smoking? Do they use scented laundry products? Do they use bleach, perfumes, or colognes? Have they recently done any renovations or painting? When I would share my condition as the reason for the inquiry, I felt more often than not, that I was a burden and an outcast. We live in a world that revolves around chemicals. Whether it be cleaning products, beauty products, renovation materials, gardening supplies...they were everywhere and trying to avoid exposure was like constantly walking a mine field in size fourteen lead shoes. My immune system was forever under attack, which caused me to be exhausted every minute of the day.

* * * * *

We decided that after living in our home for seventeen years, it was time to renovate. Though very excited, I had grave concerns. How were we going to combat the chemicals? I was assured we would be using as many "greenish" options as possible and to have faith that it would be fine. I had so many reservations about rebuilding, but I was hopeful that perhaps this would give my husband the sense of pride he never had with our existing home. Maybe it would finally be "good enough." It's important to note that although I had apprehension, I was also excited at the thought of building our "dream home" and to finally get the kitchen I had always wanted. And so, in the fall of 2008 we packed up our little home that was, "full of love and had two bathrooms" and moved in with my grandmother. I had been growing more and more nervous about the adventure as the time grew nearer, there was something looming around the whole event, but I couldn't put my finger on it. I had always been sensitive to energy and the more work I was doing on myself, the more attuned I became, the energy felt all wrong. Something was telling me no, but I couldn't articulate the reason. I can distinctly remember being in my grandmother's kitchen as we were moving our things in and stopping my husband in his tracks. I looked at him and said with such apprehension: "I have a bad feeling. I don't want to do this." His response was, "Don't worry, it's gonna be great." My gut knew better.

As unbelievable as this may sound, the same day the first brick came down collapsing our little home, my husband's company was bought out and he was out of his job of over fifteen years. Under normal circumstances, this would have been a very heavy blow, but this was an unmitigated disaster. Our demolished home resembled the three little pigs house of sticks after it had been blown to the ground and there was no going back. My financial worries grew more and more, as I'm sure his did as well. Both of us attempted to maintain a happy face, if not for ourselves, then most importantly for Joseph. Again, like all throughout our marriage, we were never there for each other as a couple, both of us suffering alone. There was way too much baggage between us to even try to get close to one another. It was like a barricade that didn't allow either one of us in.

Joseph adored being with his great grandmother whom he lovingly called BaBa. The two of them had an incredible bond. How very blessed he was to be given the chance to know her in his lifetime, just as I was with my great grandmother. While living with her, they became closer and grew an even deeper connection. They watched cooking shows and cartoons together, reading and telling stories to one another. Although Joseph adored his special time with BaBa, it was clear he was struggling with being away from our home and neighbourhood family, particularly Arman. We were both creatures of habit and routine. I tried my best to bring many of the comforts of home along with us including his bed, special toys and of course, bin upon bin of LEGO, but it wasn't the same. Living in the confines of the apartment was getting more difficult each day, so, when the opportunity presented itself to move into our Bloor street neighbour's home while they vacationed in Florida, we jumped at it! It made day to day living much easier, especially for Joseph. He could have friends over, play outside and he had his own large bedroom downstairs.

The chemical exposure from living in other people's space was taking a toll on me. Dizzy spells, nausea and migraines were daily occurrences. My husband was also under incredible stress trying to secure employment. The challenges were endless.

It was now April 2009, and we had been out of our home nearly six months. Our neighbours returned from Florida and we were now living in their basement which was a tight squeeze for the three of us. There was no reprieve from the snoring and there were many nights I never went to sleep. I sat wide awake on a futon love seat watching the hours painfully and slowly pass by, it was unbearable! When our home was almost completed, I begged to move back. My nerves and health were shot, and I couldn't take another day! Dizzy spells had been replaced by vertigo attacks which lasted for days. The migraines were getting more intense and the fatigue had turned into debilitating exhaustion. I needed my home back! I needed something that was safe and familiar to ground me, but my husband was vehemently against moving back before the house was completed. After many heated debates he reluctantly agreed.

As soon as we moved in my health immediately began to worsen. Whatever "greenish" products were used, were far from healthy for me to be around. Adhesives, caulking, paint etc., were causing reactions and poisoning me with every breath. A gas stove that I was dead set against, arrived despite my pleas. Between the gas stove and the gas fireplace, the fumes were overpowering my system. I used air purifiers constantly, but they were not helpful. I was being poisoned and re-poisoned daily. I liken it to sniffing airplane glue twenty-four hours a day. I couldn't think straight, let alone walk straight as the nausea was intense, and my concentration was terrible.

At this point, I could no longer be a passenger in a car due to the vicious vertigo and relentless nausea. Each time I attempted, my brain felt like it was in a blender, just as in the cockpit of the plane, it was a jumbled mess that I couldn't make sense of. It felt like my brain no longer knew north from south and was constantly going in a different direction than my body. Day after day, I lay on the sofa feeling like I was falling apart piece by piece. Countless times I ventured to the family doctor only to have my concerns and symptoms dismissed and belittled over and over again. He was an incredibly egocentric man without an ounce of compassion and the same bedside manner as the doctor who dealt with my miscarriage. He was disrespectful to women and used their hormones as a cause for everything. He constantly said it was nerves and stress that were making me sick. but I knew better! They were a contributing factor, but certainly not the root cause. There was something wrong! I changed family doctors only to get more of the same responses. The only one who truly understood and validated my symptoms was Dr. Ravi. He was also the one who could provide me with some relief, if only temporarily. Unfortunately, he had recently passed away which was devastating news and sent me into a whole new level of panic. Though we never got to the root cause, he helped me to live some days with at least a small degree of relief. I was desperate for understanding, for compassion, for a diagnosis and cure for my ongoing and never-ending suffering. I was desperate to find my *missing peace.*

There were days I'd be home alone, laying on the bathroom floor for hours, shaking and crying, wanting the terror in my head to stop. I was frightened by what I didn't understand and could not control in my brain. I was continually sent to my knees, collapsing in what I would call neurological distress. People reading this may wonder why I didn't keep trying to seek help from the Western Medical community, but by this time the medical world had begun to make me believe that I was crazy. I was tired of being dismissed and labeled so I stopped going. The stress and humiliation caused by these visits were not worth it to me anymore. I stopped putting myself out there again and again, to be judged and belittled. I began doing the alternative medical circuit, but still no solid answers. Though each had a variation, they all kept coming up with the same vague conclusions, my liver was overloaded with toxins, Epstein Barr Virus, severe candida, hormonal imbalance, structural issues and stress. All of these carry a myriad of symptoms that overlap and mimic one another. Nothing provided me with long-term relief, or a clear picture of what was really going on. Each practitioner would say the same thing: "Treatment should have worked by now", at which point, they would give up on me or I would give up on them.

As the mystery illness progressed, it became more difficult to conceal and going to work had now become sporadic. After Joseph and my husband left in the mornings, I laid on the sofa crying in pain, terrified by the never-ending vertigo. Joseph knew I was unwell but had no idea to what extent. He lived his entire life with mommy having headaches and I did my best to hide and disguise so much of my suffering in order to spare him the worry and concern. When Joseph returned home from school, my theatrics would commence and for the most part, I think he believed me. When Joseph asked why I had not been to work, I pretended all was fine. Strategically, I placed an array of file folders and office supplies on the coffee table in front of the sofa I had been laying on all day. I insisted I was working from home, doing paperwork and taxes.

* * * * *

Joseph was always such a very well-mannered boy, never asking for anything, ever. Never in his twenty-two years, as I write this book, has my son come up and said: "I want" or "Can I have?" If there was anything he desired, Joseph would ask permission to spend his own savings. One day, as the two of us were watching television together, a commercial came on advertising a new LEGO set. He was awe struck! Feeling not too bad that day, I asked if he would like to take a drive and purchase the new set as a special treat. He excitedly leaped out of his chair saying over and over, "Yes please Mommy!" Between the short time I asked and when we were ready to go, a major rainstorm was beginning to come through. Weather had become one of my many enemies now as the barometric fluctuations created extreme pressure that resulted in migraines and my usual vertigo would get much more intense during storms of any sort. I came down the stairs and Joseph took one look at me and knew I wasn't well. Of course, in true Joseph fashion he said, "It's ok mommy, we can go another time, I don't need it." At which point, I didn't care if I had to put him on my back and crawl the entire way, we were going! I told him to get his jacket on, there was a LEGO set waiting for us! With a huge smile, he donned his coat and we were off! With each step to the car, it felt like I was carrying my brain under my arm, it felt like my brain was no longer a part of me. All I kept thinking was: "How am I going to get there?" Growing up, Joseph was easily overwhelmed with new tasks and quickly became defeated. When he was three years old, I sat him down one day with a stack of white paper and coloured markers asking him to write on twelve sheets the saying, "I CAN DO IT!" The entire time he was creating his signs, I had him repeat the phrase over and over. Each sign was then hung up in every room of our home as a constant reminder to him that he could do anything. My son could see me sweating and struggling as we headed up the road to the toy store. In the sweetest and most unforgettable voice he said, "Mommy, you can do it!" He repeated it continually the entire trip, every once in a while, taking his small hand and rubbing my shoulder. Joseph's love and support is what got me there and back. When he was a tiny boy, I would repeat to him: "We can get through anything knowing we don't have to face it alone." He was my rock, he was my solid, that was my son.

JoJo Marie Schillaci

Chapter Nineteen

It's now 2010, Joseph is twelve years old and I had been struggling with my health for some time now, I was on a mission to find any support I could to help me get through the Hell I was living so I decided to reach out to our parish priest. I ended up placing more than a dozen calls requesting communion and prayers (more for comfort and support than religious reasons), but not one call was returned. When I questioned the parish secretary, she explained that I was not within their "service area." I never recalled them asking what area I was from when they were passing the basket or mailing me envelopes for donations. After sixty years of my family being a part of the church, I was "too far" to receive prayers. My friend Rosemary mentioned that there was a remarkable minister at nearby St. George's On-The-Hill Anglican Church. When she said his name, I giggled out loud. I remembered Father Myles from my days at the funeral home. He was an unconventional, lively-spirited humanitarian whom we all wanted to do services with. I had to reach out! I called him up at 9am on a Monday morning and introduced myself. He vaguely remembered me. I shared with him my struggles and that I was a parishioner of a church down the street. When he inquired as to why my clergy refused to visit me, I told him of my ongoing battle and I'll never forget his response… "Do you have coffee?" "Yes", I replied, somewhat hesitantly. "Good, pour me a cup, I'll be there in ten!" True to his word, he arrived ten minutes later and shared an hour with me, listening, giving counsel and communion. Father Myles was just as I remembered him. He was a musician who played in rock bands and had found his calling later in life. He was unedited and unapologetic, he was the real deal. He invited our family to join them for Sunday service. It didn't matter to him what religion you were, it was about opening your heart and coming together, and this deeply resonated with me. I never considered myself a religious person, having less interest in Bible quotes and more for living a life of compassion and connection. For many years, I watched our son "do time" in the pews at Sunday service, only to come home with nothing gained, but an hour lost. It was time for change!

The following Sunday, Joseph and I attended service at St. George's. It was unlike any service we had ever experienced before. Everyone was smiling and full of the most beautiful welcoming energy. There was music and laughter and when we exchanged the sign of Peace, I witnessed a new level of sincerity. Joseph giggled as Father Myles made the sign of the cross and said: "Without spirituality the sign of the cross is just baseball signals." This was a far cry from the sombre, monotone lectures we had been accustomed to. It felt right. I happened to look down at the church bulletin that was laying on the pew. Upon reading it, I laughed out loud: "Something To Read If The Sermon Is Boring." Oh yes, I think I'm gonna like it here!

The next week, Joseph agreed to go again. This time, before the service began, Father Myles took him down to meet James, the Youth Pastor. I had heard that St. George's had an incredible youth group run by an amazing man. Joseph reluctantly agreed to go with James, and I attended service upstairs. Afterwards, Joseph met me outside with the biggest smile I had seen in a long time. He jumped in the car and talked about the youth group all the way home. The great people he met, the games they played and the places the youth group were planning on going. He was hooked!

St. George's on-the-Hill Anglican Church, Toronto, Ontario

After that, Joseph went every Sunday, whether I was able to attend or not. Sometimes he rode his bike, occasionally his father took him and other times, someone from the group would be kind enough to pick him up. He always looked forward to it. With the incredible guidance, inspiration and dedication of James Noronha, the youth group did amazing things. St. George's believed children could make a difference and learn to live a compassionate, Christian life, not by studying the Bible, but by active, compassionate community outreach. Serving and preparing "Out of The Cold" dinners, handing out bagged lunches to the less fortunate downtown, singing at the local hospice care centre and charity drives, the list was endless. They also had great fun doing activities together such as laser tag, Canada's Wonderland, movie night sleepovers, amazing race events and so much more. Joseph absolutely thrived in this environment and loved being with like-minded kids. He fit in perfectly and for a mom who was limited in what she could give in the moment, St. George's and James were the biggest blessing anyone could ask for.

* * * * *

My life was taking on a much more isolated existence from people, from places, from movement and from experiences and, as a result, from human connection. My world was becoming smaller and smaller and so were my life experiences. Family gatherings were impossible for me to take part in. The chemical allergy was extreme and I was hypersensitive to virtually everything imaginable. The potential poisons were endless, and people's understanding and compassion was limited at best. I never knew when the vertigo would begin or end. Like a forecasted storm, sometimes it was predictable. Other times, it would approach like a demon in the night, silent and without warning. Each day, my energy was different. Some days, I managed to get by but, other days, I couldn't lift my head from the exhaustion. This made planning anything next to impossible and as a result, I inevitably would spend holidays alone. My husband would take Joseph to either his family or mine and I was left on my own, it was an all-in or all-out existence. I continually mourned what I could no longer experience with my son and wished deeply to be a part of special occasions. Though he tried to show a brave face in front of me, I could see how disappointed he was each time they left without me. Those wonderful summer days we spent together were a thing of the past. Centre Island was impossible now, despite it being a mere fifteen-minute ferry ride, the ever-present vertigo and motion sickness made the mere thought of it inconceivable. Bike rides were also out of the question and outings were subject to me being well enough to drive and there was always the threat of chemical exposure. I would have given anything for the simple life we used to share. My husband continued to take him on outings, with Joseph always bringing me back a treasure from his travels, usually a rock to add to our collection that we had amassed throughout the years, a lovely gift that was always bittersweet to receive. It was sweet for him to think of me and bitter to have a reminder of more time lost. People would send me pictures of their own travels and gift me souvenirs, I was appreciative, but a part of me did not want to be reminded of the fun I was missing. Even cooking and baking were becoming next to impossible tasks because the fumes from the gas stove caused me to collapse on the floor each time I tried. My existence and joy were derived from the time I shared with my son at home and with our beautiful Old English Sheepdog, Shomei.

Joseph and Shomei, 2009.

Shomei was the most incredible human spirit captured in a dog's body. She never knew she was a dog. I don't think anyone ever told her. Shomei was terrified of other dogs and preferred the company of humans and much like Joseph, she never caused problems and asked for nothing but love. She was the essence of pure love, in the truest sense of the word. Humans could have learned so much from Shomei.

* * * * *

My cousin Cosmo is the kindest and most gentle soul you will ever come across. Soft spoken, and just like the great grandmother we shared, a man of few words, but someone who is always listening. Growing up, after we finished work at the garden centre, most Saturday nights were spent with his family. Our grandmothers were sisters and there was something incredibly special about the mingling of four generations around the dinner table. I adored these nights.

My Aunt Lena and Uncle Joe Pusateri.

His parents, my Aunt Lena and Uncle Joe, always make you feel welcomed. There is a coziness to their home that I loved so much as a little girl. Aunt Lena is yet another female force to be reckoned with in our family. Small in size, but with a perfect mix of opinion and attitude in the most feisty form. Much like Auntie Rea, if she likes you, she loves you and she will let you know it. Similarly, if you do something that doesn't sit right with her, you're going to hear about it. A real straight shooter and I love her for it. My Uncle Joe is small in stature but ten feet tall in character. A mild-mannered gentleman who never feels the need to be boisterous or condemning. Just a sweet, quiet man whose permanent smile lights up his face and all those he encounters.

As my illness progressed, my contact with people lessened and the fear grew more each day. I ached for comfort, something familiar so I called my cousin Cosmo. He immediately came to my door spending many Sunday afternoons at my side. We discussed our belief in something higher, the power of the Universe and the energy that was constantly surrounding us. Our conversations deeply resonated with me, he was speaking my language and I loved it! Whenever I was faced with questions and challenges, Cosmo constantly encouraged me to "put it out to the Universe."

* * * * *

It was during this time that one day, my husband asked me to retrieve something from his wallet. In the more than twenty years we had been together I had never gone into his wallet, just as he had never gone into mine. There was no need, no desire. When I opened it, I was shocked to find an old picture of his high school sweetheart who had moved to Australia. It was finally confirmed and I never said another word about it. I replaced the picture, too sick and too tired for yet another battle. The ghost I had felt for all these years WAS real. She wasn't in my head; she was in his wallet all along.

Chapter Twenty

I dreaded the night. Going from a sitting position and laying my head on a pillow was impossible. The only way I could manage a bed was to be propped up like a sitting Buddha, supported by a mountain of pillows that were in every shape, size and material you could imagine. It was important that my head stay completely straight as the vertigo attacks had escalated in intensity and duration and any degree of tilting my head would initiate these attacks. When they hit, it felt like I was being suspended upside down off the edge of a cliff. My brain could not differentiate up from down and the room began to spin, accompanied by vicious nausea. Closing my eyes made it a thousand times worse. Trembling does not come close to describing what my body would go through. I could feel the bed shaking beneath me from my body trying to escape the Hell it was in. It was the most terrifying thing I had ever experienced. These attacks could last minutes or drag on for hours. As the anxiety escalated, my heart raced like a stampede of wild horses! I felt like I was going to die!

At twelve years old Joseph was far wiser and more aware than that little boy of two who used to get ice packs for mommy's head. I carried tremendous guilt for not being able to give him the childhood he had become accustomed to. One day, Joseph looked at me with the utmost sincerity and said: "Mom what does it feel like to be angry." I stopped what I was doing, stunned at such a question. "What do you mean, what does it feel like?" He explained, "I don't think I've ever felt that before." "You've never been angry Joseph? Ever?" "I don't think so mom. I've been sad and disappointed, maybe a little mad, but I don't think I've ever been angry." Sweet Jesus! Wow! After thinking about it and discussing what he had said with his father, we both could not recall seeing him angry or mad. Some who don't know better may think this was due to Joseph being a spoiled, only child. This couldn't have been further from the truth. This is a child drenched with love, safety, security, laughter and understanding from both parents. A spoiled child, he was not. This was the child who asked to go to the toy store "just to look" and would do just that and nothing more, never asking for a thing. This is the child who made band aids out of leaves for injured worms. This is the child that picked flowers for the neighbours and would check in on his elderly great grandmother to ensure she was ok. This is the child who at nine years old, insisted on getting his first job sweeping hair at a barbershop. No, this was not a spoiled child but a child who was respected, loved and whose voice was always heard. I took his question about anger to heart, but I don't think I ever did answer it.

Unlike Joseph, I was now all too familiar with anger on a daily basis. Anger at the medical profession for not believing me. Anger at the people surrounding me, whom I felt were not supportive. Anger at my body for putting me through such Hell. Anger at myself, for not being able to figure it out. Many days, my low-grade anger would boil over to full-blown rage. This was not me; this is not how I lived my life. To me, my character was becoming unrecognizable.

I didn't feel right and knew there was something else going on with my body. It was different from years previous to the wedding when I had the emotional breakdown, a complete fraying of my nerves and emotions. This time, I wasn't feeling that at all. This was physical. Something was going on, but I had no idea what it was. It felt like a low energy buzz throughout my entire body and again, I had been led to believe everything was in my head, so after a while, I assumed this was too.

I accepted the task of hiring a caregiver for my grandmother. She did not want anyone else looking after her, which made this process extremely stressful. Grandma was less then cooperative, and her anger had grown more volatile as she grew older. I was scheduled to meet the potential brave candidate at Tim Hortons and while making my way to the coffee shop, I got caught in a surprise downpour and was stopped dead in my tracks. I felt like I had stuck my wet finger into a light socket and an intense surge of what felt like electricity started to climb from the bottom of my spine and raced to the base of my skull. "Now, what was happening to me?" I composed myself enough to make it inside, but I wasn't truly present for our meeting as my mind was preoccupied with yet another worry. Over the course of several months I experienced the same thing half a dozen times. There was never any rhyme or reason, it came out of nowhere and it added to the already seemingly unsolvable mystery of my health.

I truly believed that banging my head on the treehouse many years earlier was the source of much that I was now experiencing. Even though the doctors diagnosed it as a minor concussion, the effects it had on me were anything but. My husband made a connection through work to someone who had also suffered a concussion. Paul was recovering from what I learned was Post Concussive Syndrome (PCS). PCS is defined as a complex disorder in which various symptoms such as headaches and dizziness last for weeks and sometimes months after the injury. Once again, these symptoms were extremely vague. Also, mine had not last months, but for years! I agreed to speak to him, and we had an immediate connection. Paul had done a tremendous amount of research and was very knowledgeable about the condition. He was compassionate and willing to give me insights to attempt to clarify what I was experiencing. He was not only book smart, but a wise old soul. His kindness and most importantly, his understanding were the soft place I had been aching so badly for. Finally, someone who got it! His wife Melanie was equally kind and understanding having recently gone through her own traumatic injury. We connected every week and I shared my constant battle with them. Their attentive ears were a blessing and although they couldn't explain the reason I was still suffering, they were a huge support. They continued to be an integral part of my healing for years to come.

My time with grandma was gradually becoming less and less. Grandma, like me, had mobility issues which limited her ability to leave the house. My grandmother had celebrated her ninetieth birthday and shortly thereafter fell and broke her hip. Under normal circumstances, I would have been by her hospital bedside, but this time was different. On good days, I would go for short visits, but they were sporadic. I made homemade soups and applesauce with my husband and Joseph kindly delivering them to her. Joseph would go any chance he could. She was suffering from pain and was very depressed while in the hospital, constantly saying in an exhausted voice "It's time to die." True to her stubborn ways, she began refusing to do her post-surgical breathing exercises and Joseph would get upset with her. Even at his young age, he was one of the very few to whom she would listen. Every day, he told her to do the exercises for him. If he couldn't get a ride over to the hospital, he would call her on the phone and listen to her until she completed them. Those two would do anything for each other.

She now had an around the clock caregiver which gave me some peace of mind knowing at least that she wasn't alone. It was little comfort and I missed her terribly. She worried constantly about me and called frequently just to check in. She always called them, "Those goddamn headaches" when referring to my health. She hated them as much as I did. I never went into great detail about my health with her, just like Auntie Rea, I believed the less she knew the better. Our phone calls never seemed to be enough as I was used to seeing her daily and her absence was a huge void in my life, but Joseph continued his visits after school and on Saturdays. There was always something comforting about grandma's apartment, it was like home-base to us. That warm place with a familiar smell and sweet memories.

Grandma and I going to a wedding, 1995.

* * * * *

One day, while discussing technology with Joseph, I commented that people didn't call each other anymore.

Phones don't ring, people don't truly connect any more. I was then given a lesson in millennial communication by my son. Joseph said: "Mom, that's not how people do it anymore. Ya gotta get with the times if you want to stay connected with people." Technology is not something I embraced and still don't today. I do believe it has its place and I am grateful for so much that it has brought to our lives but, at the same time, I mourn the simplicity of the old days. He said the best way for me to connect and reconnect with people is to go on Facebook. Reluctantly, I agreed to have him set up an account for me. With my outside experiences being so limited, this would give me a chance to interact with people, even if only from a screen.

One day, a name popped up on Facebook that I was delighted to see. Louie had been a very special friend from elementary school more than thirty-five years earlier. Even back then, Louie's character was larger than life. He danced, sang and marched to his own beat and he chose the volume which was always set on high! I was thrilled to reconnect! Soon after, I found another dear friend, Johnny C. Another sweet memory from my elementary days or shall I say daze. Johnny C was my grade seven and eight crush. He was a slightly ginger, Irish boy who made me laugh, made me smile and made me blush usually all at the same time. I would get butterflies standing next to him and talking to him made my knees go weak. He was also my very first kiss. It happened at our grade eight Christmas dance, right there in the 1950's style gymnasium amongst the smells of vintage wood curing, decades of sweat and a little too much "Babe" perfume. Someone decided to bring mistletoe and as they approached and hung it high above our heads, Johnny C gentlemanly gave me the sweetest peck on the lips. I felt it all the way to my toes! That was as far as the preteen romance would go, but I never forgot sweet Johnny C. After sharing phone calls with each of them, we all decided to meet for a drink (for me it was always tea) at a local pub close to where we had gone to school. This was a huge undertaking since I was rarely leaving the house amidst all the worsening symptoms. My social life was non-existent and despite what was working against me, I had to try. My efforts would not be wasted. I was met with the most beautiful, warm and compassionate energy with both of them welcoming me with their arms opened wide. I managed to last an hour before the symptoms forced me to call it a night. It was the most I had laughed in years. A very, very sweet night indeed.

Chapter Twenty-One

Looking back, the beginning of 2012 was definitely a forewarning of what was to come. I had exhausted what I believed to be, the gamut of alternative health practitioners. Even worse, the western medical world concluded time and time again that my issues were psychologically driven. I was no longer working and it was now impossible to carry out the simplest of tasks. I recall trying to sweep the kitchen floor and after two minutes falling to the ground in a crying heap. I felt like my brain was in overload! It was impossible for me to figure out how to hold the broom, walk and sweep all at the same time.

On a cold Sunday in February, my husband and son decided to go tobogganing at a park just five minutes away. I reluctantly declined even going to watch. I had a terrible headache and the fatigue was keeping me on the sofa yet again. I was very upset about missing out and after a short time, decided to surprise them. It took all I had in me to drive to the hill and as I sat in the car, I was apprehensive about taking that first unsteady step out. It felt like I was walking in a fun house with moving sidewalks and distorted mirrors, flashing lights and noise makers. This was my new normal. Joseph's face lit up like a Christmas tree when he saw me and excitedly screamed: "Mom watch me go down. Watch me!" It was worth all the pain and suffering just to see and hear my boy so happy. Shomei began leaping and bounding through the mounds of snow. She was a snow dog through and through and was equally happy to see me and have us all together. I lasted a short time until the snow began to fall heavily. Giant white flakes falling from the sky at a dizzying speed. My brain was upside down again. I couldn't keep my eyes open. It was too much! "Stop it! Just stop it!" I pleaded over and over "please make it stop." I staggered to the car and drove at a snail's pace back to the house. Finally, I made it home. I desperately needed to cut off visual and audio stimulation. I literally crawled up the staircase to my bedroom, undressing as I went and leaving a trail of clothing behind me. Making my way into the bathroom and keeping the lights off, I was now in darkness. I slid into the tub which I had filled to the brim and with every bit of energy I had, lifted one leg with the balance of a new born fawn and made it inside my cocoon of comfort. I submerged myself up to my ears with only the slight outline of my face breaking the surface. I felt my body beginning to calm down and my senses quieting. The warmth of the surrounding water provided the hug I needed to keep me together in the moment. Without knowing it, I was grounding myself and stabilizing my brain and nervous system at the same time.

* * * * *

Joseph was now in his grade eight graduation year. I had spent his entire elementary school life alongside him helping out in classrooms, heading up fundraisers and being a constant image around the school. Not anymore. The school had an idea I wasn't well, and the staff was always loving, compassionate and supportive to our family. I was no longer able to make it out to school events and social activities which broke my heart as much as I'm sure it broke Joseph's. The senior students had been working for weeks building a set and rehearsing for their first school play. The night had come and there was no way I could go. I couldn't walk, and I couldn't see straight and was sweating profusely with severe nausea. Louie and I had spoken of the play earlier and true to form, he offered to keep me company. It certainly didn't lessen my heart breaking, but it definitely warmed it. As my dear friend sat with me, I gripped his hand tighter and tighter, I had him in a human vice. I was conscious of what I was doing but couldn't help myself. I felt like I was holding on for dear life. The daily fear I had faced my entire life was hitting critical mass within me. There was a looming fear of falling off the edge of a cliff into the abyss, alone into the unknown. I had to hold on to something, to someone, to anything. If you had asked me why, the only answer I could have possibly given was, "Because the only other option was to let go and there was no possible way I could do that."

* * * * *

There was a Goodwill thrift store just down the street and it was now the only place I could manage on a good day. The two-minute drive was tolerable and even if I only lasted five minutes inside, at least it was something. The day was bright and sunny, so I ventured over. I loved their book section and on this particular day, decided to peruse the titles and see what treasures I could find. Between the many rows of books, I quickly became overwhelmed. Each title began to merge into another, each bookshelf floated into the next and my head was spinning out of control. Within minutes I was on my knees. "Now what?" The store seemed bigger than usual, enormous in fact. I couldn't manage everything that my eyes were taking in, there was way too much information. My brain was being bombarded with too much light and sound. Sobbing uncontrollably, I staggered to the car. "How was I going to make it home?" It took more than an hour to reach my driveway and I swore I would never put myself in such a vulnerable position ever again.

That night, I lay shaking in my bed, propped up by my mountain of pillows attempting to sleep and as usual, it was elusive. I kept hearing the same message over and over again in my head, "Get downstairs and don't come up again!" I felt an incredible sense of urgency. My gut was warning me that one day, I was going to get up those stairs and not be able to get back down. No way! I wasn't going to let that happen! The next night, I began sleeping on the main floor by the sliding door just off the kitchen. We had a chaise lounge, and this was where I laid my head each night for far longer than I could have ever imagined in my most frightening dreams.

Spending day after day alone until Joseph came home gave me hours to sit and ponder one catastrophic thought after another. My seclusion caused my fears to escalate. The heaviness of my thoughts weighed on me like a ton of bricks. The all-consuming questions of "how, why and what if?" that plagued me as a little girl in bed, had returned. Those thoughts had grown with me. They were a deep part of me and now they were larger and more daunting than ever before. Just as that young child, I dreaded the night. The silence brought heightened sensitivity to everything I was feeling emotionally, physically and mentally. The enemy at night was not only the symptoms, but my thoughts. Peace was ever elusive, nonexistent in any way, shape or form. I ached for just a taste of it. A morsel of calm to nourish and comfort me. There was no mommy bed to crawl into now. I had to get through each minute until the light of day signaled that I had made it through again. Nightmares were frequent occurrences but, on this particular night, I experienced one like no other. It was so vivid, so clear. In my dream, I was using my tongue to feel my teeth one by one. As I ran it across the top of my mouth, each tooth loosened until finally falling out into my hand. Then the same thing began to happen with my bottom row of teeth. While sleeping, I saw the image of myself reflected in a mirror, my mouth gaping open and blood dripping as each tooth slowly slipped from the grasp of my hands on to the ground. With that image my eyes shot open and I awoke in terror as a wave of panic washed over me. I had dreamt all my teeth had fallen out! I shrieked out loud: "Oh my God, the dream book!"

* * * * *

I had been sleeping downstairs for a few months now and could barely poke my nose out past the front door. As the symptoms increased day by day, my overall tolerance was decreasing. Over the years, my world had become smaller and smaller and I could no longer go into the living room easily, somehow the space felt too big. It felt like there was too much to see and too much to take in. The small side alcove off the kitchen where the chaise sat, felt manageable and more sheltered for my brain. I spent all of my days and nights on the chaise with my forever companion Shomei at my side. The powder room was exactly twenty-one steps away. Some days, walking was difficult. On good days, I used a chair as a walker to assist me with my balance which was terribly off. I felt like the floor was constantly sloping, causing me to often lose my footing. The not so good days, I couldn't even manage that. I resorted to keeping an emergency bucket hidden from sight under the huge round marble coffee table that sat in front of the chaise. It was my dirty secret, not unlike the pacifier I used behind the recliner as a child. My husband knew, he saw it. It made the shame that much worse. I felt so alone, so helpless and needy, like a small child crying out for help, for love, for understanding and hearing nothing but silence in return…I longed for my *missing peace*.

Shomei giving comfort, January 2012.

One day, as I was using the bucket, it suddenly collapsed from under me. My bottom abruptly met the ground and I sat startled in broken pieces of plastic amongst my own urine. I was bleeding from the sharp edges that had punctured my skin. I crawled into the kitchen to get paper towels and cleaned myself and the floor as best I could. I began to gather the pieces and the one thought that kept running through my mind was, "I've hit rock bottom." Little did I know, there was still a much greater fall awaiting me.

JoJo Marie Schillaci

Chapter Twenty-Two

It was spring 2012 and my health was crumbling. My family was crumbling. Our life as we knew it was crumbling. The marriage was severely strained as the deep mutual resentment created an even greater distance between us. Over the years, I developed a defensive porcupine mentality in the marriage as a way to protect myself. Eventually, he gave up trying to figure out how to hug a porcupine and the vicious cycle continued. He was visibly unhappy in the marriage, as was I. Joseph was also not his usual carefree, happy self. One could see that my health issues were weighing heavily on his mind. Joseph and I had always been extremely close and deeply connected, yet there was so much I had hidden from him in recent years regarding my health; there was no hiding it now. The jig was up! Somehow, despite the challenges, he remained the calm, compassionate and loving soul he had always been. He immersed himself into service, which always fueled him. Service at St. George's, at school and within our community. No matter what Joseph did, he always made us proud.

People in my life were beginning to drop away. The invitations stopped coming and the phone stopped ringing. When an offer did come up I would inevitably and respectfully have to decline. People didn't understand my illness. How could they? I didn't know what was happening and couldn't explain it myself. If you were to tell someone that you suffer from cancer or heart disease, they would be able to wrap their heads around it. My illness didn't have a name nor an IV, wound or balding head. Where there is misunderstanding there will always be scuttlebutt. The gossip soon began and was fueled by those who knew better. This was salt in my already gaping wound. The ostracism from friends and family was deeply painful and it left a massive void not just in my life, but in my son's as well.

It was May of 2012 and the day before Joseph's fourteenth birthday and whereas in previous years I would have been excited planning a party, this year I was dreading it. I felt like I was good for nothing, a complete disappointment to him. The June Cleaver image I had worked so hard to maintain during his childhood had long since been shattered and unfortunately, I didn't get the feeling that anyone was going to pick up where I left off. I tried desperately to fall asleep that night, but the resulting migraine was violent. After finally drifting off for a short time, I awoke with violent vertigo symptoms unlike any I had experienced before. There was something far deeper happening, as if something snapped inside of me. At no time did it feel emotionally rooted. I knew what that felt like from years earlier and despite all the fear and terror I was experiencing, I never had one panic attack. I couldn't move a finger without my brain fighting back, it felt like it was falling out of my head. The nausea was far more vicious and intense than before. I couldn't sit up; it felt like my body had no bones and I slumped over like a rag doll. Looking back, the feelings of electric shock up and down my spine that I had previously experienced, was a warning. At this point, an ambulance ride was out of the question. I wasn't going to endure the pure Hell of travelling to the hospital, only to be told I was crazy and to turn around and go home again. I wasn't going to put myself through that yet again. Unable to stand and barely move, I was now completely bedridden. My mother immediately arranged for a twenty-four hour caregiver.

Just like at the toboggan hill months earlier, any movement such as snow falling, leaves and trees swaying or heaven forbid, a fly in my sights, my brain would go into overload. In order to shelter my brain from any outside movement, we now had to cover the sliding doors with two heavy sheets. Television and all computer screens were absolutely impossible to look at as these items would induce immediate vertigo and nausea. Radio was intolerable as my hearing had also become overly sensitive making the slightest noise feel like an explosion of piercing pain in my head. It was so bad, that our steel cutlery had to be replaced with plastic in order to minimize its impact. My senses of taste and smell were grossly overactive. As a result, my food had to be very bland, almost tasteless, in order to be tolerated. Anything else would induce gagging. The chemical allergy had been getting worse, but it was now unbearable to have the slightest scent, natural or otherwise in my space. My senses were in overdrive and it felt like I was having a physical breakdown of my entire central nervous system.

I immediately called a longtime friend and chiropractor Dr. Ric Levenston. One day earlier, he had attended a symposium on vestibular disorders at the Faculty of Medicine Neuroscience Department at the University of Toronto. Dr. Ric now believed that I was suffering from a vestibular disorder. The vestibular system is a sensory system that is responsible for providing our brain with information about motion, head position and spatial orientation; it also involves motor functions that allow us to keep our balance, stabilize our head and body during movement and maintain posture. He said: "I know exactly who you need to see!"

Dr. K. had a PhD in vestibular medicine and he had travelled to war zones such a Kuwait and Afghanistan treating soldiers with traumatic brain injuries. His protocol is diagnostics, followed by intense computer assisted rehabilitation. The best news was that the testing was mobile! Within a week Dr. K was at my bedside ready to begin the hour-long testing of my brain and I was terrified! Both my son and husband were present to support me. I was given a pair of virtual reality-like goggles and asked to look at a screen. He directed me to tell him if I saw the green lights on the screen moving. Through my eyes, it looked like fireworks shooting back and forth and it instantly induced nausea and a massive headache that was incredibly difficult to manage. "Yes, and I can't take it. It looks like fireworks of green lights and it won't stop, make it stop!" I could hear my son say to his father: "Dad, the lights aren't moving." I later learned that this was my brain misfiring. A series of other tests were done and at the end, the doctor concluded there was definitely a vestibular issue, but he couldn't determine the extent of it until the results were analyzed. Three weeks later, he returned and announced that I had a significant left unilateral deficit of my vestibular system. In short, part of my brain had died. BOOM! The results were in and it was both objectively and medically confirmed! I was indeed NOT crazy! The symptoms were NOT in my head and I did NOT do anything to create this! Vindication at last! If I could have jumped up and danced at the news, I would have. I took a deep breath and listened as he told my husband: "Your wife is very sick, and this is going to take time." This explained why my brain continually felt like it was in a blender as well as the overload and spatial issues I had been experiencing. Dr. K. described to me that my brain could not get a clear signal from my eyes. The visual input when sent through the vestibular system to the brain, was incorrect. It was similar to a television channel without a clear signal, resulting in a snow screen. It was beginning to make sense.

The good news was that the vestibular issue was restorative and not degenerative. There was reason to believe that through rehabilitation, a different part of the brain could take over a new task thanks to the blessing of neuroplasticity. This means the brain is not hardwired as once thought and can be taught new tasks over time. When I asked how this happened, his answer clarified thirty years of confusion. He compared my vestibular system to that of a porcelain vase. When I had the terrible bicycle accident at the age of seventeen the impact likely traumatized the vestibular nerve causing a crack in the vase. The subsequent extensive dental work including root canals, braces and extractions would create a few more cracks. As time went on, my structure had been compromised by spending years sleeping in obscure positions like the car and shower stall, coupled with mounting stress, created more hair line cracks. The concussion from the tree house had created a major fracture to the system/vase and increased emotional pressure was putting an extra burden on an already taxed system. In 2011, I reluctantly had two root canals done and they were the final blow. After enduring so much damage, the vase could only stay intact for so long until finally, it fell to pieces causing a breakdown of my physical nervous system. Now it made sense! He explained it would be a very long process of at-home rehabilitation as there was no facility for such a program. I was given a computer program designed for my particular rehabilitation needs and while donning "3D like" glasses, I would have to work through several series of programs. This was the first stage, followed by physical rehabilitation. I would have to re-teach my brain how to sit up, stand, walk and multi-task all over again.

I was ill-prepared for what lay ahead for me. In the beginning weeks, rehab sessions would last anywhere from a minimum of thirty seconds to a maximum of two minutes per day, that's all my brain could tolerate. At the end of these mini sessions I got terribly ill, suffering debilitating migraines lasting more than a day, which inevitably delayed the next session. I had no idea how brutal it was going to be. Sometimes ignorance is best.

Soon after being diagnosed, I needed to find the best osteopathic practitioner to help me with manual manipulation and structural issues who also needed to have a background in traumatic brain injuries. I found a highly regarded and well sought after Toronto practitioner, Katherine Liberatore who also taught at the Toronto Osteopathic College and had extensive training in brain trauma. Katherine was at the top of her field, but her waiting list was weeks long and she didn't make house calls. I called anyway. After hearing my situation, she explained that she was in the east end and did not make house calls but would do her best to find someone to help. True to her word, Katherine called a few days later, but she had no luck finding a connection. In the interim, Katherine decided to treat me until I found a permanent solution. She arrived on her day off and found me in darkness. I was in the bed, hunched onto my right side and could barely talk from the intense migraine, so I used hand signals and scribbled on paper to communicate with her. Our first treatment lasted only five minutes and it was immediately apparent to her, the dire condition of my central nervous system in addition to the vestibular issues. This did not deter her.

Katherine came on her day off every week for three years, always with the most beautiful energy and always with a smile on her face. It took more than a year and a half before she could do a complete treatment on me without my brain fighting back. Her work was setting the stage for my vestibular and central nervous system to heal. The woman that didn't do house calls was one hundred percent committed to my case. She believed in me, in the treatment and in the rehabilitative process that had been laid out. Over time, Katherine learned more about the intricate details of my case and personal life and she not only saw, but felt the effects of the dysfunctional marriage that was in crisis along with the growing financial pressure. All of this added insult to injury and Katherine was gracious enough to offer me a sliding scale for payment. I immediately renamed her "Special K."

Chapter Twenty-Three

I had now been completely bedridden for more than five months or 150 days. It had been more than 300 days since I had a shower or bath and the bucket had been my side kick far longer. Our home had gone from one filled with fun and laughter, to a dark, almost eerie silent tomb. It wasn't just the silence around me, but also the silence within me. I had always been the clown, the jokester, the organizer and the doer. My life had taken a 180-degree turn and I now merely existed from one painful moment to the next. Breath by breath, I struggled immensely just to make it through the days. Each morning, I'd open my eyes and think: "Dear God, how do I make it through another twenty-four hours of Hell?" The thought of one more day in the bed was daunting. The only inspiration I had to continue breathing was my son Joseph.

If indeed there was a Hell, I was most definitely living in it during the last half of 2012. The first step of the vestibular rehabilitation was implemented, and it went at an agonizingly slow and painful pace. I had gradually increased the computer rehab from thirty seconds to ten minutes per day and I kept thinking the second coming of Christ would happen long before I would take my painfully awaited first step out of the bed. I was having a terrible time dealing with the illness induced by the rehabilitation exercises, and it was creating even more anxiety within me. The feeling of needing to hold on was ever present and ever increasing as the peace I longed for seemed to be getting farther and farther away from my reach.

I asked Dr. K. if he knew of any past patients willing to share their support and insight through the process. I needed to speak with someone who had been to Hell and actually made it back. He explained that unfortunately, people that make it to the other side of vestibular rehabilitation rarely if ever, want to go back to it in any way, shape or form. This included talking with patients and I was beginning to understand why.

One of the biggest challenges I faced was being in the exact same spot and in the same position every moment of every day. I ached to stand up, stretch my body and move the muscles that needed to be released from their prison of stillness which was my crypt like bed. My entire world now consisted of a 10x12 space, the bed I lay in, the marble table that housed the bucket, and the sliding door that showed me the only proof that the outside world even existed. Directly in front of my bed was what I referred to as my inspiration wall. The wall I faced day in and day out. It was covered in inspirational sayings given to me by friends and family providing me something positive to focus on each day. Some of the sayings I still remember so clearly today are:

- You've got what it takes, but it will take everything you've got.
- You don't know how strong you are until being strong is your only choice
- It always seems impossible until it's done.

- I'm not where I need to be but, thank goodness, I'm not where I used to be.
- Don't look back, you're not going that way
- Don't believe everything you think
- He is able who thinks that he is able

These powerful words of inspiration, amongst approximately one hundred more are what my eyes and my mind focused on every single day. I read and repeated them as if I were doing a ritual prayer.

The rest of my home did not exist to me, the living room which was around the corner, might well have been on the other side of the world because of my body's inability to get to it. I longed to take back my home! Watching the caregivers in my kitchen doing what I wanted to do, no, what I needed to be doing, ripped me apart inside. Oh, how I wished to cook for my son, wash a dish or sweep my floor.

Joseph had begun grade nine and as if that wasn't difficult enough, under these circumstances it must have been sheer torture for him. The boy who used to smile from morning till night had become quiet, withdrawn and sad. The pressure of seeing me desperately working through the rehab was one thing, but the tension in the house was another. It was clear to everyone that the marriage was falling apart. All the challenges of decades previous and the baggage we each walked in with, were now hitting critical mass. The marriage had no solid foundation and though we tried our damnedest to build our lives together, it was built on quicksand not bedrock. Over time, the more we struggled individually and as a couple, the further down we sank.

During this difficult time there was nothing to grab hold of, not even each other. What little communication existed had completely broken down, and I could feel his mounting anger, frustration and resentment.

The fears I carried my entire life had now transformed into terror. Everything that I had been fearful of in my past became more pronounced, more real and more imminent: finances, being alone, not being good enough and resisting the natural flow of life. All were thoughts that I ruminated on repeatedly throughout the day. I shook uncontrollably and began scratching at my arms and legs until they bled. I laid in terror from what I knew at my deepest core was unfolding but had no control of stopping. Again, if you were to ask me what it was, my reply would have been that same vague image of the monster from my childhood with no name, inching his way closer and closer.

* * * * *

Caregivers were a completely different story and a challenge of their own. Along with being costly, they were next to impossible to secure. We couldn't afford to sponsor help from overseas and even if we could, it would be a very slow process. As a result, the girls we hired used the position as a stopgap between contracts. As I speak of my experience with caregivers make note that this is my personal experience with the ones that came through my door, of which there were more than forty-five over four years. I am not painting all caregivers with the same brush. I can only speak to the ones under my employment.

To the vast majority of caregivers, this was not a highly desirable job. They preferred to work for the elderly who did not have all their faculties than for a forty-five year old woman. Regardless of the confines of my bed and my physical limitations, I was in fact, running my home and nobody's fool. Unfortunately, most of the caregivers did not provide what I would call "care." They provided the absolute minimum, devoid of kindness or compassion. Often, I would be left for hours without food or attention while they lay upstairs in my bed talking on their phones for hours. I was constantly put in a position of begging for basic care which demeaned me even more. Many times, they wouldn't show up for their shift, leaving us to frantically scour at the last minute for a replacement. The only exception to this was Gemma, my longtime weekend caregiver, who was not only loyal, but a constant source of laughter and support.

*****

It was now Christmas 2012 and under normal circumstances I loathed this time of year. but this year it reached an all-time new low. Regardless of my personal disdain for the season, in the past I had always done everything humanly possible to provide Joseph with the best Christmas experience possible. Visiting Santa, baking cookies, Christmas parties and decorating and I loved watching his Christmas performances in school plays where each year he inevitably played "Joseph." He enjoyed being chosen for the role because "Joseph" was a carpenter and my son loved to build. In kindergarten, he was insistent about bringing his toolbox on stage for the nativity scene, we finally talked him out of it.

This time, there was nothing I could do to fake the festivities, I was hog-tied. The only saving grace was St. George's. Joseph was heavily involved with all their Christmas activities and of course, the annual Christmas pageant which I was going to miss. It was bittersweet watching him so excited as part of that community and me not being able to enjoy it with him. He and my husband would set up the Christmas tree close to the sliding doors where I could see it from my bed but, in all honesty, I would have rather had it out of my sight. It was a glowing reminder of all I was missing, yet again.

It was one evening shortly after Christmas when my husband would come to my bedside and say in the heaviest tone: "I think I'm done. I don't think I'm into this anymore." and that's how I rang in the new year. A bomb drop, instead of a ball.

Chapter Twenty-Four

And that's how I started 2013. In my wildest imagination I could never have predicted the disaster that lay in waiting for me. It was better that I couldn't. The news from my husband created a tidal wave of terror within me. After twenty-two years of marriage, why now? Why in this moment? How could I possibly manage all that I was facing with divorce on top. The more I thought about him leaving, the more encased in fear I became. I couldn't breathe, it was like the world was coming down on me, my world, our world and Joseph's world. What about Joseph? This is where my panic reached a whole new level. I begged my husband to give me time, to let me at least get into the walker, be mobile and then we could figure things out, whatever that may be. I begged him in desperation not to leave. I remember holding his hand so tightly, grasping at his shirt, his arm, anything I could hold on to in an attempt to keep him close. Again, holding on for fear of letting go. Each day, asking him for reassurance that he wouldn't do anything yet: "I can't take one more thing. Tell me I have nothing to worry about. Please!" I begged him over and over again. I was like a starving person begging for food or a person in the desert begging for water. I trembled so badly that my muscles would begin to cramp, and I would again claw at my arms and legs like an animal, not feeling the breaking of my skin or notice the blood under my nails. I was clawing to get out, to get out of my own body to escape the confines of fear that held me for decades. The wall next to the bed felt like it was closing in on me, just as I clawed at my body, I tore at the wall with the hope of getting closer to freedom. Over time, I clawed the wall down to the studs as if trying to break free from Alcatraz. I had to get out and save my family, or what was pitifully left of it. Deep down, I knew I was postponing the inevitable. For many years I knew my husband didn't want to be in the marriage: always feeling the lurking ghost between us, but to have it confirmed was entirely different. I felt like I was being abandoned and this triggered a cavalcade of past emotions and fears. I felt like a baby being left on a doorstep to be someone else's problem. The words worthless, unworthy and unlovable came to mind. But, as sad as it may sound, I knew that the threat that I felt was not about losing love. It was so clear to me in that moment, that I was not in love with this man, but with the image of family we had tried so desperately to create and secure for our son. He was my friend, my longtime friend that I cared about. I didn't want to lose that, but I knew deep down I already had.

    We had defied the odds against us by persevering this long, but it just couldn't happen now. Of all the damn times, not now! Joseph's world was already blown apart, this would surely destroy him. All of this, these days and nights I was existing through had to be a nightmare. This wasn't real. It couldn't be. I kept hearing my grandmother's words over and over again as she read from her dream book when I was a little girl. Looking back at the reoccurring dream I had where all my teeth fell out, I realized the dream book was right. I WAS LOSING EVERYTHING!

* * * * *

After six months of computer rehabilitation it was now time to add the physical element. Unfortunately, a physiotherapist worked with me for over three months before I found out she had zero experience with the complex world of vestibular rehabilitation. I immediately discontinued the sessions and called my cousin Cosmo for help to fill the position. I trusted him explicity. I had one of the very best osteopaths in Toronto, now we needed to find the very best vestibular rehab specialist. Within ten minutes he called me back: "I found him!" His name was Joon Nah, the co-owner of Cornerstone Physiotherapy. Joon was not only Toronto's finest vestibular rehabilitation specialist, but highly acclaimed at being "the best" in Ontario. Upon meeting him, I had no doubt that I was in the right hands. It was obvious that he had the knowledge, capability and a clear plan to get me on my feet again.

Joon was no nonsense, but I could feel his compassion even if it was covered under many layers of practical ass kicking. He made it clear to me this was not for the faint of heart and that it would not come easy. It was going to be a long, hard process and he was fully committed to the case. He also made it abundantly clear that he expected me to meet him with the same level of commitment. There would be no wimping out on this. Through shaken voice and weakened spirit, I said without a second thought, "yes, I'm in, I can do it." When asked where a patient like me would do this type of rehab, he said firmly and emphatically: "Right where you are. You are exactly where you are meant to be." Joon openly admitted that he had never worked with a patient in these circumstances before; he was well aware of both the financial and marital challenges. The worst thing for neuro rehabilitation is stress. The brain needs calm, but it was clear that I had more going on than the average person. He suggested that I consider, what most people did, and go on pain relieving medication, as well as sleeping aids and anti anxiety pills. I flat out declined. The chemical allergy made me hyper-sensitive to all medications and I was going to manage with alternative methods. I needed my wits about me if I was going to carry on parenting my son through whatever Hell storm this was. He supported my decision and never brought it up again.

And so, our work together began. The major portion was ocular vestibular rehab using a laser pointer attached to a head band. I was to follow targets and outlines while moving my head slightly in every direction. Sometimes with eyes open, sometimes closed but, either way, it was sheer Hell. Chin tucks as well as minor leg movements began preparing my muscles for the big day when I would sit up. As with the computer portion, it would induce brutal migraines and savage sickness within me. My brain felt like it was floating in a bowl of oil and water each time I attempted the movements. I would move my head ever so slightly to the left, and my brain seemed to be five steps to the right.

Every day, I worked my hardest to reach a tipping point, trying my best to get my brain to cooperate with the rehab. It was a constant one step forward, two-steps backward cha-cha that I danced alone. I had no partner. I was mentally, physically and emotionally exhausted. My steadfast comfort was my son and our beautiful fur baby Shomei. Every day, Joseph helped with my laser exercises and encouraged me to "Just keep going." On bad days, he would sit on the bed and make me laugh as he always could. He had a dry sense of humour and a sarcastic mouth, just like his mama. I had been having a particularly difficult day when he came to my bed with a homemade sign for the inspiration wall. Joseph took a marker and wrote the same words I had asked him to copy when he was just a wee boy… "I CAN DO IT!" Through tears, I kept repeating it over and over again.

Joseph was a most compassionate soul. He was and is one big throbbing heart with incredible sensibility that you don't often see in people three times his age. He spoke little, but was always thinking, pondering and absorbing. After his studies, he spent the majority of his free time with the youth group and he was thriving. Despite our challenges at home, he was having an amazing time with an amazing group of people and doing amazing things for the community. James was taking the youth group on a mission trip to Itabo, Cuba and thought it a good idea for Joseph to join them. We agreed and in March of that year he embarked on his first adventure without us, and I had no reservations about letting him go. I completely trusted James and I knew he would be surrounded by goodness. Joseph was so excited he could barely contain himself. Again, a bittersweet time for me as I sat on the side lines not being able to help him pack or drive him to the airport to see him off. Though I missed him terribly, I took comfort knowing that he was having fun and experiencing new things away from the stresses of home. When he returned, Joseph was different. More independent, more self-assured and more confident. Again, St. George's was such a blessing.

* * * * *

Shomei always knew when I needed her most. She could sense my pain, my fear and anxiety. Standing guard at my bedside, sometimes lifting her paw and placing it upon my hand ever so gently. She looked at me with those big brown eyes and I could feel her love, her compassion and concern pour through. She had a lovely way about her. She had a human quality that was indescribable. You had to experience Shomei to fully comprehend her. I shared with her my fears, my inner thoughts and secrets and she always listened, never interrupted, and never gave advice I didn't want to hear. She just showed up and loved me unconditionally. She loved me despite the fact I couldn't feed her, bring her for a walk or have anything to give but my love. I was always enough for her. Shomei was also a source of great comfort for Joseph during this time. Whenever things became overwhelming, he and Shomei would head to the lake, it was their special place.

* * * * *

The only real distraction I had were the outside images of the world I watched through the sliding glass door. The world of which I was no longer a part, but a world for which I longed and ached. Not unlike the once breathless beings that I had witnessed in body bags at the funeral home, I too felt like breath was no longer in me. I was suffocating. Eventually, I could tolerate having the curtains opened small amounts. In order for them to be opened, the wind needed to be calm and the movement limited. Nature had always been my sanctuary and now it was a one-dimensional picture I admired like a painting on a wall. I studied that picture all day, every day. I could tell you which leaves were missing from each and every tree. I knew the habits of every squirrel and could identify them by how each one moved about differently in their own unique way. My sense of smell was heightened and each time the front door opened, a waft of outside air reached my bed. I could smell the weather and season, each one having its own distinctive redolence. I watched seasons change at a snail's pace and was learning from nature's classroom that everything evolves in the perfect time and in the perfect way. I witnessed how snow-covered ground can miraculously flourish into thick, green grass and how brown dormant sticks can blossom into lush greenery and fragrant blooms. Nothing could be rushed or wished to move at a faster pace than what was determined by the Divine. No matter the paralyzing grip of the bitter cold that seemed to keep us frozen in time, the warmth of the sun would inevitably return to usher in a season of rejuvenation and rebirth. Laying in the bed day after day, I had to keep reminding myself of this. I had to trust that my time to bloom would also come.

JoJo Marie Schillaci

At my darkest moments, I remember the feeling of complete helplessness most of all. An apocalyptic sense of loss of control. My instinct was to fix it all. That's what I do. My gig so to speak. I'm Super Mom! But not this time. Now, all I could do was breathe through each catastrophic moment, hoping somehow it would all magically fix itself. I could not move; I could barely raise my arms enough to embrace my son. I longed to, "hold him together." It was like being tied to a tree and watching your entire world, all that you have worked for, burn to the ground and being forced to watch, unable to rescue but a memory. I could not run away from it. I could not deny what was happening. The muscles in my body ached from the tension, stress and sheer panic of what was unfolding. Nail marks covered my hands and arms from trying so desperately to hold on. There was no escaping it. All I could do was let go.

Written 2013

Chapter Twenty-Five

I had spent my entire life running from my demons, immersing myself into doing and not feeling. I escaped the thoughts and fears by doing for others, by keeping my mind busy and distracted. I avoided anything that was a trigger or a source of emotional duress. These were the coping skills I had used my entire life. Where there is discomfort, run and when you're tired of running, bathe in the calm of nature. This was, quite obviously, no longer working for me. I couldn't run, there was no longer a means of distraction and the comfort of nature had become a flat screen. I was drenched, drowning, soaked to the skin in fear and enveloped by terrifying thoughts from which I had no escape.

The nights still haunted me. I hated being downstairs all alone while everyone else went upstairs to sleep. I felt left out, left behind and abandoned. Some nights, the physical pain kept me up but, most nights, it was the emotional pain, the torment and fear. One night, I noticed a bottle of Tylenol had been carelessly left beside me by a caregiver. I laid staring at it for hours with overwhelming thoughts of: "I can't do this anymore." If this was all life was going to be, I didn't want it. I poured the entire bottle of red pills into my shaking hand and stared at them while talking out loud to myself: "Is this it? Is this really how it is all going to end?" As I was asking the questions over and over, a moonbeam shone through the front window and landed on the picture of Joseph on my inspiration wall. Sobbing uncontrollably, I called out in a whisper for my mother... "Mom I don't feel good. I don't feel good." It was the little girl who still remained terrified inside me from decades earlier screaming out. I put the pills back in the bottle and threw it as far as I could across the room, well out of reach. The moonbeam was a sign. A sign from something far greater than the fear. It was in that moment I made the decision to stay. I was in this to the end and I was not going to let THIS be the end. My son was watching, he needed me and leaving would be a selfish act. I was all in and committed to Joseph and to living fully again...somehow.

In the morning, I realized more than ever, that what I had done up to now was not working. I had made the decision the previous night to stay on this earth, now I had to figure out how. A banner hung in our living room for years quoting Mahatma Gandhi that read: "Be the change you wish to see." I never believed in putting things up for show. I wanted Joseph to be reminded of those words every day and to learn to live by them. This time, they were meant for me. I needed to walk the talk and live what I had always taught him, I needed to be the change. It was time to look inward, not outward.

During the many hours of reflective thought and conversation with my cousin Cosmo, I was learning more about the power of the Universe. When I was desperate for answers, Cosmo always said: "Ask the Universe." The irony of having someone named Cosmo teach me about the

Universe was not lost on me! Though I had tried this in the past, I was now understanding the real key to receiving messages from the Divine. Previously, I had always operated from a place of fear. My constant stream of negative thoughts drowned out any possible answers that were trying to surface. It was about getting quiet long enough to actually hear the answers I was seeking. I laid quietly in stillness the rest of the day, redirecting my mind and remaining open. Sure enough, an image came to mind…Patch Adams. Patch is a US physician made famous by a movie depicting his life. He believed in treating patients with compassion and laughter. Patch founded The Gesundheit Institute in 1971, an unconventional, not for profit medical facility. He wasn't just a doctor, he was also a comedian, social activist, clown and author. He deeply believed in treating the whole person and that love, compassion and laughter were integral elements of healing. His trademark was a clown nose. I must have watched the movie a dozen times, if not more. Each time, I would have a deep visceral reaction, an emotional resonance with his message and character. In the past, I had always been the practical joker, the clown and the one that made people laugh. I had come by it honestly, inheriting it from both my aunt and mother. Watching the two of them together was reminiscent of watching Lucy and Vivian from The Lucy Show. When they were together, hi-jinx and hysteria were all in a day's play.

It had been so long since I tapped into that part of me. Did she even still exist? The message from the Universe was crystal clear to me, somehow, I needed to inject laughter into my days and tap into my "inner Patch."

That day, when the caregiver brought my lunch it came with a Babybelle cheese. Being resourceful as ever, I fashioned the red wax encasement into a cup and placed it on my nose. Voila! I did it! I had my very own clown nose! Laying in the bed, alone with nothing but the bucket and the constant pain, I was beginning to smile. It's impossible not to smile with a clown nose on. Later that day, when Joseph arrived from school, he found me with the makeshift clown nose. He immediately went to the fridge and grabbed himself a Babybelle to make his own. He took a picture of himself and it would be the first clown picture of many that would adorn my inspiration wall. Wearing a cheese clown nose became a right-of-passage for all who came to visit. Each person was fitted with their very own and their picture then added to the collage of smiles that served as both a source of good energy and a reminder of the love that surrounded me.

That night, I laid there for hours grinning and totally immersing myself in the energy that I had created both in and around me. Everything felt lighter. There was a definite shift, a change from what I had been feeling within me for so long. Best of all, I had created it myself. I was indeed the change I wished to see.

Chapter Twenty-Six

The effects of the clown nose were so profound I wanted to thank Patch deeply for the gift of his insights, so I dictated to my caregiver a letter of appreciation to him. I found the phone number, but not the address of the Geshuntheit Institute. I called to inquire and to my utter shock and awe, Patch answered the phone! I was like a giddy schoolgirl. It was surreal speaking to the man I had come to admire so very much, and he blessed me with an hour of his time. We talked at length about what I was going through physically and emotionally including my illness and the breaking down of the marriage. At the end of the conversation he said: "JoAnna, I'm going to give you a prescription." I was so excited! Finally, someone was going to provide me with the answers to escape this Hell! I listened attentively and with anticipation so I wouldn't miss a word of his magic formula! Patch said: "I want you to write this down and put it on your inspiration wall. Repeat it over and over each day." He paused and then continued in a most matter of fact fashion, "JoAnna, take charge of your response to it all." And? Go on...nothing? That was it? You've got to be kidding? That's not what I was expecting. I was looking for a step by step instruction manual giving details and guidelines to help me maneuver through this shit storm. Nevertheless, I thanked him for sharing his time and he asked me to stay in touch. I hung up the phone and laid there confused. What was I supposed to do with that? I was completely perplexed as to how I was going to execute his prescription. I did just as he asked and put his words up on the wall, staring at them and repeating them endlessly until eventually one day they would become clear. But, in the meantime, there would still be many days to struggle and navigate through.

*****

It was spring 2013 and I had been bedridden for more than 365 days and I constantly felt a growing pressure to get well quicker. Nothing seemed to be happening fast enough. After being unable to attend Joseph's grade eight graduation there was absolutely no way I was missing the next one. I made a promise to myself and I made a promise to him that I would be at his high school graduation. Failure was not an option! June 2016 was the goal and with each day that passed, I felt the date looming closer and closer. The self-induced stress and anxiety was obviously counter-productive, I knew it, but couldn't seem to gain control of the thoughts of doubt and fear.

Things had gotten a little better since I tapped into my "inner Patch." I slowly began to get my sense of humour back and it was changing things within me as well as around me. Regardless of all my efforts, the four letter "F" word was still a part of my daily vernacular and it constantly held back my progress. Fear was ever present. Rehab was moving along at a painfully slow rate due to many factors but, certainly not limited to, the marriage situation. My sound and light sensitivities were still intense and most days I would only be able to scribble my thoughts and needs on paper. Without computer, radio or television my days were spent alone in stillness and almost silence. I worked through my daily rehab routine bit by bit, but I desperately needed something to think about besides my many tasks at hand. In an attempt to shift my focus, I began writing riddles and jokes to steer my thoughts in a different direction. More importantly, I needed to say yes to laughter and no to fear. So, I came up with over 100 one-liners during some of my most trying days. Somehow, the deviation was like a pain reliever allowing it to ease its grip, even just the slightest. No one could figure out how I managed to do it and quite honestly, neither could I. I chalked it up to a survival skill. Friends would call to hear my joke of the day and I added it to my daily progress board that I sent to my rehab team. I couldn't wait for Joseph to come home from school and tell him mom's cheesy joke of the day. In true teenage fashion, he would roll his eyes, smile and hug me. He knew as bad as the jokes were, I was smiling and that's all that mattered to him.

I had a phenomenal wellness team. It consisted of the best vestibular rehabilitation specialist in Ontario, the best osteopath in Toronto and state of the art vestibular computer rehab. I also had an amazing group of people loving me and supporting me through it all. But, even with all this, I still knew something was missing. I felt that someone else needed to be on this journey with me, but I had no idea who. It was an overwhelming sense within me, a calling to someone. I was now changing the way I interacted with the Universe. Again, I would get quiet and leave my mind open to what I was meant to hear, allowing the answer to come naturally. The old, fearful and never-ending dialogue was replaced with quiet stillness. Amidst the stillness and silence the answer came to me. It was now clear that I had to call Dr. Ric Levenston again, the man responsible for my final diagnosis. He immediately said: "You need Dr. Peter!" Dr. Peter Gaibisels was both his friend and colleague, a chiropractor by profession, but he brought many more modalities to the table then chiropractics alone. Within hours, Dr. Peter was standing at my bedside. He was a very tall, broad shouldered man and I had to look up, waaaay up at him. His hands were massive and his voice was very deep, so deep in fact, I felt the vibration of it in my chest as he spoke. Through his larger than life form I could feel a gentleness come through. He reminded me of The Friendly Giant, a character from a television show I had loved as a little girl. He was the Friendly Giant, Fred MacMurray and Andy Griffith all rolled into one.

As Katherine had done almost a year earlier upon her first visit, Dr. Peter allowed my body to dictate what it was capable of receiving in that moment, which wasn't much. I looked up at him as he held my hand and with a quivering voice asked, "Dr. Peter, please, please tell me everything is going to be okay. Please, I need to know that it's going get better?" Kneeling down beside me, he held my hand tighter and replied in the softest most gentle loving tone: "JoAnna, life owes you nothing. You have to ask yourself, if it doesn't get any better than this, are you still willing to live?" I was stunned and immediately thought, "what an asshole! Was he kidding me?" With that, he stood up and said he would be back later in the day. When I asked him why, he simply and matter of factly replied: "because you need help that badly. You're in that bad of shape."

I learned over time that Dr. Peter was a wise man who spoke only the truth no matter how difficult it may be to hear. He came to my bed four out of five days a week and made himself available by phone at any hour of the day or night. Most days, he arrived to find me trembling in fear. I shook so badly he had to lay across my legs in an attempt to calm them and provide the comfort and security I desperately needed.

Dr. Peter is a renaissance man. He has more talents and knowledge than I can mention or remember for that matter. He's felled many a tree, survived in the woods by foraging, is a beekeeper, environmentalist, handyman, master mover, professional singer, piano player and landlord just to name a few. Some days were talking days in which he would share his insightful words of wisdom. Other days, he would merely look at me in my frail state and sit himself down at the piano, touching the keys ever so gently which providing a soothing sound and vibration without causing strain on my already maxed out auditory nerve. Dr. Peter never knew what modality he was going to utilize that day until he walked through my door. Each time, he allowed himself to get quiet and receive the message from his Creator for the next right step to take. There were days when my body would reject the rehab and he knew that what I really needed was compassion. These were the times when he would hold my feet to ground me or brush my hair ever so gently.

He was aware of the financial challenges and graciously gave of himself and his services freely. He was so much more than merely my practitioner. Dr. Peter helped to parent me through the storm and I could always depend on him. Just as he did that very first day, Dr. Peter never said what I wanted to hear, he said what I needed to hear. He was a very important part of my wellness team and a very important part of my life. He stood up and protected me when I needed him to. From the moment he came into my life, I never felt alone again. Not because he enabled or used his ego to take control, nothing could be further from the truth. Dr. Peter always challenged me to become my very best, to tap into my inner power, to be reliant on myself and to believe in my own resilience. He was there to support me, he was there to be my compassionate practitioner and father image, but this was my road to walk. His end goal was always to teach, guide and enable me to stand and walk it literally and figuratively on my own two feet.

Chapter Twenty-Seven

It was now September 2013 and I had been bedridden for more than 485 days. The doorbell rang and the caregiver answered it, returning with a large thick manila envelope with my name on it. My heart was beating like the hooves of a thousand Clydesdale horses as my stomach turned over and my entire body began to shake out of control. My logical self knew exactly what was inside, but yet I still held it in my hands in utter disbelief. I had just been served divorce papers.

The marriage was over. After almost thirty years together and twenty-two years of marriage, we were done. I laid the unopened envelope on the marble coffee table beside the bed. It screamed silently at me, "failure, unlovable, abandoned...again!" My gaze moved from the envelope to the bucket and back again about a dozen times or more. This was now my life. A bucket I couldn't rid myself of, and a broken marriage I could not hold on to. My mind couldn't help but flash back to that fateful day when the bucket had broken from under me. I recall thinking, "Dear lord, I've hit rock bottom, it can't get worse." Cue the doorbell to ring. Not five minutes from when the divorce papers arrived, in walks the CRA (Canada Revenue Agency). They were here to collect some unpaid business taxes which had been neglected in the chaos. Yup, it can always get worse.

The CRA agent was a short, mild-mannered, soft-spoken gentleman. I could immediately feel his kindness and his compassionate energy. He came to my bedside where I lay holding the CRA papers in one hand and divorce papers in the other and asked me to tell him what was happening in my life. I then gave him the Coles notes version of my *War and Peace*-like story. The agent understood and explained he had a similar situation happen to him some years earlier. "It does get better. You will survive this." He placed his business card on the table and said no one would be calling me again anytime soon, he would see to it and with that, he was gone and I lay in a state of utter and complete shock.

It was now time to open the Pandora's box I had dreaded for so long. My mom's dearest and oldest friend Beverly (Auntie Bev), came to support me as well as read the most intimidating contents. The first line set the tone of the entire document, M_____ vs M_____. It felt like the announcement of a boxing match, not unlike Tyson vs Holyfield or Ali vs Frazier. I felt the tears begin to fill my eyes and stream down my face. "Is this what we had become?" How was I supposed to fight when I was already knocked down for the count? It just didn't seem like a fair fight to me. As Auntie Bev read the words aloud, I felt like I was drowning. I was only hearing what sounded like garbled, muffled waves of terror. There were pages upon pages of disclosure forms asking for financial information that I didn't have. Without the funds for a lawyer, I took a deep breath and placed the papers back in the envelope and asked the caregiver to put them in the living room far away from my sight. In order to get into the ring, I needed to focus on my rehab. This was where my energy had to be.

* * * * *

The fall of 2013 brought a level of sadness I didn't think was possible. My beautiful grandmother that I had always shared so much with and loved so dearly, was hospitalized. It had been so long since we had seen each other and I missed everything about her; her feistiness, her laughter and even her temper. Not a single day had gone by that I didn't ache to be at her side in the apartment. I wanted so badly to sit together, and watch cooking shows the way we used to, laughing out loud as she critiqued the "shit" they called food. God, how I missed her.

She was coming to the end of her life's journey. Almost every day after school, Joseph traveled back and forth to the hospital on public transit. He would sit with her endlessly, one hand holding hers and doing homework with the other. They adored each other and she felt comfort with Joseph, it was hard not to. His was a soul full of love and compassion and when he was connected to you, you knew it and she knew it very well. She was always so very proud of him.

I called her on the days that my head and strength would allow, both of us were barely able to speak, but we knew the other was there and that's all that mattered. During this time, I struggled with so much anger and frustration. I felt so robbed. Robbed of the time I should have had with her, not just now in the hospital, but the years before. Some people flocked to the hospital in an obvious effort to cleanse themselves of guilt, rather than comfort a dying woman who had always given so much and asked for so little in return. Not my Aunt Lena and Uncle Joe. They had always been there for her in every way and cherished her to the end. I had the utmost respect them and always will.

When Joseph returned home each night, I watched my son's heart break a little more. He knew his time with her was limited, he knew she was leaving soon. Yet another loss and another blow to his ideal world. My dear friend Rizwana came to my bedside one night, giving comfort to me as she always did, knowing how desperately I wanted to be with grandma. Rizwana had witnessed through the years, what my grandmother meant to me. While she was with me, we called the hospital so I could at least say goodnight to her. My grandmother was getting weaker, her voice growing more faint each day and I had difficulty hearing her, so I put the phone on speaker. All of a sudden, she spoke with more strength, clarity and conviction than I had heard in the nights previous. She repeated the same question to me over and over: "Domani mattina? Domani mattina? Domani mattina? (Tomorrow morning? Tomorrow morning? Tomorrow morning?) Joe, Maria? Joe, Maria?" Rizwana and I shot a knowing glance at each other, we knew exactly what she was asking. I replied: "Grandma, do you want to go to them? Is it time?" "Yes" she pleaded. She was asking permission to go. There are no words to describe what I felt in the deepest part of my being as I said, "It's ok, we are all good here, you did your job. Go to your love, your baby, your mother, it's time." My heart was breaking, and at the same time, I knew that I had been given the most precious gift. She chose to ask me, and I was honoured.

The next morning on October 17, 2013 at 6:00am, Antonina (Lena) Badali née Schillaci took her last breath and joined her true love and baby girl. Our matriarch was gone, and it hit all of us hard. My grandmother was the type of woman you believed would live forever. Her fierce determination and stubbornness had gotten her through so much in life, but now it was time for grandma to let go. Just as with Maria and my father, I was robbed of my final goodbye.

Joseph was heartbroken at the loss of his great grandmother, the larger than life woman who had played such an incredible role throughout his entire childhood. He wrote a beautiful eulogy and prepared a picture board that was displayed at her visitation. The bravery that this young man showed during this time was nothing short of miraculous. With his mother still bedridden and his parents just separated, he not only attended the visitation and funeral, but he also escorted his grandmother (my mother) throughout the entire three day event. He was always by my mother's side and made sure she was never alone. My brother had pallbearer duties, so Joseph was the man in place of Anthony and our father. My heart bled for the loss of grandma, and for my son having to face it without me. I'll never forget the incredible kindness of my brother during this time. He knew how close grandma and I were and how much we meant to each other. Anthony also knew how isolated and alone I felt not being able to be a part of her final goodbye. He came over between visitations to my bedside to hold me while I cried and I will always be grateful for his kindness.

What came after the funeral compounded the pain of the loss of my grandmother. A "hidden" illness is unfortunately often judged and/or ridiculed. You are ostracized and abandoned. No one had ever heard of vestibular; it was foreign, unfamiliar and easily dismissed as being in my head. Ironically, it was in my head, my brain in fact, but it could not be seen. The lies fell on the ears of the ignorant and this trumped any kindness or compassion. At the funeral, there were people saying that I could have attended if I really wanted to. These are the same people that never bothered to inquire about the facts surrounding my illness and this cut me to my core. It would take some time before I could forgive such a cowardly and hurtful act.

* * * * *

It was at this time that I most unexpectedly reconnected with Gus, my high school sweetheart. As chance would have it, we were both navigating through the rocky road of divorce, and our rekindled friendship gave us both much needed support through the process. We shared hours and hours of conversation and laughter which was a welcome distraction from the daily grind of pain, rehab and the duties of divorce. Gus was and is an incredibly positive support for me. He would continually send me inspirational quotes and motivational videos. One in particular resonated deeply with me. It was a TEDTalk on "The Power of Vulnerability" by Brene Brown. The first time I listened to it, I was hooked on her teachings and sought out more of her work. One of her famous talks is called "Why Your Critics

Aren't the Ones That Count." In it she recounts the criticism she endured online and how one single quote shifted her thinking and was the game changer she needed. The quote was from the famous speech delivered by Theodore Roosevelt on April 23, 1910, The Man in The Arena.

"It is not the critic who counts; not the man who points out how the strong man stumbles, or where the doer of deeds could have done them better. The credit belongs to the man who is actually in the arena, whose face is marred by dust and sweat and blood; who strives valiantly; who errs, who comes short again and again, because there is no effort without error and shortcoming; but who does actually strive to do the deeds; who knows great enthusiasms, the great devotions; who spends himself in a worthy cause; who at the best knows in the end the triumph of high achievement, and who at the worst, if he fails, at least fails while daring greatly, so that his place shall never be with those cold and timid souls who neither know victory nor defeat."

It reminded me every day that the critics don't matter. This was my journey, my arena, my battle, and I was in fact daring greatly. My days were not for the cold timid souls.

JoJo Marie Schillaci

GRANDMA'S EULOGY WRITTEN BY JOSEPH IN ITS ORIGINAL FORM (UNEDITED)

My great grandmother, Antonina Badali, was born February 12th, 1919, in Termini, Sicily. When she was just sixteen years old, she had two men vying for her love. The better man won. Giuseppe Badali sent his soon-to-be wife to the big city of Palermo to prepare for their wedding. In 1934 the two were married in Italy, and then traveled to Canada to start their life together. The enamored couple lived with their sponsor in Toronto, and soon after started a fruit store, living in their apartment upstairs. It was there in the upstairs apartment that Lena Badali gave birth to her first three children, Anthony, Antoinette, and Josephine. I remember hearing stories of the babies being weighed on the fruit scales after they were born. Her and Grandpa Joe worked long hours at that store, children in hand. They were determined to make a life for themselves, and more importantly, a future for their children. Soon after, my great grandparents, being the businesspeople that they were, opened fruit stands on the Toronto Islands, as well as at the Canadian National Exhibition. My BaBa (what I always called her) was both a businesswoman and a mother, balancing both without missing a beat. They soon after decided they needed more room to run a family of six, so they built the Bloor Street apartment building in 1951, after the birth of their fourth child Maria. They were forced to move in before construction was complete, so Bishop Allen offered the facilities in the basement of Our Lady of Sorrows Church for them to use, almost right next to the apartment. That was the building she lived in until the time of her death, her comforting home. After settling into their new home, my great grandparents decided to take on another business idea. Her and her husband founded Islington Nurseries in the late 50s. Husband and wife, together as always, put so much effort into that business to make it what it is today. I remember hearing stories of my BaBa, outside shoveling bushels of dirt, and then going into the kitchen to make everyone the home cooked meals they so eagerly waited for. The more people sitting around that table for lunch, the happier she was. And if you didn't eat, God help you. Her mother, my great great grandmother, came to live with them in 1959 from Italy. Six years after that, my great grandfather passed away from cancer. She was heartbroken, and until the day of her death never got over the loss of him.

With the help of her children, she was able to pull herself back up and continue business at the nursery, every Sunday going to bring flowers to her beloved husband's grave. To get away from all the daily grind of running the business, she would go on her yearly trip to Niagara Falls with her daughters and granddaughters, always stopping to buy fresh cherries at the side of the road. They did this year after year. And then her youngest daughter, Maria, passed away in 1992 at 42 years old. My BaBa never really recovered from this tragedy. A large part of her still lied with Maria and Grandpa Joe up until her passing. I unfortunately did not meet either of these people. When I was young, my great grandmother and I were inseparable. I'd spend my days at the nursery with her and my grandmother Antoinette. I was happy. Halloween was my favourite time at the nursery. BaBa would be dressed up in crazy wigs and huge purple glasses, perched atop a plastic witch nose. She'd be serving customers, forgetting she was wearing that ridiculous getup. But it didn't matter. She never took herself too seriously, always laughing at the funnier things, life had to offer.

Joseph and BaBa, one month before her passing. Forever holding hands, September 2013.

I went to elementary school at Our Lady of Sorrows School, just down the street from the apartment. I'd go after school all the time to spend time with her, and she'd always come to special events at my school. Sunday dinners were by far the most memorable. Whenever my mom was yelling at me for not wanting to eat my vegetables, she'd be the first to defend me, even trying to sneak some off of my plate and onto hers. One thing that many people didn't know about my BaBa is that she was a huge animal lover. There were always dogs and cats at the nursery, and she even had a budgie bird named Joey. She absolutely loved my grandma's two dogs; Rosco and Jaco and she especially loved our giant sheepdog Shomei. We'd bring her up to the apartment, and when we weren't looking, she'd give the dog a handful of cookies. It's a wonder that dog didn't gain five pounds after every visit. When BaBa was in the rehabilitation center four years ago, we'd bring Shomei there to see her outside in the garden. We had a tough time explaining why she couldn't bring the dog upstairs and into her bed. Another special moment we shared was six years ago when we renovated our house. During the renovation, we lived with her in the apartment for four months. It was trying at some points. We'd be in the living room, and every night have to sit through another thrilling episode of C'è Posta Per Te. Let me tell you: excruciatingly boring; even worse when you don't understand the language. But she was happy, and that's all that mattered. During that time, I was doing a school project on Italy. I remember running across the street to Brentwood Library and getting the Italian books and getting her to read and translate them to me. It was great listening to her read, and even better telling stories. She always told family stories about her history coming to Canada. It is because of those stories that I feel like I know my Grandpa Joe and Aunt Maria intimately. She kept them alive through herself. She'd never tell those stories in a sad or depressing way, but rather in a way that intrigued you, that made you want to know more about where you came from. She never felt complete after Joe and Maria passed on; a piece of her always lied with them. But it was her hard-headedness and her determination that kept her strong. And now, at this time of her passing, we ask that no matter what she was to you, *mother, grandmother, great grandmother, aunt, cousin, friend; to keep her spirit alive as she always did with others that meant so much to her. Have conversations, share memories, tell stories; when you sit around the table, smile and laugh, and allow the next generation to know and to enjoy her as the true gift that she was to all of us. Thank you for all you did for me BaBa. For me; and for all of us. We'll miss you greatly. Rest peacefully.*

My Missing Peace

The silence in the darkness all too familiar much the same,

Laying in hope of the footsteps that were forever elusive & never came

As was the kiss, the embrace the ever knowing, the never showing,

To measure the pain of the heart against the pain of the form, this was not life or was it the norm

To measure the blame of each against the shame by all, the higher the pedestal the higher the fall

Where did it all go, did it ever exist, the struggle to end or to persist

The arms that came empty the promise much the same, heads held low cannot bare to continue the game

To measure the loneliness against the minutes or against the years,

so much resentment so many tears

Walk away if you must for you never truly arrived, to be in body but not soul, perhaps you tried

To measure the loss in the being or in the time, sometimes the result is not worthy the climb

Written 2013

JoJo Marie Schillaci

Chapter Twenty-Eight

Dealing with the caregivers was an ongoing nightmare which exacerbated my already constant state of stress. Often, girls would come through word-of-mouth, very seldom with patient references. In my desperation, I would have to settle for whoever showed up which in turn, left me in a most vulnerable position, as was the case in late 2013 when yet another new caregiver arrived, again through word of mouth. She was to work the Monday to Friday live-in shift. As soon as I met her, I felt something was off, but couldn't put my finger on it. I had always been a keen judge of character, very sensitive to energy and I knew something was definitely amiss with this girl. She had just arrived in Canada the week previous from China and was grateful for the job opportunity. On her first day, I awoke from a nap to find her sitting uncomfortably and unnervingly close to me. She had a gaze that made me both frightened and uneasy. When I asked what she was doing she simply replied that she was making sure I was okay and that I had someone there when I woke up. I tried my best to brush it off but, the more I thought about it, the more concerned I became. She shared her stories of working at a nursing home in China and described how they openly performed what she referred to as "mercy killings" due to the lack of space in the facilities. I can't imagine what my face must have looked like as she told her tale of horror. I had no words. I just kept staring in disbelief as she spoke with a casual, almost eerie demeanour about the way they administered lethal injections into the frail and vulnerable with a matter of fact attitude. You would think she was speaking of getting rid of pesky rodents, not human beings. Whether or not this was true, it spoke volumes of a disturbance within her. I did not close my eyes once from that moment on. As long as she was in my home my eyes were wide open day and night. It would be on her fifth and final day of work that my suspicions were confirmed. During my daily washing regime, she was insistent on cleaning my private parts, something I had always managed on my own. No matter how adamant I was against her help, she took a strong hold and the sexual assault occurred. As it was happening, I remember everything going dark and seeing spots before my eyes. Becoming overwhelmed by fear, I started to black out, a survival mechanism of the mind to block out the assault and protect itself from what was happening in the moment. With my body weak and shaking I pulled my lower half back onto the bed from the basin, not moving, not crying, barely able to think, I just closed my eyes and was devoid of any feeling whatsoever. I couldn't run from her and she knew it. I was a three-legged gazelle. As hours passed, my mind travelled back to when I was thirteen and was preyed upon. It brought back every feeling and emotion like it was yesterday. It's easy to sit in judgement and question why I didn't call the police or cry out for help, but I was alone in the house and it would be her word against mine. I didn't have one ounce of fight left in me and just wanted her to leave quietly. I didn't tell anyone until years later and as with many victims of abuse, we carry unwarranted shame and guilt. Somehow, in our mind, we feel like we asked for it, somehow, it's our fault. Self-blaming once again.

The caregiver situation had not improved nor did the money to finance it. Each day I felt crushing pressure to get well, a constant ticking of a clock that felt more like a bomb in my head, repeating over and over: "Your time is running out!" I had to be well enough to get down the street for graduation day. The short-term vision was to get in the walker and to the bathroom, this way I could rid myself of the bucket and more importantly, the caregivers.

Unfortunately, I had many other tasks that took precedence over rehab. First and foremost, I had to be there for Joseph in whatever way, shape or form I could each day. I rested as much as possible during the day, preparing for 3pm when he returned from school. Next in line was the daily running of our home, everything from figuring out the inside and outside maintenance, to household finances and practical tasks each day, which included the managing of caregivers. An enormous amount of time was taken up with the separation/divorce. Anyone who has been unfortunate enough to go through the process, knows the drain it takes on you emotionally, physically, and energetically. Lastly, whatever energy I had left was given to rehab.

*****

Most days, I was at the mercy of all that was crumbling around me. I had begun embracing humour once again, but I knew I had to begin taking control of my negative thinking if I was going to really make the necessary shift to reach my goals. A friend sent me a quote for the wall that read, "Worry is a negative prayer." It resonated with me now more than ever since sharing the many conversations with Cosmo about the power of trusting and speaking to the Universe. There was no way I was going to send the message of my fears out for the Universe to hear and from that point on, I put a gag order on myself. I spoke daily to the Universe about my desires and a clear vision of what I wanted my future to look like. I did this constantly, almost obsessively, my never-ending conversation with the Divine. Dr. Peter continually reminded me of the importance of speaking in the affirmative and beating the drum of what I wanted and not what I feared. I was blessed with an incredible group of people surrounding me with love. On the days I found myself struggling, my dear longtime friend Sharon would always answer the phone and say the same thing over and over "I don't know how you're going to do it, I just know you will." Sharon stood by my son and I from day one and was always a constant voice of reason and reassurance.

Compared to what I had done in the past, this was a profoundly different way of thinking. Fear had always been a normal state of mind for me. Thinking and speaking positively were work, hard work. The negative came easy and flowed out of me effortlessly, it was my mind's path of least resistance. I was now creating a new path, new connections in the brain for positivity and slowly allowing the old ones to dissipate. In essence, I was utilizing the same principles of neuroplasticity that I was using to learn to walk again. I was creating new neuro pathways in the exact same way, repeating commands over and over again. Working out my brain was not unlike working any other muscle in the body that had been neglected. It was exhausting and caused the brain to fight back, just as with the rehabilitation process. Brain burn and mental fatigue were constant, but I knew this was a critical step in moving myself forward and taking control of my life.

My dear friend Louie had kept in touch during this entire time. He loved my creative Babybelle cheese therapy and also knew my love for nature and the deep disconnect I was feeling without it. Typical of Louie, he showed up at my door with a roll of sod and inserted into the grass were pictures of his family and friends all adorned with cheese noses attached to sticks! Along with it was a note that read, "The grass is for your feet, the pictures are for your soul, the smiles are for your heart and the sticks are to poke the eyes out of anyone that stands in your way!" I was overjoyed! It was marvelous! Absolutely the most touching thing to receive at such a dismal and critical time.

The roll of sod was a game changer! We immediately rolled the beautiful carpet of goodness on to a sheet of plastic and placed it on top of the bed. Dr. Peter lifted my feet and lay them on the grass so gently and lovingly as I closed my eyes and let my other senses take over. The first thing I remember experiencing was the smell and the incredible scent of life, of the soil and of the earth that brought back memories from my childhood spent at the garden centre. It was reminiscent of the earthy smell of Mr. Nortime when I was a little girl planting alongside him in the summer sun. It also reminded me of standing in the topsoil pile while the dump truck delivered its load. If life had a smell, to me this was it! The rich and fragrant aroma felt like familiar arms embracing me after so very long. The bottoms of my feet had not felt anything for more than seventeen months and when they met the tips of the slender new blades of grass, it felt like a thousand tiny little fingers caressing not only the soles of my feet, but my soul at its very core. Their soft, gentle and slightly edgy touch awakened something deep within me that had been laying in waiting. It sent a vibration through me that resonated in my entire body. I felt like someone plugged me into an electrical outlet and I was receiving a positive charge from the tips of my toes to the top of my head, quite the opposite of the negative shock I had experienced in the past. We did this for as long as the sod would stay alive and each time, the experience was different, each time it was its own Divine blessing.

Louie also introduced me to his good friend James Desroches. James is a very kind, beautiful and intelligent soul. His wisdom was bountiful and came with great clarity. There were times I needed his wisdom and no matter where he was or what he was doing, he always had the compassion and willingness to take my calls. This is a man who had no direct connection to me, but a man who refused to let me struggle alone. Sitting with James can be overwhelming. So much of his wisdom and insight coming at the same time, but I did my best to remain open to all I was meant to absorb and take away in each moment. We shared many deep conversations of introspective thought. It was at one of these gatherings that he would gift me five words. He said they would guide me, but I needed to connect to them and make them my own. "Oh God" I thought, another cryptic Patch Adams prescription to freedom. Just as with Patch, I accepted the wisdom with deep gratitude and wrote them on my inspiration wall. The five words were:

Trust

Acceptance

Gratitude

Commitment

Liberation

He gave a brief description for each, something for me to ponder. It would be some time before I was ready to fully embrace them and I had no idea that they would become the biggest part of my rebirth and transformation and the greatest gift he could have given me.

JoJo Marie Schillaci

Chapter Twenty-Nine

I had now been bedridden over 600 days and another Christmas approached with the same excitement for me as a root canal. The thought of facing the holidays was always difficult, but never so much as this year. Unless you looked at a calendar, you would never have known it was Christmas by the look of our home. There were no decorations, no gifts, no tree, no sparkling lights or bows. I was very grateful to St. George's for providing Joseph with an outlet to enjoy and experience the holidays in a way that I couldn't provide. I recall he and I sitting on the bed one Sunday morning, when the front door opened and there stood my mother, my brother and his girlfriend. Their arms were loaded with decorations and my brother dragged in a tree behind him. Anthony put up the Christmas tree and they all worked alongside Joseph decorating it to perfection! They made the house beautiful and placed gifts under the tree. It wasn't about the physical adornments, but rather it was about the spirit of giving, caring and loving that brightened every branch. My chosen brother Louie would show up Christmas Eve loaded with presents. I will never forget him handing me a pen and telling me to write, "from Mom" on each tag addressed to Joseph without my son knowing. He was a real live Santa Claus in his truest form.

* * * * *

With the new year, new challenges and blessings melded together into a watercolour of emotions. I began to explore and ponder the work that needed to be done with the five words James had gifted me. I still felt lost as to how to implement the words in order to create the much-needed shift.

St. George's continued to be a blessing in our lives. Reverend Pat was the most beautiful woman with an incredibly compassionate, no nonsense style about her. She visited regularly and was a source of both peace and strength to Joseph and I. Upon her retirement, Father John would take her place. He was equally committed to visiting me and sharing both his support and prayers. One day, he came and sat next to my bed and shared the unbelievable news that some parishioners were willing and wanting to support my home care. I could hardly believe my ears! They had researched and spoken to the professionals and it was clear to them that this was where I was supposed to be rehabilitating. Without ever being asked, they poured their heart out to us because that's what St. George's-On-The-Hill is all about, compassionate community outreach and support. They truly live what they preach every day, and their generosity gave us a tremendous sense of relief.

The church hired Joseph for the summer. He would be performing maintenance work for the church property along with the adjacent private school. They were very happy with his efforts and he was equally thrilled and thrived being amongst such goodness. So impressed with his work, they hired him throughout the year as well.

Joseph reported to an incredibly kind and compassionate man named Anatoli. At a time when my son needed the influence of a good man, he stepped up and was a solid role model. He took Joseph under his wing and provided him with guidance and support, always keeping an eye out for what was best for him. To this day, I don't think Anatoli realizes the importance of the role he played in my son's life and continues to do so to this day. He is a special member of our chosen family.

With the earlier passing of my beloved grandmother came the inevitable selling of the Bloor Street building. It was a second mourning for me as the building that was a landmark in our lives and in our hearts was soon to be gone forever. My business would close its doors at the very same time and again, I felt robbed. Robbed of the opportunity to bid farewell to my second home and robbed of the opportunity to say goodbye to the place and the people that had been such a huge part of my life.

We were all feeling the losses, and no one was spared the pain, not even our beautiful Shomei. She was also feeling the changes that were so apparent around us and began losing huge patches of fur down to the skin all over her body. The vet diagnosed her with mange as a result of stress.

I remember laying in the bed shortly after the building had sold with such a profound sense of hollowness within me. It was as if with every heartbeat there was an echo of despair, loneliness and emptiness. I felt like everything was pulling away, leaving me...changing. I wanted someone to hold me together, no, I needed someone to hold not just me, but all the broken pieces of my life together. I told Dr. Peter over and over how much I ached to be held, to be hugged and comforted. He simply replied, "JoAnna, you must learn to hug yourself." Exactly what I didn't want to hear. He was the ever-present voice of reason and wisdom in my life and some days I loved him for it and some days, well, let's just say some days I didn't. Despite not wanting to hear it, I would do as I always did and take his advice. I wrapped my arm around myself as tight as I could over one shoulder and then the other. There I would lay embracing, holding and clinging to my own self for what seemed like dear life; self-soothing, attempting to take away the pain in both my heart and body. I felt crushed both physically and spiritually. I was broken. Who would ever want to play with a broken doll? Ironically, I was completely and totally lost in losses. I had lost my marriage, my business, my grandmother, our Bloor Street home, money, my security, my dignity, time, experiences...the list seemed endless.

I was no longer a wife, granddaughter, entrepreneur, community activist or volunteer. I didn't know who or what I was to myself or anyone else. I also lost my identity as I went through the divorce process and shed my married name. Shakespeare's famous quote: "A rose by any other name would smell as sweet," implies that a name is simply a label to distinguish one thing from another. I didn't have another name and I felt indistinguishable, lost. Who was I? I felt like a "Jane Doe" laying in the bed not unlike a body on a gurney in a morgue waiting to be identified.

I had my son and my inner circle of goodness along with the best rehab team possible and this is what I had to focus on, the blessings. It was imperative that I shift my mind from what was gone to what remained here and now. I also had to focus on the biggest gift that still remained...me. I was still here, alive and it meant there was reason to believe this wasn't the end for me. Instead of thinking and rethinking, "I'm still in this bed" with anger and frustration of all that I was missing, I began to change the energy and meaning behind those same words, "I'm still in the bed," acknowledging the fact that I was still here breathing and that was enough to affirm trust. There was a bigger plan in all of this, of which I was somehow an integral part. The Universal plan of life.

My thoughts became deeper as I searched for direction, where to go and what to do now. I continued to allow stillness of my mind in an attempt to hear what the message was the Universe was trying to tell me. It was in the silence of my mind that for the first time, I began seeing clearly, "the messages in the mess." The Universe had a plan, and this was all part of it. As painful as it was in the moment, I had to believe everything I was experiencing was purposeful. There had to be a purpose in the pain, this couldn't be for not. It was all part of a Divine blueprint that was going to reveal itself...eventually.

It was obvious and crucial to me that the only way to move forward would be to let go. To stop clinging to what once was, and to let go freely of the past. Releasing the fears which weighed heavily like cinder blocks that I had carried for a lifetime. I felt a calling so loud within me that I was literally physically shocked awake, awakened from the trance I had been in for my entire life. It was in that moment that I realized I was not on a road of never-ending pain, but in a labyrinth of self-discovery. This wasn't a straight line, but a circle with curves amongst peaks and valleys, it had a centre, a core. I was on a journey to find my very core being, the deepest, most genuine and authentic part of myself, my essence, my purpose. For the first time I began to realize that I didn't need to figure it all out in this moment. I didn't need to know the entire map today, I just had to keep taking the next right step and I would be guided along the way. It was now clear to me the meaning of Patch's prescription that remained on my wall for so many months. I needed to stand guard of my emotions, my words and my thoughts in order to put myself in the power position of my life and not remain a victim to all that was happening around me. It was time I took control and it was absolutely time that I, "Took charge of my response to it all."

So much of what I had come to rely on in my life was like a bouquet of balloons I clung to tightly. Not unlike a young child clinging to what seemed to be so very important in a moment in time. My knuckles were white, the sweat dripping from my palm. Slowly and methodically, I watched as the Universe would ease my grip enough to allow one balloon at a time to rise gently, almost majestically through the sky. As I watched them float far beyond my reach, they became smaller and smaller until out of sight. The distance between us made it difficult to remember my love affair with each one. Another one gone and another and another. Although they were lighter than air, as they drifted away, they felt like concrete being lifted from a tomb off my chest. The pain of releasing each one gave a contrast of both heaviness and lightness of being. In letting go freely I allowed myself to soar. Not by something external and temporary, but by the grace of that which was left behind...Me.

Written 2014

JoJo Marie Schillaci

Chapter Thirty

I had never truly lived, but merely existed through the clutches of fear and now everything in my life was at a standstill including myself. As I delved deeper into the concept of letting go, I came to realize that if I wanted to get a different result and survive, I was going to have to embrace a new way of being, a new way of thinking and a new way of showing up.

Enter the five words from my dear friend James Desroches *Trust, Acceptance, Gratitude, Commitment* and *Liberation*. I knew now, more than ever, that I needed to master these words and become fully committed to them. They began to scream out to me with an immediate call to action.

Trust was the first word listed and the first step in the process of letting go. I came to refer to *trust* as the "anchor" word as this was the first word on which to build the foundation of my future life. I had never trusted the natural flow of life and looking back, I can see that theme playing over and over and it was never more glaringly obvious, then during the birthing process of my son. Life was not to be trusted it was to be feared. That had been my lifelong belief instilled from childhood that held me back from experiencing so much...fear of death...fear of highways...fear of water... fear of flying...fear of finances...fear of abandonment. The list was never ending just like the fear. Each one was a direct result of not *trusting* something higher than myself and not *trusting* the flow of life. Fear is what was keeping me suspended within this living Hell in the bed, but I knew no other way of being. I had never entertained the thought of there being an alternative, my brain was hardwired for fear.

It had come down to either turning left and doing what I had always done or turning right into the abyss of the unknown. This was about *trusting* in myself, *trusting* in a power higher than myself, and also *trusting* that something better was awaiting me. The choice really happened that quickly. In an instant, we can alter our trajectory by changing one simple thought. The magical solution I had searched high and low for, turned out to be in my very own thinking.

And so, the work began on developing *trust* in myself, my gut and my inner voice. Genuinely and deeply believing that my mind and my body had the power to conquer and overcome anything and everything. I recalled Dr. M saying many years earlier: "You have a remarkably powerful mind. Just imagine what it could do for you if you put it to use positively instead of always to the negative." I now made the choice to focus on my positive abilities and dismissed every negative thought that was contradictory.

Beyond *trust* in myself, this was also about building an intimate *trust* with my Divine power that I believed in, which for me, is the Universe. It's easy for us to believe in a higher power when things are going well. The true test of our faith is in times of struggle and darkness. We are quick to say that we believe, but what exactly does that mean? We tend to believe that when things are going well, a higher deity is responsible, but when we don't get what we want, our faith plummets and we believe the world is against us. This was about embracing my higher power and truly believing in the deepest part of myself that everything good and bad was happening for my highest good. Even if I couldn't see it in the moment, the Universe was always working for, not against me. It was safe to let go because I was held in the capable and loving hands of something higher. I needed to commit to building an unshakable foundation of *trust* with the Universe. This was going to be a daily discipline, a new way of thinking from that which I was accustomed. Doubt had been with me for as long as fear. Doubt is the precursor of fear and without doubt, fear cannot exist. I had to stand guard against my two demons. I needed to believe the Universe had already figured out what I couldn't wrap my head around. This was indeed a labyrinth of self-discovery and the Universe was guiding me every step of the way. It knew best.

While discovering the meaning of *trust*, it was clear what my next right step needed to be. I made the decision to put down my armour and be brave. I was exhausted from the defensive stance I had taken my entire life. I was exhausted from shielding myself as a way of protection. In short, I was exhausted from fighting, from running and from managing. I was finally ready to be vulnerable, I was finally ready to let go and release my lifelong grip, knowing deeply that I was safe. I *trusted* that letting go didn't mean giving up. I began to realize that the Divine spirit that resided in me was constant; it was always at work and I was always safe. Everything was going to happen in the perfect time and in the perfect order. I meditated deeply on this meaning of *trust* every day, allowing it to sink in and resonate true in every part of my being. I began *trusting* the process of life...my life. As I did this, my brain began rewiring itself for faith and *trust* and dissolving the old synapsis of doubt and fear.

I then began working on making meaning of the second ***Pillar**, acceptance.* To me, on the surface, it meant acknowledging and allowing myself to be in the moment as it was without resistance. I had fought my reality every step of the way by constantly fighting being in the bed, battling through the divorce and in fear of my reality. Clearly, I had not yet accepted myself or my current situation. My MO (Method of Operation) was to deny and run. If I was to allow myself to accept my reality, I would have to deal with all my demons and face them head on with all their scary moving parts. These parts included the reality of being single and living life alone, the financial mess and my uncertain future health, all of the unknown. Fear was scary and dysfunctional, but it was familiar. I knew how to live in fear, but I didn't know how to live with *acceptance*. I had spent my life swimming upstream against the natural current, trying desperately to avoid the uncomfortable, attempting to hold on to things that were obviously meant to leave. It was exhausting and unproductive, it used an incredible amount of energy and in the end, nothing I wanted was upstream. When the fear hit, I never went through it, I went around it, under it, against it, but never through it to the other side. By avoiding it, I placed myself in a constant struggle, drowning in the deep end instead of allowing the natural current to take me effortlessly downstream where I was meant to be. In the words of the infamous British army General Sir Winston Churchill: "If you're going through Hell, keep going." I began to realize that *acceptance* meant going through, not avoiding it. It was time to *accept* where I was, who I was and how I was meant to be. As soon as I was able to actually say out loud and believe deeply, "This is what's happened and it's ok", everything changed within me and around me. I began to let go and feel myself floating downstream, *trusting* that the Universe was bringing me exactly where I was meant to be in the perfect time. *Acceptance* was about feeling with my entire being, my current state and *trusting* it was okay. In no way did it mean that I was giving in to demons, challenges or fears. What I was doing was allowing my body, my mind and my spirit to not fight but instead to preserve its energy for good. This allowed my body to heal, to breath and to move forward; *accepting* where I was in life as well as *accepting* people and circumstances for what they truly were, not on the surface, but deep within. *Accepting* that at the root of all conflict and experience I would find that I received exactly what I needed in that moment, even if painful. It was necessary in order to propel me further toward my greatest self and best life.

The Universe is always conspiring to help us complete the "incompletions" in our life and give us closure. Sometimes the gift is disguised in painful experiences. Ironically, many of my lifelong fears were presented to me while I was in the bed which meant I could no longer run from them. The Universe was at work giving me the opportunity to finally face them once and for all. We must remember that pain is never about punishment, but purpose. Each experience good or bad, can either paralyze us into a state of "why me" or propel us into a state of "for me."

It was now time for the third *Pillar*, *gratitude*. I had done all the proverbial exercises on *gratitude* before without feeling anything life changing. We all know the drill, wake up and find five things we are *grateful* for. The sun is shining, I'm alive, I have a roof over my head, I have family that loves me, and I have wonderful friends. Done. How many times had I done the exercise, only to feel nothing. I was going to have to look much deeper to figure this one out.

What I began realizing was that I was focusing on the surface gifts, the sunny days, the flowers, the great company I had that day. Not to discount *gratitude* on any level, but the surface scraping wasn't going to suffice. There was something more to uncover. What if it was about being *grateful* for all that wasn't perfect, all that was not going as planned? For the struggle? What if it was about being *grateful* for, of all things, the shit storms? Somehow, in my mind I needed to reformulate the challenges. There must be a blessing in all of this. For me, deep *gratitude* was about being able to look at each storm as its own unique and Divine blessing. There was a purpose and a gift, a lesson to uncover with each one that presented itself. It was never about punishment, but about purpose. When I positioned myself in a place of *gratitude* and realized that everything put before me, every challenge and every obstacle was for my greater good, something happened energetically. It was as if my knees hit the ground and I released, realized and gave thanks for the opportunity to grow, thanks for the wisdom, thanks for the people that came into my space and yes, even thanks for the people that had left my space. In that moment I experienced a state of grace and energetically, grace is deeply healing. By taking on a new perspective and being truly and deeply *grateful*, I released the need to be in a constant exhausting state of defensive bitterness. This third *Pillar* of *gratitude* allowed positive energy to go into my cells and generate a vibration of peace. I reformulated my struggles, obstacles and challenges from hurdles into gateways and as I opened the gates of *gratitude*, I could see that there was always, always something to be *grateful* for on the other side. In some way and in some form, it is a blessing, even if I couldn't see what it was in the moment, I *trusted* that it would reveal itself. Being *grateful* put me gracefully into the power position and took me out of victim mode.

It was now time to implement the fourth *Pillar*, *commitment.* I thought I was already committed. I was still here, I hadn't checked out, I wasn't giving up. I was committed to the rehab program, to my son and to getting better. What was I supposed to be committed to besides the obvious? The message slowly began to reveal itself. Perhaps it meant being *committed* to the *5 Pillars*. What if it meant being *committed* to being *trusting*, *accepting* and *grateful*? This meant being fully *committed* and disciplined to my thoughts, my words and actions every minute of every day. I had to be fiercely *committed* to being positive, to my goals, to the energy I put out as well as the energy I allowed into my space. My entire life, my thinking automatically went to the negative, it was the path of least resistance. I had to be *committed* to changing, *committed* to my goal so fiercely that I was willing to be vulnerable and embrace a new way of doing things. This also meant that I had to be *committed* to thinning the herd which meant letting go of people that did not serve my highest good, the ones that weren't in my cheering section. It was in that moment that I decided to adopt the famous saying: "If you're not on my side or by my side then you're in my way." It was of the utmost importance for me to guard all that I would allow into my sacred space of healing, and more importantly, my sacred life.

The fifth and final *Pillar*, *liberation*, would be the gift I would receive after implementing and living the first four. I needed to be patient as I waited for the light of *liberation*, *trusting* it would come in its own Divine time.

The bridge to peace is gratitude…

Written 2019

JoJo Marie Schillaci

Chapter Thirty-One

By spring 2014, I had been bedridden for almost 700 days. I had not seen my reflection or had a bath or shower in many more than that. I longed to sink deep into a tub and allow the water to embrace every part of me. I ached to cleanse myself of the layers of fear and torment, to submerge myself into the water and once again feel its safe embrace.

My reflection was an entirely different matter. I had no interest in facing whatever it was I had come to look like. I knew I had physically changed and not for the better as I could feel the rough, dry chaffed skin on my face and arms as well as the deep sores from where I had scratched and picked myself raw. The fear and anxiety had ravaged me in so many ways. I ran my fingers along my forehead and down my cheeks, across my lips not unlike a blind man reading a face for the very first time. It felt different, aged. I could feel the deep furrows on my forehead and the profound creases between my eyebrows. My hair, that had always been thick and healthy was now thin and straggly, reaching more than halfway down my back as it hadn't been cut in years. I had gained significant weight from my immobility and could see it in my legs and around my middle. I could feel it as I exerted myself to turn from side to side. No, I could not bear to look at my reflection, I could not face the reality of what I had become. Some things are better left unseen.

The words which I would now refer to as my "*5 Pillar Words*", were a huge part of my life and my go to for daily meditation. I was feeling the benefits of focusing on each one with both intention and **commitment**. Fear was lessening its grip ever so slowly, and peace was gently stepping forward in my mind, body and soul.

Rehabilitation was still moving forward but, again, it was slow and excruciatingly painful. I was now able to stand for up to thirty seconds at a time and on particularly good days, sit on the chair next to the bed for three to five minutes. These feats did not come without a price. With each new, exciting step I had to endure the brain's retaliation, its continual fighting back against the new task it was being asked to perform. Some days, a two minute stand would leave me with a crippling migraine that would last for days which put me back in the fetal position awaiting the brain to settle down. As the new synapsis were working to connect it felt like my brain was a piece of cheese being pulled along a grater, I would refer to this as brain burn. I experienced the same when I did the emotional work, again, creating new synapsis and disconnecting the old. The physical fatigue was debilitating, and severe atrophy had set into my muscles from lack of use, coupled with Epstein Barr virus. The slightest exertion would leave me feeling like I had completed a ten kilometre run.

With Joseph in front of me holding my hands and Shomei at my side, I finally took my long awaited first step. I could see and feel in Joseph's eyes his deep love, support and his belief in me. He knew how hard this was for me as I clenched his hands with the tightest grip and shakily stood up. With tears streaming down my face, I looked into my son's eyes and asked, "Joseph what are you doing?" He simply and lovingly replied, "Teaching my mom to walk, just like she taught me." Keeping my head completely still and my eyes focused on his, I lifted one foot and gently brought it forward and then the other. I did it! I finally did it!

Once I took those first two steps, I longed for more! It was impossible to push the brain to do more than it was ready for and I was reminded of this time and time again by my team. They repeated that it was about continuing to work patiently and methodically at the rehab routine and trusting that the brain would let me know when it was ready for more. The brain would always determine when the moment was right for the next step forward both literally and figuratively, but I yearned to walk just a few steps more to see the other side of the wall. It had now been two and a half years since I saw the lost land of my living room. Knowing how badly I wanted to walk, Dr. Peter came to my bedside and while holding his hands out in front of me he asked me to stand and to place my feet upon his. I'm sure I must have looked confused as he gave me one of his loving, reassuring smiles and gently motioned me to rise. I gently rose and placed my bare feet on top of his and held his arms as he held mine. He began to walk backwards, giving my brain the benefit of forward motion and ever so slowly, together we took seven strides to the kitchen counter. It was both terrifying and exhilarating! I grabbed hold tight of the counter and explored every inch with intensity, feeling its coolness, its curves and edges and its slight imperfections that now seemed so much more pronounced. I stared at it from the bed for years, wondering when I would be at it again, and here I was! It was surreal! From this vantage point it also allowed me to see my entire living room. It looked so big, enormous in fact. The windows were allowing in the most beautiful sunlight that lit up the entire room, and I felt like I was seeing it all for the very first time. Before too long, Dr. Peter gently turned his human bus around to begin the return trip to bed and as we passed the sliding door, the one I spent each day gazing out of, he opened it wide to give me my fist real breath of fresh air. It was crisp and cool! The air had the scent of newness and rejuvenation of spring and I too was feeling a newness sprouting within me and a deep rejuvenation of my soul.

* * * * *

The emotional stress of the separation and ongoing divorce negotiations were causing a myriad of physical symptoms. The worst thing for neurological rehab is stress and I had a boat load of it! Each day, I was forced to deal with lawyers and learn the process as I went along…13.1 filings, affidavits and court orders, it was never ending. All the while I made sure to do my own due diligence and I never took anyone's word as truth without doing my own research to verify. I was constantly reminded of my mother who had been cruelly taken advantage of by her lawyer when she was at her most vulnerable. There was no way I was going to look back with regret of any sort.

I had so many challenges swirling like a tornado in my mind. I easily and inevitably became overwhelmed with how to figure them all out. Dr. Peter's wisdom would again guide me. He explained that once we make a decision and set an intention the "how" will always answer itself. We don't need to know how, we just need to set the intention with deep trust that it will happen. The "how" will be revealed naturally in the Divine time. I began setting deep intentional thoughts each day pertaining to each obstacle I was facing. Again, this was a profoundly new of thinking, but an incredibly freeing way of existing. Knowing deeply I just needed to keep taking the next right step and the "how" will answer itself.

I was continually making a conscious choice to keep my intentions and karma clean, as well as working on fact and not emotion, more often than not, easier said than done. When people ask me how I managed to continue a positive path throughout the process my answer was always the same: "My son is watching my every move and listening to my every word." I was never going to jeopardize the respect of my son by behaving in a way that would dishonour myself or his father. I kept reminding myself of Patch's prescription: "Take charge of your response to it all" and remained on guard of my thoughts and words. I focused on my **5 Pillars** and reassured myself that I didn't need to figure it all out at once. All I needed to do was take the next right step.

I was missing so much from my previous life but, one of the things I missed most of all, were Sunday dinners at my moms'. Her house was always the place to laugh out loud and forget what was troubling you; there was always something comforting about going back home. Now, most

Sundays she picked up Joseph to spend the day and have dinner. My brother would of course be there taking him under his wing, spending time and being the crazy uncle for which he was known to be. You never knew what the two of them would get into. It was reminiscent of the days when he and our father would get into mischief, but on a much more understated and safe scale, to say the very least. My mother and brother were there for us in every way and every day, somehow always knowing what we needed long before we did. As much as I was grateful that Joseph was with them and having fun, each Sunday I would end up being the only guest at my very own pity party. I felt left out with abandonment ringing loud in my head like the bells of St. Mary.

At this point, I still had no television, radio or computer and the silence was deafening, not to mention the hours and hours of undistracted time. Desperate times called for desperate measures. In the Patch Adams movie he suggests ringing up strangers on the telephone to make them smile. One day when the silence was particularly maddening and I was at my wits end, desperate for human contact, I picked up the phone. What the heck was I doing? Was I losing my mind along with everything else? Through the questions I continued to dial a random number, making up a name and asking if they were in. The person on the other end inevitably said wrong number and after apologizing, I'd ask if they would like to hear a joke. I then proceeded to share a riddle or two I had written and each time they would giggle out loud, followed by a thank you. Each person was genuinely happy to have received a wrong number and this little gesture gave me someone to talk to, as well as a little distraction. It always made me smile to hear laughter that I had created.

My brother Anthony, 2015.

Music has always been a huge part of my life and these days I was missing it more than ever. In the past, I had used it to help me through the rough days and trying times. The words of a song can bring connection to our struggles, our pain and often our loneliness. Music has a unique way of healing and its vibration can provide comfort, unfortunately for me, not this time. My auditory nerve was still in hypersensitive mode and a mere whisper felt like a jack hammer in my head. Every noise was exponentially louder, not to mention the new age technology that had a much higher pitch causing terrible dissonance throughout my entire, very frail central nervous system. One day Anthony walked in with a transistor radio and in his true inner rock star form, handed it to me and said: "Here, listen to some tunes, you'll feel better." When it came to music, Anthony had always been a huge influence. I grew up as his little sister who loved to sit on the basement stairs listening to him and his buddies play their garage band tunes. He brought me up with an appreciation for many different genres of music and artists alike, rock and roll, country, blue grass, jazz and even classical. Many times, he showed me videos of the amazing banjo pickings of Roy Clark and it now seemed appropriate that he would be the one to bring music back into my life.

At first I was hesitant, but I was so excited at the thought, that I eventually felt the fear and did it anyway and tuned it to its lowest setting. As I placed the radio on my chest I could scarcely make out the words and could just slightly feel the vibration. After thirty seconds, it was too much as my head began to hurt, the brain burn began to set in and I felt my nervous system running for cover, but those thirty seconds were magical. The next day I attempted another thirty seconds until I established a tolerable baseline. Over a few weeks, I built up a tolerance for several minutes at a time which enabled me to enjoy at least a couple of songs per day. My ears had been starving for this!

During the ongoing circus of divorce, I hung up with my lawyer feeling totally exasperated. I laid back, took a deep breath and turned on the radio for a little distraction and Don Henley's, "End of the Innocence" began to play:

Remember when the days were long
And rolled beneath a deep blue sky
Didn't have a care in the world
With mommy and daddy standin' by
But "happily ever after" fails
And we've been poisoned by these fairy tales
The lawyers dwell on small details
Since daddy had to fly.

Each word made my eyes fill up and before long, I was crying out loud. Music is a remarkably powerful force and with each word of that song, I felt a direct hit to the pit of my stomach. Henley's lyrics said it so perfectly…Joseph never did have a care in the world and now the fairytale was over. The fairytale his parents tried so desperately to act out and carry on for many years, was over. That innocent boy who never felt anger, who believed all was good and perfect, could now see the world and our family as it truly was. We do such a disservice to our children when we raise them on the "happily ever after" principle. I cried for Joseph, I cried for myself, I cried for the man I married so many years earlier, which felt like a lifetime ago.

JoJo Marie Schillaci

Chapter Thirty-Two

At the end of 2014, Joon requested I go back on the iPad and connect to social media and my first response was: "No thanks, I'll take a hard pass." Technology had never been my thing, and the mere thought of my eyes moving around a screen induced stress and nausea. He explained that going on the iPad was about ocular movement and brain connection therapy. Watching short videos, reading text and looking things up on the web were all part of getting the brain reconditioned and functioning normally again. This was all part of the bigger rehab picture and connecting to social media was about resocializing myself into a world from which I had for so long, been literally and figuratively disconnected from.

Slowly I began the process on the iPad and the symptoms it created again made me feel like I was plummeting off the side of a roller coaster while hanging upside down. Just as I had done with the radio, day by day I would spend a few seconds more until I made my way up to minutes. I re-established my Facebook account and enjoyed connecting with a very small select group of people again. Social media has a natural way of making us feel inadequate in our looks, our lives and our love, always focusing on people's highlights and the sweeter moments of life. The act of "busy" is not just glorified but rewarded. For some people, Facebook "likes" can be compared to a "hit of crack." It can become an addiction for our ego and a way to validate our existence and importance. To someone whose existence was from a bed, it was getting more and more difficult to emotionally maneuver through, and difficult to not feel like I was missing out on so much of life. Regardless of the obvious challenges it brought forth, I was enjoying reconnecting with the outside world. I was now active in discussions and learned about all that had changed since being in the bed. I finally felt like I was a part of something, even if only a part of a virtual world. The technology I had always complained about had actually become a blessing. Firstly, it allowed me to rehabilitate my brain from my bed and secondly, by bringing a collection of friends back into my life that otherwise would not have been possible. I continued to post my progress and exciting achievements each day, despite how small they seemed in comparison to others. I was overwhelmed by the amount of love and support I received from my small inner social media circle and they became a huge part of my daily life and remain so today.

The *5 Pillar Words* were helping me put each challenge into perspective and allowed me to *trust* that things would somehow always work out in Divine time and order. This freed up an enormous amount of otherwise wasted energy from worry. *Accepting* each obstacle as it was, and not acting like it was catastrophic was key. This kept things in a reality-based state, as opposed to the self-induced fear mongering, to which I had been accustomed. With each hurdle put before me, I tapped into deep *gratitude* and worked at uncovering the gem I was meant to find. Every day I stayed fiercely *committed* to taking the next right step towards my awaiting *liberation*.

It was now time to begin sharing the words of wisdom with Joseph, sharing with him my thoughts on each one and how they related to absolutely everything in life. He seemed open to the concept and ready and willing to learn more. Joseph and I shared a remarkable bond that was only strengthened more by my years in the bed. That bed was the birthplace of the most deeply intense and emotional conversations about life, our life, his life and life in general. This is where the most critical and challenging role of my parenting took place. This was our sacred space where we shared our thoughts, fears, opinions, joys and struggles. We both enjoyed diving into the deep end of conversations as we looked to gather a clearer understanding of our purpose through it all. Never with judgement but, rather, with compassion, respect and brutal honesty. It was obvious Joseph was looking for a light to follow, I could see it in his eyes. My role as a mother had been redefined, no longer the physical caregiver who cooked, cleaned and drove him to school. My role was not to be his rock, but his boulder, his anchor each and every day, just as he was for me; a constant light despite the darkness that seemed to be all around us. I had to show him by example, not just how to live in joy, but how to thrive in times of conflict and despair. I had to step up my game and live the words I was teaching, he trusted me and letting him down was simply not an option. He soon began implementing the words into his own life and his own challenges, allowing himself to take comfort in the Universe and in the fact that we didn't need to figure it all out in this moment. We both just kept taking the next right step, individually as well as together. Not one day did we have an argument or disagreement as it was always about working together and never against one another. I reminded him of Martin Luther King's famous quote: "The ultimate measure of a man is not where he stands in moments of comfort and convenience, but where he stands at times of challenge and controversy." It was through the importance of my new role that I not only parented my son, but myself as well. The book *The Prophet* by Kahlil Gibran is my favourite and I often turned to it in times of confusion when I lacked clarity. I also introduced Joseph to the writing of Gibran and he too sought comfort in its pages, many times taking it from the shelf as he headed to the water where he sat and read with his constant furry companion and sidekick. That old soul I gave birth to is a seeker of wisdom, a doer of good deeds and he is built of character, integrity and compassion at his very core.

  He continued to immerse himself into community service with St. George's, his high school and on his own. As far back as I could remember, Joseph had always been happiest when he could be of service to others. I was grateful that his present circumstances had not changed or hardened his beautiful open heart. I told him to give what he had freely, trusting that all he needed would always come to him. I truly believe the moment you hold your hand closed to give, you also close your hand to receive. He lived this principle absolutely every day and always drew to him all that he required.

  I had been taught by a dear Buddhist friend many years earlier, the basic principles of energy and how it affects us. As I learned, I taught Joseph along the way. I felt it was important for him to understand energy's role in forming our reality in every moment and I spent many of our bedside gatherings explaining the Universal law: "What you put out is what you will receive back." Our energy is a constant echo of what we speak and think on a daily basis. We set the vibration through our actions, words and thoughts and it resonates like a beating drum. If we put out fear and scarcity, we will without a doubt, create and receive more of that very thing. I shared with him our responsibility as individuals to stand guard against the vibrational energy we put out to the world, as well as our responsibility to stand guard against the vibrational energy we allow into our space, we must be vigilant. I was reminded of my great grandmother and the beautiful life she lived, her positive attitude and her prayerful lifestyle, which enabled her to live a most peaceful existence. This was a beautiful example of a blessed life lived. Joseph and I as a team, were very mindful of this basic theory. We were there to remind each other if we saw old patterns of thinking coming to the surface. We had become aware of the need to speak as if our goals had already been achieved, our problems already resolved and the deep belief that we already had all that we required in this moment. It was tough! It was the preverbal, "fake it till ya make it" mindset, and that was ok. Each day that passed we became more disciplined, more aware, and more determined with this new way of thinking, new way of being and new way of showing up. It was for us, a totally new way of existing. The positive energy it created within us, within our home and around us was undeniable and things were finally shifting. The vibrations of love and laughter began to fill our days and we both experienced a surge of energy. We could hear the drum of our desires beating and although still a distance away, we heard them, nonetheless.

*****

It was now time for Joseph to begin searching career options for university and he continuously repeated that he had no idea what he wanted to do with his future. Joseph, as I'm sure the majority of young people, felt completely overwhelmed with having to make such a huge decision at such a young age. I decided to break it down and simplify the task. Joseph sat with me and we did an exercise on happiness. What did a happy day look like to him? What would it include? What would it not include? What activity brings you the most joy? What do you despise doing? It was an amazing conversation and great opportunity for introspective work on his part. Building had always been his passion and a source of happiness from the time he could drag a hammer behind his diapered bottom. Many mornings as a toddler, he would wake and exclaim with the determination of an old man: "I must build today mommy!" I would laugh and ask what it was he had to build? He would matter of factly reply, "I don't know, but something!" By the time he was five years old his father had taught him how to use a drill and he had his own toolbox that he kept at his bedside. All that LEGO sure helped develop his building and design interests, truly the best toy on the market! After completing our exercise on happiness, Joseph's decision was clear, he was going to pursue a career in engineering. We knew what he wanted to do, now I trusted that the "how" to pay for university would answer itself.

JoJo Marie Schillaci

Chapter Thirty-Three

By December 31, 2014, I had been bedridden for over 940 days. Another year was ending, and I was *grateful* to close its door. I was *grateful* for the lessons I had learned, the wisdom I had gained and for each and every shit storm that propelled me further along the labyrinth. I was *grateful* for all my strides forward, and there were many. I was *grateful* for the beautiful people that had come to my bedside with their love, support and their deep belief in me. The outpouring of love, not just to me but, to my son as well, was remarkable and truly humbling. I was *grateful* Joseph had used every crappy situation as fertilizer and allowed it to help him grow more each day. I was deeply *grateful* that I had found the path leading to my own self-discovery and I now realized I wasn't, "being buried" but in fact, "being planted," I had been given a second chance at life. There was definitely a death in progress, the death of the old, fearful, powerless self and the planting and rebirthing of my true, most fiercely independent and authentic self that lay in waiting. For the first time in my life a peacefulness had begun to envelope me like a warm blanket fresh from the dryer on a cold, damp day. It was a deep comfort from within me, not from something external and I felt an incredible sense of control of my thoughts and my emotions, a deep inner peace was being established and with that, I was handling life differently. I was showing up differently, instead of the usual exhausted, emotional and fearful responses, I was showing up peaceful, calm and levelheaded. I had developed a remarkable self-propelled faith and belief in myself. It had always been there, buried under years and years of layered fear waiting for the Divine time to be uncovered layer by layer. It was through my disciplined *commitment* to the *5 Pillar* words that I was *liberated* into a state of self-generated inner peace. I felt like Dorothy in the Wizard of Oz, always believing that the power I was searching for was being governed by something external. It was not unlike the extraordinary wizard that was far from reach and seemingly ever elusive, until finally realizing: "I had the power all along." I had been shackled and chained to my thoughts, my fears, my past and it was now my choice to put myself in the power position and let them go. I soon realized I actually held the key to freedom all along. "What's the difference between a king and a slave? Courage." I was no longer the cowardly lion frightened by every bump in the night or by the darkness. As I faced the darkness of my fears with *trust, acceptance, gratitude* and *commitment*, they simply melted into the light. As I released the shackles, I also freely released the need to blame others. This was not only about facing fear, it was also about taking ownership. This was about taking responsibility for me, my life, my thoughts, my actions and inevitably, my reality. When I could say I created my past and present reality equally, it meant I could also create my future by design. We cannot choose to be responsible only when it feels good or when it's convenient. Deep self-discovery for me was realizing that at the end of the day, I was the creator of my life in every moment in how I chose to speak, to listen, to love, to hold on, as well as how I chose to let go. It was about embracing and allowing the natural flow of life to take me to the right place at the right time as the Universe saw fit. When we reach a level of personal ownership, love and acceptance, we realize this is where the vow: "In good times and in bad, in sickness and in health, for richer or for poorer," needs to be promised. With no other does this pertain more than to ourselves. Without a vow of independence, acceptance and love for yourself, a vow of any kind to another is virtually impossible. I vowed to never be a slave to fear, to others' actions, words or beliefs, and to always remain in the power position of my life.

Me while bedridden, 2014.

There was also no denying the effects of pouring love on absolutely everything that was good, as well as bad in my life. I was consciously choosing to release the anger and bitterness and turn to love and prayer. I prayed and meditated daily for those I loved and more importantly, for those that presented the most challenges in my life. To hold loving space for your "perceived" enemy is to sit in grace. To love is to be vulnerable and as Brene Brown has said: "Vulnerability is the birthplace of love and inclusion." Her research shows that people who are able to experience deep connection are the ones that showed courage to be authentic. They let go of who they thought they had to be, and were vulnerable enough to show up and be seen as they truly were, knowing they were enough and believing that they were truly worthy of love. This was all part of the journey to discover my core truth at the centre of the labyrinth, breaking out of the mold of what I thought I had to be and standing in my most imperfect self, knowing deeply that I was worthy just as I was. I was shedding the need to fill my aunt's enormous shoes, releasing the need to be June Cleaver and letting go of the guilt of other's transgressions as my own. I was acknowledging that each battle we have with another is actually a battle we continue within ourselves, it has absolutely nothing to do with external stimuli. It is finding out the true enemy within and working through the wall that incapsulates fear, anxiety and dis - ease. When you reach inner peace, you are not at the mercy of those or circumstances around you. There was now no doubt in my mind I was going to emerge out of this and I was now choosing to do it by pouring more love on absolutely everything and everyone, but most importantly, I was finally pouring more love into me!

* * * * *

By the end of the year I felt like I was emerging from the tar pit, slowly, very slowly, but emerging. I was sleeping well, and rehab was progressing beautifully. I had finally hit the sweet tipping point we had all been anxiously awaiting, and I was now using my walker to take more steps and I had begun relearning simple tasks such as folding laundry. Each task represented a collection of smaller tasks for the brain to perform. I would speak aloud with a running commentary in order to assist the brain through each command. For instance, the day I washed my first dish I would tell my brain: "I am putting soap on the rag, I am running the water, I am wiping the dish, I am rinsing the dish, I am placing the dish on the counter." Things that had been second nature to me now had to be relearned in the smallest of baby steps. It's like reciting the alphabet. It rolls off your tongue with ease forwards from A to Z, but now try to recite it backwards from the middle with the letters upside down. You have to sit and think about it right? That's how every task was for me, that was my vestibular challenged brain. Nothing flowed with ease and movements were ridged and disjointed. Another day, I was given the task of peeling an apple, something I had been proficient at from a young age cooking with my mom. Now, the dialogue was: "I'm holding the apple, I'm placing the knife against the apple, I'm turning the apple." I didn't care how long it took to perform each activity; I was overjoyed to finally be able to do everyday blessings that many people take for granted. Moving my head while walking was still not mastered, nor the journey to the bathroom, but I was able to walk the five steps to the back door which was a blessing unto itself. At the beginning, I sat in a chair with the door open feeling the fresh air on my face, other days, I would sit with my arms and legs sticking straight out to catch rain drops or feel the snow melt as it hit my skin. It was all simply magical to me. It would take some months before my brain could handle stepping down onto the deck but, when I was ready, Dr. Peter would be right at my side. On my first venture outside, I remember noticing the vastness of space most of all. It had been so long since I had experienced the limitless sky instead of the ceiling over my head. The sky was massive and the sun and moon were remarkable to witness again. Dr. Peter sat me in a chair as he lovingly buried my feet into a container of earth. As I rubbed my feet deep into the dark soil and let it squeeze between each of my toes, I was back in the dirt pile at the nursery! Dr. Peter just sat quietly at my side allowing me to take in the experience through all of my senses. Every chance I could I'd poke my nose out of the sliding door to drench my senses and rejuvenate my spirit.

* * * * *

During this time in bed, if there was ever a word that evoked the most negative response in me, it was the word hope. Hope to me is a four letter word I can do without. People would visit, write or call and inevitably end the communication with: "I do hope you walk again and get better soon." Each time I felt like screaming at the top of my lungs… "NO!" Each time I heard it I felt like a wounded animal at the side of the road, left to the mercy of circumstances and actions of others. I felt powerless and weak, I despised that word. People in my inner circle knew it and would never utter the "H" word, at least not in front of me. For me, it was about trust, deep inner trust. Trusting that I *would* walk again, trusting that I *would* function again and trusting that I *would* live fully again. Trust put me in the power position where there was no doubt, it was already determined, it was going to happen. The Universe was listening.

*****

On a cold March day in 2015, after more than 1,100 consecutive days in the bed, I realized my biggest goal. The day that I had dreamed, ached and prayed for. I had finally increased my steps enough to make the twenty-one step journey to the powder room. It wasn't planned, Joseph was again helping me in the walker that day as he always did. My brain felt solid and I was feeling particularly strong, when I turned to him and said: "I think I can do it. I think I can make it to the washroom." Striking while the iron was hot with Joseph on one side and Shomei on the other, I held the walker in my tightest grip and slowly and methodically put one foot in front of the other. I let my eyes guide both my wheels and brain all the way until finally, I was there! In my head there were trumpets playing and confetti falling from the sky! I felt like I had just climbed Mount Everest and it was time to put my flag in the ground claiming my victory over the odds that had been stacked against me. I would have shouted from the roof top had my neurology allowed. Joseph took the walker as I pushed the door to my freedom open. As I closed the door behind me, I was ill prepared for what awaited me. Standing in the small 3x5 space I turned my body slowly to sit on the toilet. My eyes went from looking at the floor to looking directly forward. This is where my gaze met my reflection in the mirror for the first time in more than three years. As my eyes locked onto my image, I felt all the blood drain from me. I grabbed the sink in an attempt to lessen the impact, as I fell to the ground in a heap. In the excitement and serendipity of reaching my goal, I had forgotten about the mirror. How could I have forgotten about the mirror? What looked back at me was a thousand times worse than anything I had imagined laying in the bed. My skin was grey and flakey resembling stone or shale. The mental and emotional fatigue had aged me a decade, maybe two. My eyes had lost their sparkle. It was as if I was looking into two murky pools of emptiness. They were completely void of the spirit that once shone through. My face was marked with scratches and scars like deep battle wounds. The weight I had gained showed on my face and I now sported a second chin but, what stood out most in that moment, was the permanent frown lines that appeared on either side of my mouth. They were so deeply cut in from years of crying, fear and deep profound pain and sorrow. I looked like one of those clowns with a permanent expression of sadness. Joseph came in and helped me back to the walker and eventually the bed. "I look like a monster. I'm so ugly. Who is that person? I don't even know who I am." Joseph sat holding me while I processed the shock and horror of the woman I once was and had now become. Instead of this being a time to rejoice and celebrate my victory, I would cry myself to sleep, mourning the old image and terrified of the new. I had done so much work during these years in bed, working at uncovering and unraveling the fear and falsehoods that kept my truest self from being seen but, now, my physical self was the complete antithesis of this. How was I to accept this? How could I possibly meld these two together when they were so starkly different? How could I possibly become at peace with my physical self? Clearly, there was more work to be done.

As I welcomed 2015, a new year, I did not look back with regret. I had been given a gift this past year, wrapped in an unlikely disguise. No shiny paper, curled ribbon or bow. My gift was wrapped in tears, torment and doubt. Inside, under all the fear and uncertainty, this package hid a priceless treasure. Something no amount of money, planning or wishing could buy. I was gifted a second chance at life, a self-propelled faith and an incredible love for myself. They were never on my wish list. I never truly knew that I desired them. When the gift arrived, I realized it had always been there, waiting on the doorstep for the moment I was ready to welcome it fully into my life. Often, the gift is knelt before us for a lifetime, and sadly, sometimes never opened. For with the gift comes a responsibility. The responsibility for both one's happiness and one's destiny. In taking on this responsibility, you release the option of blaming others. Your life is your own, fully and completely. Not when it is convenient. Not just for the good times, but for "ALL" times. When we reach a level of personal ownership, love and acceptance, we realize this is where the vow, "in good times and in bad, in sickness and in health, for richer and for poorer," needs to be promised.

With no other does this pertain more than with ourselves. Without a vow of independence, acceptance and love for yourself, a vow of any kind to another is virtually impossible.

Written 2015

JoJo Marie Schillaci

Chapter Thirty-Four

It had now been more than three and a half years since my body was immersed into water. Finally, I was mobile enough and my brain was stable enough to have a bath. The problem was, I didn't have one on the ground floor. I was a long way off from being rehabilitated to make the seventeen stair climb to my tub upstairs. I felt layer upon layer and year after year of emotional soot and residue just waiting to be literally washed away. Once again, Dr. Peter would walk in and make my dream a reality. One of the many things I loved about this man was that to him, nothing was ever black or white, yes or no, possible or impossible. He would always say: "let's see what we CAN do." It was through that thinking, he would arrive at my door with an enormous, portable fiberglass bathtub.

It was long enough to enable an adult to stretch fully out inside and approximately three and a half feet deep. My team brainstormed the logistics and Joseph executed the mission of both filling and emptying it from in front of my bed. As I sat on the edge of the bed watching the process, I kept shaking my head in disbelief. Was I really going to have a bath? In my living room no less? It had been the wish that ran through my mind every day and now, it was finally happening. With each minute that passed, I watched the water rise higher and higher and my anticipation grew just as quickly. A caregiver helped me make the leap in, which was actually more of a gentle slow glide. As my body slowly submerged into the water, I instantly felt my entire nervous system react. Every cell was getting stimulated! The sensation of the water cascading over my body felt like a tidal wave hitting every nerve ending. I felt pins and needles from head to toe. Just like old times, I submerged my entire body including my ears in an effort to calm my nervous system. I needed to calm my body down in order to allow me a few more minutes in my baptismal font. I lasted a short, but magnificent five minutes until my system and brain became over loaded. Even in the short amount of time, I felt the previous years heavy, sorrowful energy wash away, leaving a fresh clean slate behind. Oh, this was much more than just a bath! This was a deep cleansing of my soul and spirit. Washing away the old and a purification and rejuvenation into the new.

* * * * *

I was going through a terrible time with my identity. Many things had changed around and in me. I had evolved so much from whom I used to be and so many of the hats I had previously worn, just didn't fit anymore.

Beyond the obsolete roles of wife, granddaughter, entrepreneur, volunteer and community activist, came the aspect of my legal identity. When I married my husband, I took on his name with great pride, but it no longer applied. I no longer belonged to that tribe and sadly, never did. People assumed I would return to my maiden name but, to me, that seemed just as much of a misfit. Though I was struggling with my identity through this transition period, my spirit was growing more and more each day. Through the journey along the labyrinth I was opening up and allowing myself to own all of me. I did this by being vulnerable, shedding my armour of defensiveness and by listening deeply to my inner voice, not the voices of others. By embracing stillness and quiet, the messages were received.

For the first time, I began tapping into my thoughts, dreams and deep beliefs without the echo of expectation from others. As I made my way to the centre of the labyrinth, I also reached my epicenter, which is where I uncovered my core truth. After living my entire life small, not being good enough and feeling like a misfit, I realized I was more than plenty as I was. I am a woman of incredible strength and fierce independence. A woman whose character has many fascinating sides. Some serious and full of the wisdom of an old soul. Another, a playful child with a hint of innocence. My character was big and my heart even bigger. No longer was I editing my thoughts or beliefs to suit other's comfort zones. I set healthy boundaries around myself and my energy without accepting guilt for doing so. Dr. Peter would tell me many times: "JoAnna, you're a lot of woman for the right man." The days of living small and feeling "not good enough" were a thing of the past. I came to realize that I had been living other people's falsehoods about me. A falsehood by definition, is a statement that distorts or suppresses the truth. Sometimes, others can lead us to believe falsehoods about ourselves. We slowly become brainwashed by these falsehoods and they begin to create limiting beliefs within us. This can happen quickly, or slowly over time. As we travel the road of authenticity and uncover our core self, we begin to recognize these falsehoods for what they are, merely reflections of others' opinions, perceptions and the shortcomings as well as the fears that reside within them, not us. This is how through the years I began to see a distorted image of my true self. Others falsehoods were not going to define me. They didn't belong to me. They never did. The fear stricken young girl was dying off and I was rebirthing my most genuine, womanly self. Truly a labour of self-love. I discovered there was a beautiful soul under all those falsehoods. At my most authentic core, I believed I was not just lovable but, deeply deserving of love. A beautiful soul.

No, I would never be able to take back my maiden name, nor did I want to. That ship had sailed. Taking on my maiden name would be like trying to fit ten pounds of character into a five pound casing. There was no way it was going to fit.

As much as I was taking control of my life, I felt lost without a name. I was in a constant state of limbo. People don't talk about this part of divorce. Many women, after dedicating themselves including their identity, to another, are left to piece back together some semblance of themselves as a person. Many of us suffer a real identity crisis as our roles, purpose and names suddenly change.

I decided that if I was now living my life by design, what better way to begin, than with a new name! I wanted my name to be not only a reflection of who I was today, but also how I got here. I chose to honour the women of influence in my life. I would take the name of Auntie Rea who taught me how to be a lady, to laugh at life, appreciate every little thing and that if you have to crawl, crawl with grace. I took the name of my mother who taught me to never give up, to be fiercely independent and that life is always better with lipstick on. I took the name of my grandmother who taught me what true love looks like, as well as how to be stubbornly determined. And last but, most certainly not least, I took the name of my great grandmother who taught me that a blessed life comes from speaking less, listening more and to believe in something higher than ourselves. I'm the woman I am today because of these women and the true gifts they brought to my life. I became JoAnna Maria Antoinina Schillaci!

JoJo Marie Schillaci

Chapter Thirty-Five

Joseph was very fortunate to have an incredible support system, my brother being at the top of the list. He also had Uncle Joey, James, Cosmo, Anatoli and Dr. Peter. A beautiful group of respectful men who lived respectable lives. But there was a *missing piece*. I felt he needed a male closer to his age and physical abilities to take part in the active portion of his life. Despite the odds, I decided to put in an application to the Toronto chapter of the Big Brothers mentoring program. Within a surprisingly short amount of time, he was accepted, and a Big Brother was found. As a single mom, I was thankful for the added support and blessing to our lives. Little did we know how truly big a blessing Big Brothers would become.

* * * * *

As 2016 began, I had been bedridden for more than 1,300 days. This is when I turned my attention to my biggest goal, Joseph's high school graduation. I was now walking small distances in the walker throughout our first floor and increasing my nervous systems' tolerance to stimulus. In order for me to reach my goal, I needed to be able to get in a car, travel the five minutes to his high school as well as be able to sit through various stimulus for at least thirty minutes. Clearly, I had my work cut out for me.

Rehabilitating for my first real adventure out in more than four years would be not unlike all my other achievements, arduous, methodical and painfully slow.

 I simply began by sitting in the car for five minutes at a time on good days. Joseph, again my constant rehabilitative sidekick, would bring me out to sit in his car with Shomei full of excitement in the back seat. She adored car rides but, little did she know, we weren't going to leave the driveway. My son and I laughed together at the sheer ridiculousness of it all. Joseph timed our rehab sessions and I felt each minute pass like an hour. I know it's hard to imagine, but this had a huge impact on my brain. My eyes were required to take in a tremendous amount of information and then transfer it to my brain. Houses, trees, moving cars not to mention all the birds and squirrels actively moving around me. Added to that were the sounds of traffic and children playing in the street. I could smell the scent of nature pollution, and I could feel the vastness of space all around me. To my system it felt like I was sitting front row centre at a rock concert. When the five minutes were up, I returned inside to go through the usual calming of the brain and nervous system. I laid back in bed where the brain knew what was familiar, away from all the stimulus. After a couple of weeks, it was time for the next right step. On a good day, we would move the car ten feet to the end of the driveway, I would then slowly get out and walk back to the house. The brain would have gone into immediate shock had I stayed in the car while it was in reverse. This was rehabilitation on a whole new level as the vestibular system was now being challenged with movement other than my own. I was instantaneously nauseous, followed by dizziness and brain burn. After a few more weeks, it was time to drive two houses down the street and then come back, all the while, my brain felt like it was being pushed into overdrive. The loading of new information was a challenge but, even more so, was the eye movement. Each time the car moved, I felt like I was back on the rollercoaster ride. While in motion, I had to make certain not to move my head and to keep my eyes fixed on a target in order to lessen the symptoms.

Within a couple of months, I graduated to going around the block. It was wonderful to see my neighbourhood again, the community I had been a part of for so many years and worked on helping to evolve. It all looked so different. Many houses had been rebuilt, new stores opened and old ones had closed. The volume of traffic is what I remember being in awe of the most. There was so much! I felt like Rip Van Winkle awakening from a decade of slumber. Everything seemed so different, the pace was much faster than I remembered. I was totally in awe and amazed that I was now a part of it all, even if only in a small way. I kept thinking: "this was what was happening each day I laid in the bed. Everything kept going and at light speed."

My brain was beginning to accept the short rides and I was grateful. I enjoyed the little bit of relief it provided from the confines of my usual walls and bed, not to mention that the fresh air was great therapy. No matter the strides forward, I heard the ticking of the clock getting louder and louder and the words "not good enough" beginning to echo yet again. Doubt was rearing its ugly head, always the instigator, but never the ally. Each day I turned to my *5 Pillars* words to guide me through and quiet the fear and doubt. ***Trusting, accepting,*** being ***grateful*** and fully ***committed*** and knowing deep down, one day I would be fully ***liberated***. I kept focused on the image in my mind of sitting in the audience, watching Joseph walk across the stage and receive his diploma. I *trusted* the "how" would answer itself.

It was already April and I only had until June 29th, Joseph's graduation and my 48th birthday to reach my goal. I was going to be there, that's all there was to it. Each day, Joseph invested so much of his own time working on my rehab and encouraging me every step of the way. I knew how much having me attend the ceremony meant to him, though he never said so. He always said it didn't matter, but mama knew better.

During one of our usual evening bedside chats, I felt confident enough to tell him: "I think I'm good Joseph. I'll be able to get to the school and sit for the ceremony for sure." The school was less than a five minute drive from our home and I had been doing so well with my endurance exercises. I was proud of myself and overjoyed with the thought of finally realizing my four year goal. Joseph stared at me with a look of shock and dismay. Quietly, he said, "Mom, it's not at the school. It's at the Canadian National Exhibition." I felt like I had been thrown out of plane without a parachute. "What are you talking about? Why? How?" The fact was that the school did not have the space to accommodate the graduates and their guests, so it would be held at the Queen Elizabeth building on the CNE fair grounds. This was an almost eight kilometer drive! How could I ever make it there and then manage sitting for the ceremony? My heart was breaking, and I began to cry. It was then that we realized we had been working on a completely different goal this entire time. We sat and held each other knowing full well how much this meant to both of us, but not wanting to admit it to either one. As much as we were working on *trusting* the process, it looked pretty damn bleak. But we didn't stay there. We couldn't. The next day, I began my new rehab goal: the CNE fair grounds. My mother came several days a week after work, Sundays and Saturdays to go for drives with the CNE always as our goal. We went a little further each day, until finally, we arrived. I also worked on practicing increasing my endurance to sit and be stimulated by lights and sounds, in anticipation for what would be facing me in that building come June 29th. That was the day I *trusted* both Joseph and I would finally be *liberated*.

JoJo Marie Schillaci

Chapter Thirty-Six

The big day arrived and it felt like my graduation day, as well as Joseph's. The culmination of four years of blood, sweat and tears. Every minute on the computer program, every laser exercise, every lifting of my head for ten seconds, every micro step forward and every drive around the block was to get me to this exact moment.

    We arranged with the school staff a plan that would enable me to see Joseph on stage with as little waiting time as possible. My brain could only manage a maximum of half an hour at the ceremony plus the sixteen kilometre drive there and back. Dr. Peter, who had celebrated so many major milestones with me, had offered to drive. I sat beside him in the front seat while my ever present support system, my mother and brother, would be leaving before us with Joseph and awaited our arrival. Before Joseph left, he came to the bed and hugged me tight. Looking deeply into my eyes he said: "Mom, see how you feel. If you can make it great and if you can't, that's ok too" and gave me a kiss on the cheek. He was the most selfless child, never asking or demanding anything. Joseph never put pressure on me and somehow always made peace with the lot he had been given. My mindset was the same as it was when we went to buy the new LEGO set, I was going! If I had to crawl the entire way, I was going!

The drive to the CNE was incredibly nerve-racking! I was concerned about the traffic and not arriving in time to see Joseph on stage. I felt better as we rounded the corner into the CNE grounds and made our way to the Queen Elizabeth building. Dr. Peter helped me out of the car and into an awaiting wheelchair. I couldn't contain my excitement as we entered the auditorium which was packed to the rafters with graduates and proud parents. The space was just as I had remembered it from when I was a child. Growing up, I had watched many shows in this building during the summer runs of the fair. It was familiar and it gave me comfort. There was a sea of blue in the front rows from the graduates in their ceremonial gowns and the band was playing in the orchestra pit. I saw my mom and brother waving me in, smiling from ear to ear as they saw my wheelchair make its entrance. I can't tell you how my brain felt with all the stimulus because I was so excited and overjoyed taking in every beautiful second. If I was going into overload it would just have to wait and I would deal with the aftermath later. This was my son's moment and I was here in "real time", experiencing it with him. Not through pictures or FaceTime, but in real-life time. Joseph was unaware I had made it. It wasn't until he walked in the procession past our seats that he realized I was there. The moment he saw me, his face lit up and his eyes and smile as were as big as could be. He put his arm on my shoulder as he walked past and I felt his loving, reassuring energy.

As they called his name and I watched him walk across the stage, I saw a movie reel in my mind. The eighteen years it took to get him to this point seemed to flash before me. It had all happened so fast. As they handed him his diploma, they also announced he would be awarded two scholarships. I was beaming with pride! This was not just about what he was able to achieve, but that he had achieved it through the most challenging of circumstances. Throughout all these years, Joseph continually strived to be his personal best and to give freely and be there for others in the face of his own adversity. There could be no better birthday gift!

Joseph and I on his graduation day, June 29, 2016.

*****

Joseph submitted his university applications in January of 2016. Although he applied to several, Ryerson was his first choice. The entire time, my brother as well as many others, kept asking me: "How are you going to pay for his tuition?" I insisted that it would all work out...somehow. Joseph and I were **trusting, accepting, grateful** and fully **committed** to this. Our intention was pure, our karma was clean, and we were going to manifest all that we needed. Years previous, I would have been up at night with worry and preoccupied all day with stress. I now released the need to, "figure it all out." I stayed **trusting** and in constant positive communication with the Universe, confirming that it was already taken care of. I deeply believed the "how" had already answered itself. Sometimes, people had trouble understanding how Joseph and I remained so calm while we transitioned through the dark and uncertain times. We both had days when the questioning thoughts would come up, but we both quickly deleted them and reconfirmed our belief that things would happen exactly as they needed to. We consciously worked hard at keeping our karma clean, always taking the higher road. Many times, I would say to Joseph: "Have you ever wondered why there is only one donkey at a petting zoo? Because you never need more than one jackass!" It no longer mattered what was being said or done around us. We chose to carry ourselves with dignity, never sinking low enough to play in the mud of gossip and controversy. We were mindful of the energy we put out knowing full well that it was a boomerang delivering the very same back to us. The goodness we put out, always returned tenfold.

Soon after his university applications were submitted, we received notification from Big Brothers that there was a scholarship being awarded to one boy and one girl covering their entire four year degree, including books and fees. Applications were now being accepted. Both Joseph and I were required to write essays outlining his academic career, as well as any information explaining why he was the best choice for the scholarship. We immediately decided to apply. Once again, we began beating the drum of our desires.

It was now mid-March of that year when I heard Joseph uncharacteristically honking his horn in excitement! His face was beaming! "I GOT IT!", he yelled over and over again. "Mom, I was awarded the Clifton Family scholarship from Big Brothers!" He ran into my arms and we both clung tightly to each other as we collapsed on the sofa. Our feelings flowed from joy, to relief, to excitement and gratitude. He did it!

Joseph also received his acceptance letter from Ryerson. I was beaming with pride! Pride for what he was able to achieve but, more so, for the mindset he continued throughout the entire process.

Over and over, time and time again, we witnessed one miracle after another. Blessings of people and circumstances continually surrounded us. We were manifesting. The dark days were finally over, and we could see the light and it constantly guided our way.

In September 2016, Joseph began university at Ryerson for Civil Engineering and with the blessing of five scholarships. Although I was extremely grateful, I was ill-prepared for the cavalcade of emotions that would follow. One day it was nursery school and all of a sudden he was off to university. I had missed so much in between. Though he wasn't staying in residence, I saw him perhaps, only for an hour on a good day, but most days not at all. It was a grueling course load which would have him coming home at all hours, well past the time I called it a night.

Once again, I was feeling a sense of loss, emptiness, and a tremendous lack of purpose. The preverbal empty nest of emotions was compounded by an already intense lack of meaning and direction in my own life. It was clear to me, my role yet again, was changing. For more than eighteen years I dedicated every moment of every day to the raising of my child and now that was shifting and shifting quickly. No longer was I needed for everyday necessities. He was more than capable of taking care of himself.

I missed Joseph not being around. We had always been there both physically and emotionally, facing it all together. The house was quiet, so damn quiet. Thankfully, I no longer required caregivers. I was capable of caring for myself and the house on my own. I not only enjoyed, but took immense pride in getting back to cooking small simple meals. Though at a snail's pace compared to my usual speed, everything got done in the Divine time. The house felt so empty now. Most days, I felt like I was wandering in the dark not knowing what I was supposed to be doing or who I was supposed to be doing it for. My responsibility and role each day, had been to be Joseph's mom and if he didn't need me the same, what exactly was my purpose? I struggled with pride for the independence he had achieved and the guilt I felt for wanting him to still need me.

So many answers I sought during the bed years had come to me through the glass doors I gazed out of each minute of each day. Nature had always provided me the answers I was seeking and this time would be no different. One morning, I went into the powder room and there upon the windowsill sat a robin fledgling. He looked terrified, but not of me. He looked at me with eyes that sought comfort. He sat staring at me as I talked in a soothing voice, reassuring him that he was safe. He followed me from window to window for days, taking comfort in my presence. I spent the next several days observing the dynamic between he and his mother. I heard him call out to her and watched as she came to nuzzle and reassure him for brief spells, then off she would go again. Each day, I noticed her flying farther and farther away and increasing the periods of time between their visits. She was allowing him to explore his independence and to learn the skills he needed to be self-sufficient. I watched him grow more confident, brave and daring with his flying and landing, as well as his ability to forage for food. He no longer followed me from window to window as he no longer needed my reassurance. It was an incredible process to witness and the clear message I needed to receive.

I would once again recall the book *The Prophet*:

"*On Children*" by Kahlil Gibran

Your children are not your children.
They are the sons and daughters of Life's longing for itself.

JoJo Marie Schillaci

They come through you but not from you,
And though they are with you, yet they belong not to you.

You may give them your love but not your thoughts.
For they have their own thoughts.
You may house their bodies but not their souls,
For their souls dwell in the house of tomorrow,
which you cannot visit, not even in your dreams.
You may strive to be like them, but seek not to make them like you.
For life goes not backward nor tarries with yesterday.

You are the bows from which your children as living arrows are sent forth.
The archer sees the mark upon the path of the infinite,
and He bends you with His might that His arrows may go swift and far.
Let your bending in the archer's hand be for gladness;
For even as He loves the arrow that flies,
so He loves also the bow that is stable.

  Letting go is a very natural and necessary part of loving our children. Nature always provides the answers when we become still and conscious to the beauty that constantly surrounds us. It is always sending us subtle but distinct messages. Nature is an incredible classroom, with a library of wisdom and knowledge. It was from that little fledgling and his mom that I found peace with my new role in Joseph's life. This had nothing to do with loss, on the contrary, this was about liberation. Joseph was on his own journey and walking his own labyrinth of self-discovery. He was going to find his core truth, free from the thoughts, beliefs and falsehoods of others, just as I did. The fledgling had made it not just out of the nest, but he soared into the sky.

JoJo Marie Schillaci

Chapter Thirty-Seven

Joseph's first semester of university was brutal. He had an insane schedule and course load, which I believe, is all part of the weeding out process to see who has the "right stuff." It was obvious to me he was struggling and trying hard to adjust. I knew Joseph would figure out a system that worked for him but, as his mother, it was difficult to watch. He was barely sleeping and ate no more than the fledgling on the windowsill. He had lost fifteen pounds and it showed.

I was still adjusting to our new schedule and so was Shomei. I could see she was feeling the changes happening around her and she missed Joseph terribly. They had always been very close. All these years, she knew when three o'clock came and off to the porch she went, waiting for her best friend to come down the street calling her name. As soon as he called out to her, she bounced toward him like he had just come home from months away, not hours.

Lately, Shomei had been acting differently. She wasn't that happy puppy with a sparkle in her eyes. There was a visible sadness about her, and she seemed depressed. We chalked it up to her adjusting to Joseph not being at home and missing him. Slowly, her eating began to change, and she was barely interested in her usually favourite foods. It was time we took her to the vet. Her bloodwork showed abnormalities and she was then sent to a specialist across town. Thank goodness for my forethought of purchasing health insurance for her. It was a blessing that almost everything would be covered. The vet called and broke the news that our dear girl had stage four cancer throughout her body. The news hit Joseph and I very hard. She was one-third of our team, an integral part. My confidant and constant companion, the one that never left my side and never asked for a thing. We were going to love her through and let her stay home with us for her final days. This all came at the same time as Joseph's first semester of final exams. He cared for her through the night, changing her diaper, cleaning the vomit and holding her as she slept. He did all this with his textbooks open at his side, just as he had done with his great grandmother during her last days in the hospital, holding her hand with one and typing essays with the other.

December 18, 2016, Joseph had held her through the night as he had many nights before, but this night was different. Shomei had stopped breathing and gasped for air several times during her sleep. Both Joseph and I knew that it was time…the time we were dreading in our hearts when we would have to let her go. In true compassionate Joseph form, he insisted on taking her to the lake one last time. It was something they had always done together. But how? It seemed impossible as she could barely stand. How would she be able to walk? He looked at me and simply said: "Once you set the intention, the how answers itself." He had already claimed his intention. Joseph insisted that he could do it, believing deeply that it needed to be done for her. The lake was her happy place and he wanted to give her one last chance to experience it, together. He borrowed a wooden sled from a neighbour, attached her dog bed to it with bungee cords, then loaded warm blankets into the trunk and lifted her into the backseat of his car. I wasn't able to manage the almost two kilometre walk but, even if I could, I would have let them go alone. This was their special time together. As they began their final walk, Joseph sent me a video showing her face lit up! Her eyes looked clear and bright, though you could still see the fatigue and pain within her. She had been so listless when they left the house, but Shomei looked like she had gotten her second wind. I'm sure she could feel his commitment and love for her as he pulled her along the lakefront trail. Her face exuded pure happiness. Shomei knew this was her last go and was taking in every minute of it. He had lovingly tucked her in with blankets keeping her warm and comforted. Joseph had an amazing look of peace and love on his face. He was giving his best friend what she wanted in the most compassionate and loving way.

When they arrived back home, we knew it was time and we would do this together. I sat in the back of the car with her on my lap, talking to her the entire time while holding her close. I reassured her that she was safe, and the pain would soon be gone. The soothing talk was more for me than her as I attempted to bring reason to my brain for what seemed unfathomable to my heart. Her face was soaked from my tears. She and I stayed in the car while Joseph went in and got things sorted with the vet.

As I held her, I reminisced about our life together. Shomei never knew she was a dog and her soul was of a compassionate human past-life encapsulated in the physical form of Mr. Mugs. Her eyes had a depth to them. The entire time I was sick she never left my side and gave me unconditional love. She encouraged me with every single step of my rehab and celebrated every victory alongside me. She loved and supported me through some of the ugliest times of my life, without judgement. A quintessential true best friend. Now, I was losing her. Yet another loss. As I sat in the car, I kept repeating and implementing the *5 Pillar* words *trusting* that it was time, the Universe was calling her. I *accepted* that our time together was nearing an end. I was *grateful* for every moment we shared and *committed* to allowing her to go in peace.

I saw Joseph come out of the vet and it was clear to me he was in task mode. This was typical Joseph. He always found incredible strength to do what needed to be done, to do it right and to do it with love and compassion. He opened the door and said, "Mom it's time." I kept holding her tighter, not wanting to let go. Joseph would eventually loosen my grip and I watched them walk away together. He stayed holding and loving her in his arms as she closed her eyes one final time. He kept reassuring her it was okay, and he was there with her. He came out and we held each other for a long time and then drove home in silence. We walked in the door, not accustomed to the quiet. Joseph had a remarkably healthy way of dealing with loss and with death. He faced it head on with love and compassion, trusting and rejoicing in the love that he shared with the person and then was always courageous enough to let go. He processed death beautifully. I never wanted him to feel the fear of death that I had been accustomed to but wanted him to deeply rejoice in the celebration of life.

JoJo Marie Schillaci

Chapter Thirty-Eight

Joseph and I remained open and **_grateful_** to all the goodness that was around us. We were slowly being **_liberated_** time and time again as we remained **_committed_** to the **_5 Pillar_** words, reminding ourselves and each other, that every experience good and not so good, had been brought to us with purpose. We no longer looked at challenges with frustration or bitterness but, rather, with openness. We looked at them as building blocks preparing us for something that lay ahead. If something didn't work out as planned, we **_trusted_** it was because we were being put in alignment with what was best and meant for us. Peace began taking over our space and our thinking. The positive energy and mindset we created each day acted as a magnet for goodness and the Universe kept bringing the right people and experiences to us at the right time. It was 2017, when Gavin Ashley walked into our lives and nothing would ever truly be the same.

Gavin Ashley is an intuitive healer. He is the real deal. Gavin is not someone with a passing interest in energy, or someone that has taken a weekend course to make some money as a side hustle. This is a man who was born with a true Divine gift. From childhood, he had deep intuition and has spent his life honing his craft. Gavin's innate power has been gifted to him by a force far greater than anything found on earth. He is masterful and remarkably accurate at diagnosing people's ailments as he can get to the root cause by determining the emotional connection to physical disease. I have learned though his work, each time we have physical issues it's our body crying out to heal emotional traumas and triggers from our past. Once the emotional energy is discharged, the body can then heal itself. Gavin would call this, "a clearing." It wasn't only about clearing energy, though that was a huge part of his work. Gavin has a deep inner wisdom about him. When he talks it's like sitting with a sage, a shaman and Yoda all at the same time. He has an incredible power of human connection and a more compassionate and true heart you will never find. Despite his uncanny abilities, Gavin operates free of ego and lives a life of humility. He cares deeply for his clients and invests his heart in each and every person. He became my partner in healing, my dear friend and chosen little brother. We shared epic transformational conversations and healing sessions, enabling me to heal far beyond my wildest dreams.

The first thing I recall working on with Gavin was forgiveness. While in conversation, he pointed out to me that I couldn't say my former husband's name. I never realized it but, now that he pointed it out, he was right. When I made reference, he had taken on the name of "Him." Why was that? Gavin could see there was something far deeper laying below the surface that had to be released. He could see that I was holding bitterness in my heart. My subconscious had not let go of what I perceived had been done wrong against me. On the surface, I had consciously done the work of forgiving but, subconsciously, believing if I fully forgave it would mean I was granting a free pass, I was saying it was okay. Gavin helped me to see that deep forgiveness is the greatest gift of love that we can give ourselves. It really has very little if anything at all, to do with the other person. It's about releasing the hold of someone else's actions and freeing yourself from the negative charge associated with it. Until we do, we are tethered not only to their transgression, but to them and their energy as well. If you look up the meaning of forgiveness on the Web you will find the following: *"A conscious, deliberate decision to release feelings of resentment or vengeance toward a person or group who has harmed you, regardless of whether they actually deserve your forgiveness. Forgiveness does not mean forgetting, nor does it mean condoning or excusing offenses."* Somehow, as a society, we have adopted the belief that forgiveness means excusing the behaviour. We also get caught up with trying to determine if they are worthy of forgiveness. It is not ours to deem who is deserving, ours is to forgive freely.

In forgiving and truly releasing, I allowed myself to be fully and completely be free. The past does not define me, nor does anyone else's words or actions. There is never a free pass for bad behaviour, but it is up to the Universe (higher power) to see to that, not us. Forgiveness is about putting yourself karmically in alignment by creating an energy of love and compassion. The other person has paved their own karmic road and it is theirs to walk. Hate hurts and forgiveness heals. It's that simple.

I was now ready to release the past and deeply forgive. When I did the work of ***accepting*** the experience for what it was, merely an experience and not attaching emotional meaning to it, I was able to release the need to hold on to anger, bitterness and resentment. Meaning is the emotional charge we attach to a fact. An example of attaching meaning would be that I now carried excess body weight. The emotional meaning I attached to that fact was that I was unlovable, undesirable and undeserving of love. By doing this, I was negatively charging the experience and that negative energy resonated throughout my body.

Sometimes, we hold on to things that have been done to us like a medal worn around our neck. It's a symbol that we survived and perhaps, we use it as an excuse for our own short comings. A payoff that we receive. Our work is to release the need to blame others and dig deep within ourselves to uncover the root. We attract people and experiences in our life for a reason. Often, it is the Universe's way of showing us what we need to learn. Until the lesson has been uncovered and accepted, the Universe will continue putting the same in your path. It is about looking deeply into the mirror of self and not through the windows of others behaviour.

Through my work with Gavin on forgiveness, attaching meaning and releasing blame, my mind became clearer and my heart more peaceful. I felt an incredible lightness throughout me. I was able to not only say my former husband's name, but I was also able to say it without an emotional charge attached. I had become what Gavin would refer to as, neutral. The biggest blessing I received by forgiving, was that anger was replaced with compassion. Compassion for someone who had been a huge part of my life and the co-creator of the most incredible human I know, our son Joseph. I never wanted anything to taint that.

JoJo Marie Schillaci

Before we can master our power, we must first master our peace. We can be preoccupied with attaining power, but the true birthplace of inner power is the quiet humble stillness of inner peace. When we can self-generate peace and remain at still-point no matter what is thrown at us, we are naturally aligning ourselves into the power position of our life. Until we can master our emotions, we will remain at the mercy of people and circumstances which constantly undermines our power. It is a game of cat and mouse.

Written 2019

Chapter Thirty-Nine

It was now 2017, Joseph had found his groove at university and was excelling on multiple levels. Academically he was doing great. He had developed a time management system that was working for him, as well as connected to a social network that provided the camaraderie and support he needed. They were a wonderful bunch of young people with big minds and even bigger hearts. He fit in beautifully. Each day, he implemented the **5 *Pillar*** words to keep him grounded and at peace. He engaged in many extra circulars both charitable and competitive in nature that would help him round out his already impressive resume. This gave me peace of mind, as well as peace in my heart to see him excelling and enjoying life once again. He believed he was given a tremendous gift through his scholarships and was committed to making the most out of his university years. Clearly, he was. Joseph continued working part time at St. George's and was still very connected to the youth group as well as to James.

    I continued to work diligently on my daily rehabilitation. Though I had completed my formal rehab with Joon, there were still daily independent tasks to relearn on my own. I had finally been given the all clear to drive again and began the same process as I had as a passenger. It took many months with Joseph once again, helping me through each and every step as my driving instructor. Each venture out inevitably ended up with the two of us laughing out loud, as we did with most everything in our lives. He always started out as the serious one and I would break the tension by cracking jokes. He'd look at me and with a stern smile and say, "Hands at ten and two mom!"

It would take the better part of 2017 to become fully independent behind the wheel. It is very different rehabilitating as the driver than the passenger. As the driver there was a tremendous amount of eye movement and information to take in. Our eyes are constantly scanning, and information is continually streaming through to our brain. There is no option to shut our eyes while things calm down when behind the wheel.

When I was able to drive short distances, Sunday dinner at my mother's was top of my list of places to go. I made sure my first visit was unannounced. I wish someone had taken a picture of her face when she saw me walk through the living room to where she was sitting. She was beaming! I could see the joy and relief on her face that I was up and mobile enough to visit her. As a mother, I can only imagine what it was like for her to see me in that bed, so helpless for so long. Such a stark comparison to what she had always known me to be. My mother is my lighthouse. A constant beacon of light showing me the way through her own stubbornness and hardheadedness that we both came by so honestly.

Her house seemed smaller than I remembered. There was so much more, "stuff" then I recalled. Many of my grandmother's china and trinkets found a new home at my moms'. It was bittersweet seeing it all again for the first time since losing her. Thankfully, Sunday dinners hadn't changed in the more than five years I had been away. Tons of food and roars of laughter were being served up and I was plenty hungry for both!

I remained in treatment with both Dr. Peter and Katherine. I was in constant pain from my structure having been under strain for such an incredibly long period of time. Years of being in one position caused damage to the cervicals and the severe atrophy of the muscles surrounding them caused them to constantly shift out of position. Though it was getting better, there was still much to work through. Lacking insurance, professional physiotherapy was financially impossible. I would have to do what I could myself from home to recondition the muscles and regain my strength.

The most exciting and comforting thing I had been able to achieve this year, was climbing the stairs to the second floor of our home. Again, it took months to make the climb up the entire seventeen stairs but, when I did, I knew I had reached a new level both literally and figuratively. I was met by my bedroom and beautiful ensuite. I was now blessed to bathe and shower without the need of the portable tub! It also meant that I could finally sleep upstairs, no longer sequestered alone to the main floor.

This year was about fine tuning much of the emotional work I had been doing for several years now. I was deepening my faith and trust in the Universe. I allowed myself to surrender to its innate wisdom and timing. I found no need to fret or spend my days in worry, constantly reminding myself that worry was a negative prayer. No more wishing time to move faster or slower. I stayed **committed** daily to building an unshakable foundation of **trust**. It was a discipline, a new way of thinking. As I did this, my brain was rewiring itself for faith and **trust** and dissolving old synapsis of doubt and fear. This was an integral first step towards creating deep self-generated inner peace. Many years ago, in the bed, was when I first embraced the concept, it was difficult and felt forced and insincere. Now, it was becoming second nature and **trust** was flowing through me as easily as fear once did. The positive thoughts came freely and took very little effort. It was incredibly freeing to live a life of **trust**, knowing and **accepting** deeply, that all was good in the moment.

    I had a deep sense of **gratitude** for absolutely everything in life. After all those years in bed, barely existing, I learned to appreciate every little thing more than I ever had before. I kept reminding myself that my Auntie Rea was never given a second chance. I wasn't going to take that, or anything else for granted. Washing dishes was a blessing, never a drudgery. A rainy day was magical as it provided a natural cleansing of all that surrounded us. It was beautiful to be able to stand in a storm and feel the drops pour down on my face and remind me of the limitless sky. While waiting in line at the grocery store, I would feel the energy of frustration from people around me as they huffed and puffed in impatience wishing for things to move quicker. I would stand with the biggest grin, taking it all in. I rejoiced in my ability to stand, to smile and to be a part of the experience, while my brain accepted it all beautifully. I was grateful for the challenges that came up and there were many. Each time giving thanks and looking deeper for the opportunity and the wisdom I was meant to uncover. It was always there, bringing me to the next level of growth and awareness.

Acceptance was the most challenging ***Pillar*** for me. I was still working on *accepting* the fact that I was starting my life again from scratch and exploring, as well as uncovering my life's purpose moving forward. I had begun writing down my thoughts and lessons learned, knowing that one day I would share them with the masses. I had no idea how, but *trusting* the "how" would answer itself.

My new physical body, which my rebirthed soul resided in, was where I encountered the most dissonance in my thinking. I was absolutely falling in love with the person I was becoming and had found deep peace in the authenticating process. I was genuinely shedding the need to fit in and embracing the unicorn I was always meant to be. I embraced the empathic introvert and the hilarious extrovert I was at my core, the woman who felt deeply and shared intensely, the little girl who still loved to pick wildflowers and put them in her hair and the sensible stable rock who was often the voice of reason. I was the free spirit that walked through downtown fountains and the lady who valued and respected her body. A fiercely independent female and a woman with a most gentle touch, the pioneer who loved the simpler things and the deep soul who embraced the complexities of life and the depth of the subconscious. I was all of these and together they made the beauty of me. I began to not only embrace my vulnerabilities, but celebrated them as well, knowing that these are where my truest gifts reside.

Unfortunately, all I had to do was glance in the mirror and the constant feelings of unlovable, undesirable and "not good enough" came flooding back. Part of me was aching for the ignorant bliss I had during the years without a mirror. I had become highly critical of myself in a way I never had before. I loathed my body, the shell that encapsulated that, "whole lot of woman" Dr. Peter would continually remind me of. I loathed touching it, I loathed bathing it. The luxury and blessing I had gone so long without and now, I dreaded it. I despised touching my body and feeling so much more of me. I was proud of my spiritual expansion, yet so shameful of the physical expansion, feeling curves that were never there before. Each day, I had to muster the courage to disrobe and face the task that should have been a blessing. I hated to get out of the shower and see my reflection which would inevitably bring me to tears. I didn't know that person reflecting back at me and I resisted getting to know her. I couldn't face her, not yet anyways. I took the most beautiful vintage satin shawl and draped it over the entire mirror. I knew very well it was an exercise in denial, but I wasn't ready for her. I felt like an unfinished piece of artwork that remained a secret until the official unveiling…whenever that may be.

I remained fully *committed* to my thoughts, words and actions. As the negative thoughts came in, I acknowledged them and release them lovingly. I continued to be responsible for the energy I put out to the Universe, as well as the energy I allowed in. I remained *committed* to keeping my karma clean by living a life of love and compassion for myself and for others.

Gavin and I began working on opening my heart to love again, breaking down the walls that I had erected, some consciously and some subconsciously in order to protect myself from further hurt. Regardless of the unsuccessful marriage, I still believed in love. My grandmother proved to me that it did in fact exist through the telling of her own love story with Grandpa Joe. Did it exist for me somewhere out there? I wasn't sure. But I did know that I had too much love inside me to keep it all to myself. I wasn't going to close myself off and become bitter because of what hadn't worked out in the past. Again, the first step in healing and opening my heart was to accept the marriage as an experience in my life to assist me in growing, learning and achieving the next level of authentication. It was not about punishment and it did not hold negative meaning unless I chose it to. I was a profoundly different person now and was ready for a different experience.

JoJo Marie Schillaci

The critical self is insatiable. The constant hunger for more, for perfection, for a model of self which is only able to exist in a dream state of being. For our reality is marked with scars and imperfection, with darkness and shadows where we hide from the light, not just from others, but from ourselves.

Written 2016

Chapter Forty

It was 2018 and slowly, ever so slowly, I was working towards accepting my new physical form. I definitely wasn't there yet, not by a long stretch, but I was working diligently at embracing myself as I was in the moment. Although the veil remained on the mirror each day, I felt myself emerging into the woman I knew I was deep down inside. This allowed me to slowly get more comfortable with my external self. During this process I also began comforting my fearful, insecure little girl that had always lived within me. She would forever be a part of me but, would no longer cry out, she was now at peace. My little girl understood that she had never truly been alone and that she had always been good enough. The actions and abuse from other were not her fault and she no longer had to carry their shame. She took her place as a part of my past, allowing the awaiting woman inside to step up into full view. I began embracing what I found at the centre of the labyrinth, my core truth. I am a beautiful soul. I am good enough. I am lovable and deserving of love, curves and all.

It was the winter of 2018 when my lawyer placed before me my final divorce decree. The marriage was officially over. It had taken years to get to this final place. This final place of peace, not just on paper, but truly in my heart. I gained peace of the past through deep forgiveness for both sides. If a marriage succeeds it is because of two people and if a marriage ends it's because of two people. I had many shortcomings and I know there were many times I could have done better. We had the best of intentions, I truly and deeply believe that but, in the game of love, intention will only get you so far for so long. I am grateful that I was set free, it was a blessing to both of us. I give thanks for the years we were together. A major reason the Universe brought us together was to bring our son into this world. Joseph has a clear mission on this earth, and we were chosen to deliver him here. There are no mistakes in life and I certainly do not look at my marriage as one, it was simply a blessing with a timeline that had been reached. I had my son by my side, and it was now time to begin the second half of my life.

As the divorce decree arrived, so did my legal name change. The process had taken years. Due to the divorce, it was best to save confusion and wait until all the papers were signed off and I could begin my new life fresh. The day finally came when I looked in my mailbox and inside I found...me! My brand new, clean slate, fresh off the shelf self! I finally had a name, no longer Jane Doe! It was exhilarating and strangely odd at the same time. This was going to take some getting used to. I was proud to see the names of the women who influenced and helped me save my own life. I was determined to do them proud both in Heaven and here on earth.

I was now knee deep in the process of figuring out my life's purpose. The blank canvas was overwhelming and daunting, knowing that it was fully up to me to create my own life, free of blaming others as I moved forward. No longer a life lived by the default of fear and the self-limiting beliefs of others. It was simply going to begin and end with me. Through recent years, my writing and life coaching had begun, and people wanted more. My writing came from a most organic source, that to this day, I attribute to something higher than myself. I could never force it, it came naturally and usually, in the wee hours of the morning. Each time the messages were clear and were based on the *5 Pillars* of my transformation. **Trust, acceptance, gratitude, commitment** and **liberation** were the building blocks of my work and foundation of the message I believed I needed to share. The "how" was still yet to reveal itself.

JoJo Marie Schillaci

Chapter Forty-One

2018 was also the year I embarked on my biggest adventure yet. I began a long-term relationship with a high school friend who serendipitously came into my life and heart. There is no doubt in my mind that we were definitely joined at a soul level. When we think of our soulmate, I think we collectively believe that it's the "one." The person we are meant to be with forever, that we have a past connection to and have finally been reunited with. I believe part of that to be true of this relationship. I believe what we were experiencing was a "soul connection", but not a "soulmate." I believe we can have many, many soul connections in our lifetime, each one brought to us for a specific Divine reason. Sometimes, it is to assist one another in learning a life lesson, to finish up an incompletion from a past life, or merely to provide much needed love and support to an old friend.

Over the course of our time together, I would learn much about myself that I could never otherwise have uncovered. I realized that regardless of my past, the hurt, the pain and the fear of loss, my capacity to be vulnerable and love with all my heart was immeasurable. Through all the work I had done in the bed and since, my level of ***trust*** that I had with myself and the Universe, allowed me to truly stay vulnerable and open up to an unknown and indeterminable experience. The bitterness and fear were gone and were replaced with a beautiful open willingness to love, regardless of there being no guarantees. There are no guarantees in life and certainly not in love. I loved in the moment and lived with compassion and kindness as my goal, free of expectation. *Accepting* that this was my experience here and now and immensely *grateful* for my ability to let it into my sacred space. I was *committed* like never before, being guided by nothing but the purest of love. In sharing and allowing another to see me, all of me, I gained a loving *acceptance* of myself. This was the moment I had been waiting for. The image that had been hidden for so long was finally unveiled and as the beautiful satin veil fell from the mirror and I was able to finally gaze at myself, a peace washed over me. No longer tears of shame, but of joy would flow. I was rejoicing in my ability to embrace, accept, love and allowed myself to be seen as I was and believed that I was enough.

As the relationship came to an abrupt halt, I could clearly see that the length or end result of a relationship was never what matters. What matters is our ability to see it as a purposeful interaction. This was all part of my journey to authenticate. It was the most intense and yes, without a doubt, the most painful culmination of lessons I had to learn.

When another shows a lack of integrity and respect it is easy to become a victim of their actions and turn to old thinking patterns of "why me" instead of "for me." I was never going to play victim again. That is the quickest way to surrender your power. Instead, my focus had to be on uncovering the message in all of the mess. One day, as Joseph and I were both navigating through the hurt, he shared with me such clarity and wisdom saying: "Mom, sometimes the sum value is not so much about a person as it is about the experience." Joseph's message profoundly shifted my thinking. For me, it allowed me to reflect and realize my capacity to love, to be vulnerable, to be faithful and absolutely committed. Sometimes, people will attempt to harden you. Don't let them. Instead, seek to learn from them. Allow them to show you what you don't desire, exactly what you don't want to become. Then pour so much love into yourself, that you evolve into an even more loving, open and beautiful soul then before. Never allow anyone or anything to change the beauty and openness of your heart, soul and spirit. They don't deserve that power. It's about seizing our power, digging our heels in and becoming an even better version of ourselves because of the experience.

This was also about owning the choices I made during the relationship and the responsibility I had to myself in owning my part. This is not to say that I own another's actions. The saying: "you can't suck and blow at the same time" is very true. You cannot perform two incompatible actions or hold two views that are in contradiction. Betrayal hurts. It scars you deeply and there is never, ever a reason or justifiable excuse for it. But I did realize that I had allowed myself to over give and perhaps, over understand because I was falling in love with potential instead of what was showing in the present. I also had a need to be a caregiver, a fixer and an excuse maker. This showed me where my own work needed to be done in defining and erecting healthy boundaries for myself and my energy. I had to really examine what I desired so I would not just accept what I was given. Again, I was placed in the position to choose forgiveness and release another's sins and sever the tether of shared energy and co-dependency. I will never regret loving as much as I did, the way I did or for as long as I did. How you choose to love and treat others paves your karmic path. What they do with it, paves theirs. Your love will never be wasted when given from the purest part of yourself and with the only intention being to bring joy and comfort to another human being. I take comfort in thinking that perhaps I made someone feel special and loved even if only for a portion of time.

I don't believe in the "happily ever after" fairy tale. I believe in the "Here and now." This doesn't come from a place of bitterness, but rather a place of learned wisdom, as life is ever changing as are we. Just as a tree in the fall can't promise it will bloom in the spring. It can't promise its branches will not break in a winter storm or that the bitter cold won't take its toll and cause an unexpected death. Nature makes no promises past now. Everything has the intention of returning but is so often left to the mercy of the forces which surround it. No one is able in any circumstance, to promise tomorrow. That's just reality. A fact. We may wish to and have the intention to but, when it comes down to it, there are too many variables to know anything for certain past this present moment in time. This is not to be confused with a lack of commitment. That's an entirely different matter. Commitment equals intention and any relationship absent of intention is a relationship doomed right out of the gate. Promising something that you can't see, and have such little control over, in my opinion, are just words that have no reality base. So many of us want to hear the promise of forever because of the fear within ourselves of abandonment, to be alone.

We cannot bear a life where we are not loved by another, by an external. Our faith and our promise need to shift from external to internal. The only one you truly have for a lifetime is you. Get comfortable with yourself. Really, deeply get to know and fall in love with yourself. At the end of the day, we must be our own Prince Charming because anything else would be a grim tale.

Written 2014

Chapter Forty-Two

As I write this final chapter of my book, I can say that I am finally free. Free from the fear, the guilt, the shame as well as the falsehoods of others. Free of the feelings of not being good enough, being unlovable and undesirable. Released from the need to be accepted by others and able to rejoice in my special gifts that allow me to stand out on my own. Free of the defensive armour that weighed me down and free of the resistance that stopped the natural flow of living. Through the gift of the *5 Pillars of Transformation* and the collective wisdom shared to me by the most beautiful rebirthing coaches throughout the past twenty-five years, I have found what I had come to believe would be forever elusive, *My Missing Peace*.

I no longer fear death but celebrate life for the true gift it is each day. *Trusting* the process of living and embracing the inevitability of one day dying. I no longer resist its natural flow and allow myself to be carried in each moment to exactly where I am meant to be. I *trust* in myself to be able to handle whatever life may bring and my ability to let go of those who are meant to move on to the next, knowing deeply that the little girl inside me is safe. Despite a loss, she is resilient and never abandoned and never was because I was and always am with her. Believing that we live on far past our time here on earth and carry with us the lessons and karmic experiences of this present lifetime. Appreciating all those that are in my life today and ***accepting*** that every person and connection has a life span and that's ok. Realizing that in fearing death, we never fully live and ***accepting*** that we were all born to one day eventually die.

    I now see myself not as the black sheep, but as the unicorn I always was. Taking pride in the fact that my differences allow me to stand out and not fit in. I no longer try to be like another by making myself small in order to wedge myself into an uncomfortable space in someone else's existence. I now choose to follow my own path of uniqueness and know that my tribe will naturally gravitate and walk along side. I celebrate my feminine softer side and wear with pride my inner Tom boy. I live as a sensual woman and a playful child. I don't control my laughter and I cry without shame. I have learned that once you find your true self and embrace who you really are at your deepest core, nothing will ever be forced and you will begin to attract like-minded energy, people, love and experiences effortlessly.

    I now know that it's about dropping the veil and being seen. I can see and ***accept*** myself in my truest authentic form of mind, body, soul and spirit. Gazing into my own eyes, lovingly feeling my own curves and deeply listening to the thoughts that run through my mind. The loving begins with me. The ***accepting*** begins with me. As the veil fell to the floor and I stood in my most raw and naked form it transformed judgement into self-love. By embracing myself fully, I set the stage for my deepest healing. Through the years, society has amplified the objectification of women. A woman is far more than a vessel of pleasure. We are so much more than our physical form and should never be judged by our dress size but appreciated and admired for our heart size. True beauty is shown through our ability to not only feel empathy and compassion, but to perform it: how we hold a hand; the words we speak; the acts of kindness we perform with no other goal than to comfort and console. The purest beauty is not what you see with your eyes open, so much as it is what you feel when they are closed. You will always be enough for the one that is worthy, and you will never be enough for the one who is not. This is a deep reflection of their issues, insecurities and short comings, not yours. Our sensuality and sexuality are the end result of a state of mind not body. It is determined by the *acceptance* and unconditional love we have for ourselves and should never be measured by another's opinion or judgement. It's about *accepting* and celebrating each imperfection as proof of victory of a life lived. It's about aging not only gracefully, but **gratefully** and falling in love with every beautiful, imperfect piece of ourselves.

I now embrace and celebrate my inner clown and the gift of laughter and humour handed down to me by the women of influence in my life. My mother and aunt showed me how to not take life too seriously and if life made it difficult to smile, smile anyway. The career counseling session in high school would turn out to be a complete bullseye and not a reason for embarrassment as I once thought. There is no shame in being told that you are destined to make people happy. There is no better feeling then seeing a smile as a result of your efforts and kindness. It feels natural for me to hand out clown noses as I teach people the powerful healing of laughter as medicine. Smiling always feels better and if you have the opportunity to make someone happy, do it. It's that simple. My dear friend Paul once told me, "Smiling works in reverse." The more we smile for no reason, the happier we become. Happiness is not an end result, but a conscious decision in the moment to choose joy.

I am released from the burden of guilt and shame and stand in my power with my head held high. There is no person or experience that can strip me of my dignity or worthiness unless I allow it. We must never take on another's transgressions as our own. There is never a reason or excuse to harm another and to look at the weaker as prey. The innocent did not ask for it in any way, shape or form and there is never a reason to believe that we deserved a wrongdoing against us. Victim mentality weakens us and only glorifies the predator. People's actions are a reflection of them, and them alone. As we gain confidence and inner peace we naturally shift from the position of prey to the position of power.

I *accept* myself as a loving, caring and imperfect mother. I take comfort in the way I raised my son to find beauty in the perfectly imperfect. I now *accept* that a parent is fallible, not flawless and it is sometimes in our weakest most exposed imperfect moments that we can teach our children the most valuable lessons. When we spare a child the struggle, we also spare them the victory. Joseph sets the bar high for himself and the way he lives his life encourages me to expect more from myself. When I was pregnant with him, my very early ultrasound barely showed what looked like a lima bean pulsating on the screen. When I asked the technician what that was, she said: "That is your baby and that's your baby's heart beating." To this day, I still see that image in him. Joseph is just one big throbbing heart motivated by wisdom, compassion and love, with an unshakable moral compass. His closest friends refer to him as the "sober second thought", always the voice of reason and direction in a most humble form. I knew from the day Joseph entered this world there was something different about him. He came in an old soul with many lifetimes of wisdom, but it has also been through this present lifetime that he has chosen to learn as well. He has utilized each obstacle as a gateway to something better within himself and every shoddy situation as fertilizer to enable him to grow into an even kinder and more compassionate human being then before.

    I have learned patience through my forever comforting friend nature. Realizing that everything unfolds in the perfect time. Nature never hurries yet everything gets done. After the coldest of winters, the ground eventually softens, the grass begins to rejuvenate, and the buds begin to sprout on the twigs that had been barren so long. No matter how long and hard the winter, spring always arrives. When things in life get complicated, I do the same as I did when I was as a little girl, I retreat to nature. I observe all that surrounds me and take it in through all of my senses. When I remain quiet and open the answers always appear. When I begin to feel disconnected from myself, I automatically retreat to the outdoors and walk with bare feet to connect to the purest source of Divine energy that we have been gifted and it works every time.

Through writing my story, I have come to see how the beautiful puzzle of my life fits together. Each encounter with another, each challenge and experience play a part and represent a piece of the bigger picture of my life as a whole. Everyone absolutely necessary and purposeful. I have learned that some walk the road in its entirety, some come along for a portion of the ride and some meet you at the end to welcome you. Everyone for a reason, but not necessarily for a lifetime. Each has brought me another step through the winding path of the labyrinth. They say there are three stages to a labyrinth: releasing on the way in; receiving in the centre and the taking back out into the world that which you received. A current day labyrinth walk is used to quiet the mind, recover balance in life, self-reflection and insight. It integrates the body with the mind and the mind with the spirit. I never consciously chose to enter the labyrinth, I just somehow found myself in the midst of it and at the centre, I would find my core truth. A direct result of all the work, people and experiences along the way, I discovered that at my core I am a beautiful soul whose inner peace always existed within my deepest and truest self. As I walk out of the labyrinth, this is the gift I take with me, as well as a profound connection of my mind, body, soul and spirit finally united as one.

Through my inner peace I find a quiet place within myself. No words can explain the paradigm shift. There is something so beautiful about being able to stand within your own self with a complete and utter calm of the soul, learning that each battle we have with another is actually a battle that originates and continues within ourselves. It has absolutely nothing to do with external stimuli. It is finding out the true enemy within and working through the wall that incapsulates fear, anxiety and dis-ease. When you reach inner peace, you are no longer at the mercy of those or circumstances around you. This is not to say that I am in a perfect place and nothing upsets me. I am ever evolving, ever changing and ever improving. Through this I am becoming the woman I am meant to be, ready to take on what I am meant to do.

The rehabilitation years served as my resurrection and awakening, and the bed would serve as my hatchery. In no other way could I have uncovered the truth behind the fear, the purpose in the pain or the strength under my weaknesses. It was when I could no longer run away that I was forced to do one of two things…either face it all head on and finally conquer or lay down and die. Though I would never wish it on my worst enemy, I would not change one single day, one single experience or one single person that crossed my path, good or bad. It all happened exactly the way it was meant to, the way it had to in order to bring not just me, but my son as well to a beautiful and peaceful existence within ourselves.

As I begin the second half of my life, I embrace the purpose of the pain and the gift of the storm. I am meant to share the wisdom of life that has been gifted to me. To spread the message of peace, love and gratitude. We can achieve and overcome anything when we operate from our highest existence. Karma is always listening, always watching and as we do good, it is like a boomerang that returns the goodness to us. As we focus and pay close attention to the words we speak, the thoughts we think, the images we look at and the people we surround ourselves with, so sets the vibration around us and within us. I can honestly say I am now living my best life thus far. I am committed to the lifelong journey of bettering myself a little more each day. There is no end to self-discovery, it is a lifelong evolution that begins the day we take our first breath to the day we breathe out our last. We do not arrive so much as we "travel through." I deeply believe that life is not something to merely survive as society has led us to think. Life is to be experienced and devoured for the sweet gift it is each day.

No matter how much work I have done on myself there are still challenging days and issues that come to the surface. The difference now is that I face them with an open and *trusting* heart. I am *grateful* for the opportunity for more expansion and *accepting* that my life is a journey that is changing in every moment. I stay *committed* to the experience and willing to allow learning in. Every day I am *liberated* when I face fear in the eye and say, "I will move forward despite."

My son, my rock, my reason for always taking the next breath.

June 29, 2019.

I am...

Not defined by the one who left, but by the many who came;

Not by what I lost, but what I gained;

Not by my weight, but by my wisdom;

Not by my net worth, but by my self-worth;

Not by my setback, but by my come back;

Not by my fall, but by my rise;

Not by the lies, but by the love;

Not by the heartbreaks, but by the heartbeats;

Not by my fears, but by my forgiveness;

Not by my past, but by my passion;

Not by my anger, but by my love;

Not by my insecurities, but by my integrity;

I am not defined by who I was, but by who I choose to become.

Written 2019

Epilogue

What I learned while bedridden for over 1,460 days...

I wouldn't be where I am today, if I didn't ***accept*** where I was yesterday.

Whatever my greatness, I need to own it and just as important, I need to own my shortcomings.

Material things are not important to me. People and life experiences are what I choose to invest in.

Not to look to change, but to evolve. Change happens on the surface. Evolving, is the deep, dark visceral work.

Hate hurts and forgiveness heals. Forgiveness of others frees you. Forgiveness of yourself, is humbling.

There is fact and then there is the emotional meaning that we put to fact. How we choose to define an experience will inevitably form our experience.

Expectation leads to disappointment. Expect nothing and be pleasantly and gratefully surprised with all that comes naturally.

People meet you from where they are, not from where you are.

You don't find love, inclusion and happiness by putting up armour and being defensive. We create the opportunity for love through the bravery of vulnerability when we show up and allow ourselves to be seen as we truly are.

When you pour love on others, you naturally drench yourself.

Loving someone is never time wasted, no matter the outcome. To live without regret and to love without looking back.

To live each day with love as my goal, kindness as my default and gratitude as my go to.

Goodbyes are redirects to awaiting hellos.

To be a sovereign being. My power and strength are derived from my ability to stand in my own truth, energy and independence. My happiness is not dependent on the actions or words of others but comes from the peace I generate within myself. I am whole and complete on my own.

At the end of the day, I must be able to live with myself. That's really all that matters. That I can get up in the morning, look in the mirror and be proud of the choices I made and the person I am. Then put my head on my pillow with a deep sense of peace for my actions and words.

* * * * *

And suddenly, I realized I had arrived. Not at a place of perfection, but at a place of peace. The battle is over, the struggle has ended. That constant and what seemed like never-ending road of pain, hardship and sacrifice does in fact stop. It came out of nowhere. I couldn't have predicted how the veil of joy would look or feel. I needed to experience it fully in the Divine time, in the Divine way. As I reached such a monumental achievement as deep inner peace, the Universe blessed me once again by diminishing the memory of my pain in a most gentle way. I still can't quite wrap my head around what I have done. Deep down at my core, I just knew I always would. And so, the next journey of life begins and with it comes new challenges and obstacles. I continue winning despite what is put before me because each time I choose to show up, face fear and pour more love, I continue to beat the drum of inner peace and with that, anything is possible!

If you find yourself on your own journey of self-discovery, you may find that you are in a space between where you were and where you desire to be. This is sacred space, healing space, growing space. It is usually deeply uncomfortable and can be a great source of angst, but it does not have to be. When we can embrace the discomfort with self-love and patience and reformulate it as our possible hatchery, it can be an exciting part of the journey. Don't get discouraged by the length of time or growing pains. Your rebirth will be magnificent and will happen in the Divine right time. Keep trusting the process and welcome it with grace. Choose to show up differently and see it change you and all that surrounds you.

Allow yourself to feel the vibration, that undeniable sensation that stirs your soul. That! That is where you need to focus your attention and listen. What is it saying to you? Where is it calling you? You have greatness within you and the Universe is beckoning you to answer the call to your truest authentic self. Embrace the most vulnerable part of your being and allow your thoughts, desires and visions to emerge into the light. Voice them loud and clear, declare them, honour them and yourself. It is time to own your greatness! It is time to soar without the limitations of falsehoods and the beliefs of others. This is your life! This is your call to action!

What is important is that you begin now where you are. Begin today just as you feel. Launch that one new thought in this moment that will propel you into the terrifying and exciting new life that has been waiting to embrace you. Do this despite the fear; despite the sweat on your brow; despite your knees going weak and despite your heart pounding through your chest. Fear is your bully and he must be stood up to now, in this very moment. Fear is the emotional extortionist that has stood in your way and robbed you of the true peaceful happiness that you long for. As soon as you stand up to your bully, they lose their strength and you realize that they have their own weakness. Ironically, their weakness is always your true strength that they made you believe you had lost. Your strength is your ability to be vulnerable. Deep down fear hates vulnerability. It loves armour. It loves high walls and darkness. Shine the light, put down the shield, tear down that wall! It's time to claim back your life today!

The most important lesson I learned while bedridden for over 1,460 days...it always ***simply begins with you***!

My Missing Peace

JoJo Marie Schillaci

JoJo Marie Schillaci is an author and motivational speaker. Through her work she shares her personal story of breaking free from a life riddled with fear by utilizing her *5 Pillars of Transformation*. JoJo Marie teaches people to embrace their vulnerability as a catalyst for change, setting the stage for them to begin living their best lives free of fear and falsehoods.

She lives a simple, peaceful life in Toronto, Ontario Canada with her son Joseph.

JoJo Marie Schillaci

My Missing Peace

Printed in the USA
CPSIA information can be obtained
at www.ICGtesting.com
LVHW010208250124
769930LV00026B/442

9 781777 340902